international
review of
social history

Supplement 9

Petitions in Social History

Edited by Lex Heerma van Voss

T0351994

CAMBRIDGE
UNIVERSITY PRESS

University Printing House, Cambridge CB2 8BS, United Kingdom

Published in the United States of America by Cambridge University Press, New York

Cambridge University Press is part of the University of Cambridge.

It furthers the University's mission by disseminating knowledge in the pursuit of education, learning and research at the highest international levels of excellence.

www.cambridge.org
Information on this title: www.cambridge.org/9780521013222

© Internationaal Instituut voor Sociale Geschiedenis

This publication is in copyright. Subject to statutory exception and to the provisions of relevant collective licensing agreements, no reproduction of any part may take place without the written permission of Cambridge University Press.

First published 2011
Second Edition 2012
Reprinted 2013

A catalogue record for this publication is available from the British Library

ISBN 978-0-521-01322-2 Paperback

Cambridge University Press has no responsibility for the persistence or accuracy of URLs for external or third-party internet websites referred to in this publication, and does not guarantee that any content on such websites is, or will remain, accurate or appropriate.

CONTENTS

Petitions in Social History

Edited by
Lex Heerma van Voss

Private Matters: Family and Race and the Post-World-War-II
Translation of "American"
Nancy K. Ota 209

NOTES ON CONTRIBUTORS

Marcia Schmidt Blaine, Plymouth State College, Social Science Department, MSC 39, Plymouth, NH 03264, USA; e-mail: mblaine@ oz.plymouth.edu

Oleg Bukhovets, Russian State University for the Humanities, 6 Miusskaya Square, Moscow 125267, Russia.

Ann Day, School of Social and Historical Studies, University of Portsmouth, Milldam, Burnaby Road, Portsmouth, PO1 3AS UK; e-mail: ann.day@port.ac.uk

Lex Heerma van Voss, Internationaal Instituut voor Sociale Geschiedenis, Cruquiusweg 31, 1019 AT Amsterdam, The Netherlands; e-mail: lhv@iisg.nl

Liang Hong-ming, Department of History, Washington University, One Brookings Drive, St Louis, MO 63130, USA; e-mail: hmliang@erols.com

Lothar Krempel, Max-Planck-Institut für Gesellschaftsforschung, Lothringerstrasse 78, D-50676 Köln, Germany; e-mail: Krempel@ mpi-fg-koeln.mpg.de

Carola Lipp, Seminar für Volkskunde, Universität Göttingen, Hermann-Föge-Weg 10, D-37073 Göttingen, Germany; e-mail: Carola.Lipp@ t-online.de

Ken Lunn, School of Social and Historical Studies, University of Portsmouth, Milldam, Burnaby Road, Portsmouth PO1 3AS, UK; e-mail: ken.lunn@port.ac.uk

John Markoff, Department of Sociology, University of Pittsburgh, 2G03 Wesley W. Posvar Hall, Pittsburgh, PA 15260, USA; e-mail: jm2@ cis.pitt.edu

Rebecca Nedostup, Department of History, Purdue University, 1358 University Hall, West Lafayette, IN 47907-1358, USA; e-mail: rnedostup@sla.purdue.edu

Cecilia Nubola, Istituto Storico Italo-Germanico di Trento, Via S. Croce 77, 38100 Trento, Italy; e-mail: nubola@itc.it

Nancy K. Ota, Albany Law School of Union University, 80 New Scotland Avenue, Albany, NY 12208, USA; e-mail: nota@mail.als.edu

Gilbert Shapiro, 4625 Fifth Ave. #503, Pittsburgh, PA 15213, USA; e-mail: gns@vms.cis.pitt.edu

Potukuchi Swarnalatha, Department of History, University of Mumbai, Kalina Campus, Mumbai-40098, India; e-mail: pslatha@rediffmail.com

Andreas Würgler, Historisches Institut, Universität Bern, Unitobler, 3000 Bern 9, Switzerland; e-mail: andreas.wuergler@hist.unibe.ch

NOTES ON CONTRIBUTORS

IRSH 46 (2001), Supplement, pp. 1–10 DOI: 10.1017/S002085900100030X
© 2001 Internationaal Instituut voor Sociale Geschiedenis

Introduction*

LEX HEERMA VAN VOSS

On 31 December 1870, the Swiss philosopher, Henri-Frédéric Amiel (1821–1881), petitioned the municipal authorities of Geneva on behalf of his neighbours and himself. They lived in a street called the Rue des Belles Filles ("beautiful girls' street") and wanted to have the name of their street changed because it alluded to prostitutes.[1] This is just one among a multitude of historical facts that have come down to us because humble (or not so humble) suppliants put them on paper in the form of a petition, and the authorities to which these petitions were addressed took care to preserve them. Writing petitions was a common human experience. "Everybody is free to write petitions and have a drink of water", as a traditional German saying would have it.[2] However, as opposed to drinking water, writing petitions is an act which produces historical sources, many of which have survived. The aim of this volume is to give an overview of their importance as sources for social history.

PETITIONS

Petitions are demands for a favour, or for the redressing of an injustice, directed to some established authority. As the distribution of justice and largesse are important parts of ruling, rulers can hardly deny their subjects the right to approach them to implore them to exercise justice, or to grant a favour. And subjects have done so from Egyptian building workers in pharaonic times to illiterate Ecuador Indians in 1899; from anti-Catholic English women in 1642 to French workers asking for the repeal of the *livret ouvrier* in 1847; from Italian peasants complaining about noble banditry in 1605 to Brazilian slaves vindicating their rights against their owners in 1823; from western European early modern guild members to

* I thank Michiel Baud, Maarten Prak, Klaus Tenfelde, and Willem Trommel for helpful suggestions for this introduction. The usual disclaimer applies.
1. Philippe M. Monnier, "Amiel et les 'belles filles': bibliothèque publique et universitaire", *Musées de Genève*, 221 (1982), pp. 3–7.
2. *"Supplizieren und Wassertrinken sind jedermann erlaubt"*, quoted in Otto Ulbricht, "Supplikationen als Ego-Dokumente. Bittschriften von Leibeigenen aus der ersten Hälfte des 17. Jahrhunderts als Beispiel", in Winfried Schulze (ed.), *Ego-Dokumente: Annäherung an den Menschen in der Geschichte* (Berlin, 1996), pp. 149–174, 152.

German Democratic Republic workers demanding improvement of economic efficiency, or voicing consumer demands.[3] As this short overview shows, petitions seem to be a global phenomenon, stretching back in time almost as far as writing.

Many of the documents which are treated in this volume were not designated as petitions historically. In many languages and periods, different kinds of petition-like documents were distinguished by different terms. These could reflect the body which wrote them, whether they were aimed more at attaining justice or a favour, or juridical technicalities. In this collection of essays, we have adopted the general term "petitions" to underline how much these documents have in common.[4] The only exceptions are the contributions by Würgler and Nubola, which treat the differences between the different kinds of petition in some detail, and therefore cannot manage with one generic term.[5]

In choosing one generic term for petitions, we also dispute the argument that petitions are somehow a nineteenth-century invention, dependent on written constitutions.[6] It is clear that the character of a petition depended much on the circumstances in which it was presented – whether by an individual or by a group – and whether it addressed to a democratically chosen parliament or an autocratic ruler. The prescriptions laid down for the form the text of a petition should take could also be very influential.

Whatever form or context, petitions were usually written in a deferential style, showing that the petitioner did not intend to question the established power structure. As the petition was usually addressing higher levels, if not the apex of the power structure, this made sense. As the example quoted by

3. A.G. McDowell, *Village Life in Ancient Egypt: Laundry Lists and Love Songs* (Oxford, 1999); Michiel Baud, "Libertad de Servidumbre: Indigenista Ideology and Social Mobilization in Late Nineteenth Century Ecuador", in Hans-Joachim König and Marianne Wiesebron (eds), *Nation Building in Nineteenth Century Latin America: Dilemmas and Conflicts* (Leiden, 1998), pp. 233–253; Patricia-Ann Lee, "Mistress Stagg's Petitioners: February 1642", *Historian*, 60 (1998), pp. 241–256; Madeleine Rebérioux, "Pétitionner", *Mouvement Social*, 181 (1997), pp. 127–132; Jaime Rodrigues, "Liberdade, humanidade e propriedade: os escravos e a assembleia constituinte de 1823", *Revista do Instituto de Estudos Brasileiros*, 39 (1995), pp. 159–167; C. Povolo, "Processo contro Paolo Origiano e altri", *Studi Storici*, 29 (1988), pp. 321–360; Henk van Nierop, "Popular participation in politics in the Dutch Republic", in Peter Blickle (ed.), *Resistance, Representation and Community* (Oxford, 1997), pp. 272–291; Jonathan R. Zatlin, "Ausgaben und Eingaben: Das Petitionsrecht und der Untergang der DDR", *Zeitschrift für Geschichtswissenschaft*, 45 (1997), pp. 902–917.
4. The volume even includes a contribution by Shapiro and Markoff on a kind of document which has become famous under its specific name, the *cahier de doléances*, but as the authors explain, there are good reasons to see this as a kind of petition.
5. Würgler also treats the historiography in some details, which makes it unnecessary to repeat that in this introduction.
6. Helmut Ridder, "Petitionsrecht", in *Staatslexikon. Recht Wirtschaft Gesellschaft. Herausgegeben von der Görres-Gesellschaft* (sixth edition, Freiburg, 1961) vol. 6, pp. 230–234; Charles Tilly, *Durable inequality* (Berkeley, CA [etc.], 1998), p. 217.

Nedostup and Liang Hong-ming shows, this deferential attitude towards the powers that be could also take the form of adopting the jargon of the party in power.

THE USES OF PETITIONS

Petitions are social history in the sense that a social history of the petition could be written, showing the evolving ways in which individuals and social movements used petitions.

Where petitions became an accepted tradition, they could evolve into an institution which not only catered for the wishes of individuals, but also was used to elicit general legislation. Not only in Britain, but also in countries like Germany, Russia, and Japan, where rulers laid claim to absolute power, petitions were used by broad layers of the population to influence legislation.[7]

The right to petition could easily develop into a crystallization point for other popular rights. This happened in Western countries from the seventeenth century. The right to petition easily brought about the right to assemble in order to draw up, discuss, and sign the petition. This could involve masses of subjects in the discussion of petitions.[8] The meeting in which a petition was debated was an exercise in politics, as was the soliciting of signatures. This could involve large numbers of citizens. The Chartist petitions of 1839, 1842 and 1848 each had well over a million signatures to it. If numbers of subjects were allowed to sign a petition, and have it presented in their name, it was hard to see how they could be denied the right to present their petition themselves. But if a number of signers presented a petition to a ruler or a representative body, this resulted in a demonstration. This happened, for instance, in 1779, when Lord George Gordon introduced a petition against the relief of anti-Catholic measures in the British Parliament, and took 14,000 supporters with him to Parliament to deliver the petition.[9] The 1894 and 1932 marches of

7. Beat Kümin and Andreas Würgler, "Petitions, Gravamina and the Early Modern State: Local Influence on Central Legislation in England and Germany (Hesse)", *Parliaments, Estates & Representation*, 17 (1997), pp. 39–60; L.S. Roberts, "The Petition Box in Eighteenth-Century Tosa", *Journal of Japanese Studies*, 20 (1994), pp. 423–458; James W. White, *Ikki: Social Conflict and Political Protest in Early Modern Japan* (Ithaca, NY [etc.], 1995).
8. Charles Tilly, *Popular Contention in Great Britain 1758–1834* (Cambridge, MA [etc.], 1995); Jonathan Scott, *England's Troubles: Seventeenth-Century English Political Instability in European Context* (Cambridge, 2000); David Zaret, "Petitions and the 'Invention' of Public Opinion in the English Revolution", *American Journal of Sociology*, 101 (1996), pp. 1497–1555; David Zaret, *Origins of Democratic Culture: Printing, Petitions and the Public Sphere in Early Modern England* (Princeton, NJ, 2000).
9. Tilly, *Popular Contention in Great Britain*, p. 160.

unemployed veterans on Washington were legitimized as the presentation of petitions.

The usual way out for rulers was to forbid collective petitions. These were, for example, illegal in prerevolutionary France. In 1648 in England, where petitioning was by that time regarded as an established right, the Long Parliament laid down that petitions could not be submitted by more than twenty individuals. Under Charles II, petitioning to convene Parliament was punishable as high treason. James II had bishops confined to the Tower for petitioning against his religious policies. These attempts on the right of petition led to its being included in the Bill of Rights in 1689. In the eighteenth century, the right to petition was included in listings of individual liberties like the Bills of Rights of most American states and the *Déclaration des droits de l'homme et du citoyen* of 1791. In England, by the late eighteenth century, petitions had become the normal way in which the unfranchised could make their opinion known.

Even if authorities frowned upon petitions as a way to voice demands and to mobilize and demonstrate popular support for them, this does not mean that they did not heed the opinions uttered in them. In fact, even the most autocratic of governments used petitions as a source of information about popular feeling.[10] In the present collection, this is made clear in the essay by Nubola, who looks as the reasons Italian princes had for taking notice of the opinions brought forward by petitioners. There seem to have been at least three. First, petitions offered a window upon the mind of the general population for contemporary statesmen, in much the same way as they do to latter-day historians. This alone, as Nubola shows, could be enough reason for rulers actively to stimulate their subjects to write and present petitions. Secondly, behind the deferential facade of a petition always lurked the threat that the population might revolt if a justified demand went unheeded. The right to petition thus worked as a safety valve.[11] And thirdly, petitions could sometimes be read as an offer by a local population for a coalition with the centre of the state to work against intermediate power holders. In a recent overview, Wayne te Brake has called attention to the role of ordinary subjects in shaping early modern European politics, together with local rulers and national claimants to power. Petitions by ordinary people to political leaders at national level were one way to outmanoeuvre local elites, and thus contribute to the formation of national states.[12] It might be useful to compare the

---

10. This is of course even more true of the *cahiers de doléances* analysed by Shapiro and Markoff, the drafting of which was obligatory.

11. K. Tenfelde and H. Trischler (eds), *Bis vor die Stufen der Throns. Bittschriften und Beschwerden von Bergarbeitern* (Munich, 1986), p. 14.

12. Wayne te Brake, *Shaping History: Ordinary People in European Politics, 1500–1700* (Berkeley, CA [etc.], 1998).

centralizing and state-building effects of the right to petition national rulers with those of the establishment of juridical courts of appeal at national level.[13]

Nubola's attention to the bureaucratic and political process petitions went through leads to more insights, which should be kept in mind when analysing petitions. For instance, even if the idea of a good person heading the state was a myth, it may well have been recognized as a useful myth at both the writing and reading ends of the petitioning process. In a similar way, even if mighty and rich petitioners with good connections at court stood a far better chance of being heard, petitions nevertheless offered a way to the centres of power which was also open to those without money and influence, not because the ruling father figure was good, but because it made good sense to him to keep this way open.

Revolutionary situations, like the French Revolution, or the revolution of March 1848 in Germany, went hand in hand with waves of petitioning. These two waves are here represented in the studies of Shapiro and Markoff on the national level, in the French case, and Lipp and Krempel on the local level of Esslingen, in the German case. In the situation where workers' organizations were not yet formed or recognized, petitions were used to voice workers' demands.[14] Here, Swarnalatha gives an example of this in the colonial context, where other forms of resistance were explicitly forbidden. Usually, when other forms of voicing workers' demands became accepted, petitions became less important in this respect. However, they could linger on in situations where trade unions and workers' representation took longer to establish themselves. This was often the case within the military – where, for example, Brazilian officers in the nineteenth century had to send in petitions to get promotion – or in the British naval dockyards, as described here by Lunn and Day. Their example also shows how trade unions could use petitioning up to the point where there no longer seemed a point in keeping out the unions and full negotiations. Both this essay and Swarnalatha's show how the development of labour conditions and labour relations can be followed through consecutive petitions. The deferential mould in which the petitions were cast could convey the true feelings of the author of the petition, but, of course, did not necessarily do so.[15]

As the example of the British naval dockyards shows, petitions could lose their importance as other ways of representing interests came to the fore. In the West during the twentieth century, their important remaining role was in introducing private legislation, as in the case described here by

---

13. Wolfgang Reinhard, *Geschichte der Staatsgewalt. Eine vergleichende Verfassungsgeschichte Europas von den Anfängen bis zur Gegenwart* (Munich, 1999), pp. 291–304.
14. Tenfelde and Trischler, *Bis vor die Stufen der Throns*.
15. Ulbricht, "Supplikationen als Ego-Dokumente", pp. 169–170.

Ota. Petitioning also remained a vibrant activity in the form of soliciting signatures under a political statement and presenting these to political powerholders to show public support for political positions.[16] For individual appeals to justice, an ombudsman has, in some cases, taken over the role that petitions used to have.[17] That is not to say that the classical petition has lost its importance always and everywhere. Bukhovets draws our attention to the fact that the First Congress of People's Deputies in 1989 received 300,000 letters and telegrams. In present-day Mexico, petitions are still a living right. In many other developed democracies, whether republics or monarchies, a feeling remains that the ordinary citizen has a right to address the head of state with his or her personal problems, if other ways to find a solution to these problems have failed.[18]

RULERS

To be effective, a petition has to mention the ruler or ruling body it is addressed to, the request, perhaps a motivation and certainly the name (and often some other qualities) of the petitioner(s). These data make petitions a powerful historical source. All formal elements of the petition, as described above, lend themselves to historical analysis: the ruler or ruling body the petition is addressed to, the request and its motivation, and the name and other qualities of the petitioners.

As to the ruler or ruling bodies, here petitions tell us something about the way government was perceived by petitioners. They must have seen government as something which could be moved to decide in their favour – perhaps as a multilayered formation, in which one layer could be encouraged to operate against another.[19] Petitions tried to use perceived fissures within ruling classes, for instance, by addressing a central authority with complaints about a local authority, or addressing a colonial power with demands based on the metropolitan system of justice.[20]

16. Jean-François Sirinelli, *Intellectuels et passions françaises. Manifestes et pétitions au XXe siècle* (Paris, 1990).
17. Jaap Talsma, *Het recht van petitie, verzoekschriften aan de Tweede Kamer en het ombudsvraagstuk. Nederland, 1795–1983* (Arnhem, 1989).
18. In a number of late twentieth-century cases, the question of whether petitioning was still a meaningful individual right was debated on the occasion of the rewriting of constitutions. If political and juridical theory wish to justify this right to address the head of state, they usually find justification in the idea that it is useful to supplement other, more specific, rights of appeal, with a general right to be used when more specific procedures are lacking.
19. Rodrigues, "Liberdade, humanidade e propriedade".
20. C.R. Friedrichs, "Anti-Jewish Politics in Early Modern Germany: The Uprising in Worms, 1613–17", *Central European History*, 23 (1990), pp. 91–152; Lidwien Kapteijns and Jay Spaulding, "Women of the Zar and Middle-Class Sensibilities in Colonial Aden, 1923–1932", *Sudanic Africa*, 5 (1994), pp. 7–38.

The segment or level of government to which a petition is addressed may give a clue here. Different segments of government may put petitions to quite different uses. Radical Members of Parliament in the early nineteenth-century United Kingdom used petitions to stage debates in Parliament, thus obstructing the functioning of Parliament. Their supporters fed this strategy with a stream of petitions. When new Parliamentary rules of order (1832, definitively in 1842) made this kind of obstruction harder, the number of petitions remained high, especially petitions carrying more than 10,000 signatures, as assembling large numbers of signatures was, in itself, a way of making political opinion visible.[21] As suffrage spread, this changed the meaning of petitions, which developed into a way of showing elected representatives which way popular feeling ran.

THE REQUEST AND ITS MOTIVATION

The request and its motivation can also be used for analysis. Of course, some motivations stated can have been given only for tactical reasons. The petition may borrow the language of the ruling classes to defend subaltern ways of living. In some cases, like the Dutch Republic in the eighteenth century, the rules for petitions were so complicated that specialists were needed to draw them up. If the petitioners were illiterate, the help of a literate writer was *per* definition necessary. But whatever influences the way in which demands are voiced, demands have to be voiced as that is the point of a petition. If the obstacles are taken into account, petitions lend themselves to linguistic or rhetorical analysis as texts.

In some cases, bringing forward an argument is the sole purpose of the petition. This applies, for example, to the lengthy petition of Wang Mingding to the 1934 National Congress of the Kuomintang, analysed by Nedostup and Liang Hong-ming. Its original aim was to present its author's view on education to the congress. Even if it was not noticed there, it has enabled Nedostup and Liang Hong-ming, two generations later, to reconstruct the world view of rank-and-file nationalists.

When petitions are available in large enough numbers, they can be analysed statistically to determine the social and spatial distribution of grievances.[22] This line of analysis is represented here by Bukhovets, who uses petitions to gauge anti-Semitism in Byelorussia in the first decade of

21. C. Leys, "Petitioning in the Nineteenth and Twentieth Centuries", *Political Studies*, 3 (1955), pp. 45–64.
22. Kari Helgesen, "Supplikker på 1700-tallet: et lite brukt kildemateriale", *Heimen*, 19 (1982), pp. 93–100; Kristian Hvidt and Hanne Rasmussen, "Socialistenadressen i November 1872", *Arbejderhistorie*, 3 (1995), pp. 22–32, Gilbert Shapiro and John Markoff, *Revolutionary Demands: A Content Analysis of the* Cahiers de Doléances *of 1789* (Stanford, CA, 1998).

the twentieth century. Shapiro and Markoff discuss an important question which arose during the French Revolution. Would the popular will only be expressed in electing the people's representatives, or would electors send their representatives to Paris with a binding mandate? They show the power of content analysis and of petitions as a serial source, especially their databank of the demands brought forward in the *cahiers de doléances* in giving a precise answer to the question of who held which position in this debate.[23] Bukhovets's analysis of ethnic and national stereotypes, as embodied in his Byelorussian petitions, leads to an unexpected conclusion regarding the importance of Jewish stereotypes. Ota analyses in depth the way petitioners presented themselves and their relatives to gain American citizenship, and the stereotypes of "American" involved.

THE PETITIONERS

Especially interesting are petitions produced by subaltern groups in colonial situations. In Asia, Africa, and Latin America, the indigenous population was quick to adopt petitions, perhaps because petitions resembled oral or written appeals they were already familiar with.[24] This encounter is described here by Swarnalatha for handloom weavers in the north of Coromandel (India) in the late eighteenth and early nineteenth centuries. Soon, these weavers amazed the colonial authorities by the quality of the argument in their petitions. However, as Stern has argued for Peru, the use of petitions may have integrated native society more tightly in the colonial power structure.[25]

When reading a petition, it is not always easy to decide whom one is reading. Before the rise of mass literacy, many petitioners were unable to write, let alone write a petition. The fact that petitions had to conform to formal requirements, or had to be written in official language, often required a professional hand even if the petitioner was able to write.[26] Still, it is generally possible to determine what was the influence of the

23. As argued above, it is worthwhile to look at the *cahiers de doléances* as petitions, but, as the whole of France was supposed to produce *cahiers*, as a source these have a coverage only rarely attained by petitions.
24. Carmen Nava, *Los abajo firmantes. Cartas a los presidentes*, 2 vols (Mexico City, 1994); John Kwadmo Osei-Tutu, *The Asafoi (socio-military groups) in the History and Politics of Accra (Ghana) from the 17th to the mid 20th Century* (Trondheim, 2000).
25. Steve J. Stern, "The Social Significance of Judicial Institutions in an Exploitative Society: Huamanga, Peru, 1570–1640", in George A. Collier, Renato I. Rosaldo, and John D. Wirth (eds), *The Inca and Aztec States 1400–1800: Anthropology and History* (New York, 1982), pp. 289–317.
26. Ulbricht, "Supplikationen als Ego-Dokumente", p. 154.

professional scribe (preacher, schoolmaster), and what is the voice of the real petitioner.[27]

Petitioners usually had reason to highlight one side of the story, and an analysis of the arguments and facts presented in a petition therefore requires the usual critical attitude towards argumentative historical sources. One of the best known studies of petitions, in this case petitions aimed at a pardon, underlines the fictional element in these petitions in its title.[28] But even if we see them as fiction, these life stories had to be credible to be effective, and thus give us information about the lives of the historical petitioners. Petitions share with other autobiographical sources a certain element of fiction and the need for historical criticism, but the difference is that petitions are more concentrated in time than most autobiographies.[29] Even given these limitations, it still is worthwhile to stress how often petitioners, in the course of their pleas, find occasion to describe their lives and everyday circumstances.[30] Examples of this can be found in the essays by Blaine, Nedostup and Liang Hong-ming, and Ota.

Life stories naturally have a place in petitions brought forward by individuals. However, many petitions were produced by groups. This holds true for the European *ancien regime* and comparable societies, which were seen by its members as composed of corporate bodies. These could have good reason to send in petitions, and also were supposed to represent their members to the authorities. The collective petition also comes to the fore after the establishment of parliamentary democracy and right up to the present day, as a large number of signatures under a petition becomes an important way to influence Parliament. As Shapiro and Markoff point out in their essay, such collective petitions may choose to remain silent on issues which might divide their supporters.

Petitions identify those in whose names they are made. This enables us, in turn, to identify the signatories historically, using the information in the petition and/or what other sources tell us about them.[31] In this way we can analyse the social and economic position of the signatories, and determine the social profile of the supporters of different points of view.[32] It has, for

27. *Ibid.*, p. 157–159. See also the discussion of the role of scribes in the essays by Bukhovets and Würgler.

28. Natalie Zemon Davis, *Fiction in the Archives: Pardon Tales and their Tellers in Sixteenth-Century France* (Stanford, CA, 1987).

29. Ulbricht, "Supplikationen als Ego-Dokumente", pp. 155, 170.

30. Tenfelde and Trischler, *Bis vor die Stufen des Throns*, pp. 27–28.

31. Bernard Laguerre, "Les pétitionnaires du Front Populaire: 1934–1939", *Revue d'Histoire Moderne et Contemporaine*, 37 (1990), pp. 500–515; Nicolas Offenstadt, "Signer pour la paix en 1938–1939: Pétitions et pétitionnaires", *Cahiers de l'Institut d'Histoire du Temps Présent*, 26 (1994), pp. 249–263.

32. Oleg G. Bukhovets, *Sotsial'nye konflikty i krest'ianskaia mental'nost' v rossiiskoi imperii nachala XX veka. Novye materialy, metody, rezul'taty* (Moscow, 1996); Mark Knights, "London's 'Monster' Petition of 1680", *Historical Journal*, 36 (1993), pp. 39–67.

instance, been possible to determine that in Germany in the sixteenth century all social classes presented petitions, but that the large majority were from ordinary people.[33]

The contribution by Lipp and Krempel shows how the identification of petitioners in other sources makes it possible to paint the whole landscape of the social groups signing different petitions in one of history's significant waves of petitioning: the 1848/49 Revolution.

Among the ordinary citizens petitioning, we find both men and women, if usually far more men than women.[34] As is clear from Blaine's study of women petitioning the New Hampshire government, the caring role of women was a basis for petitions. So were widely shared assumptions of dependence and helplessness. The provincial government of New Hampshire felt as much obliged to assume paternal care for these women as the Italian princes described by Nubola. This was especially the case when female petitioners could claim that their men were gone, dead or missing in action, or had treated them badly.

As is clear from the above, petitions were used by subjects, including quite humble subjects, in various cultures and political settings to voice their demands. Their ubiquity suggests that petitions are responsive to a need felt by individuals and human societies across cultural boundaries, perhaps something as fundamental as the need for justice.[35] However that may be, this collection shows that petitions certainly enable present-day social historians to hear the voices of working-class and middle-class men and women of the past, who would otherwise remain silent.

33. Ulbricht, "Supplikationen als Ego-Dokumente", p. 152, based on Helmut Neuhaus, *Reichstag und Supplikationenausschuß. Ein Beitrag zur Verfassungsgeschichte der ersten Hälfte des 16. Jahrhunderts* (Berlin, 1977), p. 299.
34. For Restoration France, Odile Krakovitch counted that petitions by women were between 2 and 4 per cent of the yearly number of petitions presented to the *Chambre des députés*; Odile Krakovitch, "Les pétitions, seul moyen d'expression laissé aux femmes. L'exemple de la Restauration", in Alain Corbin, Jacqueline Lalouette, Michèle Riot-Sarcey (eds), *Femmes dans la Cité 1815–1871* (Grâne, 1997), pp. 347–371, 351. A similar number was counted for the July Monarchy period by Riot-Sarcey; Michèle Riot-Sarcey, "Des femmes pétitionnent sous la monarchie de Juillet", in *ibid.*, pp. 389–400, 389.
35. Barrington Moore, Jr, *Injustice: The Social Bases of Obedience and Revolt* (New York, 1978).

IRSH 46 (2001), Supplement, pp. 11–34 DOI: 10.1017/S0020859001000311
© 2001 Internationaal Instituut voor Sociale Geschiedenis

Voices From Among the "Silent Masses": Humble Petitions and Social Conflicts in Early Modern Central Europe*

ANDREAS WÜRGLER

Social historians have quite frequently referred to the "silent masses" in history.[1] They have thereby hinted at the problem that most preserved documents derive from a tiny elite. The great majority of the people, being illiterate, only very rarely left private letters, diaries, autobiographies and testaments, or official acts, charters, statistics, and reports.[2] Besides the source problem, this view reflected concerns of structuralism and Marxism, both very fashionable among social historians up to the 1970s, who related the masses' interests to socioeconomic conditions. Ordinary people thus appeared rather as objects of economic structures than as subjects of historical processes.[3] Though some German-speaking social historians integrated the anthropological category of "experience"[4] into their studies in the 1980s, they assumed that ordinary people had interests in, and experiences of, but still no influence on historical processes. Merely local and reactive early modern social protest thus remained historically unimportant – in sharp contrast to the nineteenth-century working class movement.[5] During the 1990s, studies of social conflict focused on the

*Abbreviations: StABE = Staatsarchiv Bern; StAF = Stadtarchiv Frankfurt (RS = Ratssupplikationen, BMB = Bürgermeisterbücher); StAM = Hessisches Staatsarchiv Marburg; StAZH = Staatsarchiv Zurich. Many thanks to my colleague, Beat Kümin, for linguistic support.

1. Hans-Ulrich Wehler, *Deutsche Gesellschaftsgeschichte*, vol. 1 (Munich, 1987), p. 194; Wolfgang von Hippel, *Armut, Unterschichten, Randgruppen in der Frühen Neuzeit* (Munich, 1995), p. 57.
2. Natalie Zemon Davis, *Der Kopf in der Schlinge. Gnadengesuche und ihre Erzähler* (Frankfurt, 1991), pp. 19–20.
3. Fernand Braudel, *Die Dynamik des Kapitalismus* (Stuttgart, 1986), pp. 15, 16. But there are some exceptions, e.g. George Rudé, *The Crowd in the French Revolution* (London, 1959); E.P. Thompson, "The Moral Economy and the English Crowd in the Eighteenth Century", *Past & Present*, 50 (1971), pp. 76–136; Peter Blickle, *Die Revolution von 1525* (Munich, 1975), [cited hereafter the 2nd edn, 1983].
4. Jürgen Kocka, *Sozialgeschichte*, 2nd edn (Göttingen, 1987), pp. 162–174; Jürgen Schlumbohm, "Mikrogeschichte – Makrogeschichte: Zur Eröffnung einer Debatte", in *idem* (ed.), *Mikrogeschichte – Makrogeschichte* (Göttingen, 1998), pp. 7–32, 20, 24–28.
5. Jürgen Kocka, *Weder Stand noch Klasse. Unterschichten um 1800* (Bonn, 1990), p. 32; Arno Herzig, *Unterschichtenprotest in Deutschland 1790–1870* (Göttingen, 1988), pp. 21, 114.

concept of agency and discussed the influence historical actors had on processes such as modernization.[6]

In order to study ordinary people as historical actors, petitions provide considerable qualitative and quantitative advantages. *Petitions, grievances,* and *supplications, Gravamina, Suppliken,* and *Beschwerden, doléances, requêtes,* and *représentations, gravami, petizioni,* and *querele, clamores, greuges* and *griefs* – or whatever they have been called in changing times and regions[7] – were produced by individuals or groups, regardless of their age, status, class, ethnicity, religion, or sex. As they were composed in the most varied situations of life, they document needs and interests, hopes and experiences, attitudes and activities. Although these sources were written by ordinary people (mostly with a little help from a professional writer for a modest fee), state, church, or other institutions dealt with them carefully – and preserved them in their archives.

Up to now, several historical disciplines, from ecclesiastical and legal to cultural and gender history, have occasionally used these petitions.[8] The new history of crime, with its focus on law suits, discovered multiple extrajudicial proceedings (*l'infrajudiciaire*) by analysing petitions and supplications;[9] studies in administration, law, and government labelled "*Gute Policey*" try to measure state efficiency by means of supplications and petitions;[10] the

6. Andreas Würgler, "Das Modernisierungspotential von Unruhen im 18. Jahrhundert", *Geschichte und Gesellschaft*, 21 (1995), pp. 191–213; Andreas Suter, *Der schweizerische Bauernkrieg von 1653* (Tübingen, 1997); Wayne te Brake, *Shaping History: Ordinary People in European Politics, 1500–1700* (Berkeley, CA [etc.], 1998).

7. Cf. Antonio Marongiu, *Il parlamento in Italia nel medio evo e nell' età moderna* (Milan, 1962), Index s.v. "Gravami"; Andreas Würgler, "Beschwerden", in *Historisches Lexikon der Schweiz*, www.dhs.ch.

8. More details in Andreas Würgler, "Suppliche e gravamina nella prima età moderna: la storiografia di lingua tedesca", *Annali dell'Istituto storico Italo-germanico in Trento*, 25/1999 (2000), pp. 515–546, 521–527.

9. Gerd Schwerhoff, *Aktenkundig und gerichtsnotorisch. Einführung in die Historische Kriminalitätsforschung* (Tübingen, 1999), pp. 85–91; Andreas Würgler, "Diffamierung und Kriminalisierung von 'Devianz' in frühneuzeitlichen Konflikten. Für einen Dialog zwischen Protestforschung und Kriminalitätsgeschichte", in Mark Häberlein (ed.), *Devianz, Widerstand und Herrschaftspraxis in der Vormoderne* (Konstanz, 1999), pp. 317–347, 346; Karl Härter, "Strafverfahren im frühneuzeitlichen Territorialstaat: Inquisition, Entscheidungsfindung, Supplikation", in Andreas Blauert and Gerd Schwerhoff (eds), *Kriminalitätsgeschichte* (Konstanz, 2000), pp. 459–480; Carl A. Hoffmann, "Außergerichtliche Einigungen bei Straftaten als vertikale und horizontale soziale Kontrolle im 16. Jahrhundert", in *ibid.*, pp. 563–579; Benoît Garnot, "Justice, infrajustice, parajustice et extrajustice dans la France d'Ancien Régime", *Crime, History & Societies*, 4 (2000), pp. 103–120.

10. Cf. the contributions in Peter Blickle (ed.), *Gemeinde und Staat im Alten Europa* (Munich, 1997); André Holenstein, "Die Umstände der Normen – die Normen der Umstände. Policeyordnungen im kommunikativen Handeln von Verwaltung und lokaler Gesellschaft im Ancien Régime", in Karl Härter (ed.), *Policey und frühneuzeitliche Gesellschaft* (Frankfurt, 2000), pp. 1–46; Achim Landwehr, *Policey im Alltag* (Frankfurt, 2000), pp. 281, 311–312.

history of early parliaments and studies of social protest and revolt have the longest tradition of analysing petitions.

After introducing the key concepts of "social conflicts" and "petitions, *gravamina* and supplications" – very often triggered by conflicts – the main part of this essay will discuss the potential contribution of collective and individual petitions and supplications for research on social conflicts.[11] Examples will be taken from the German-speaking central European area which was – in contrast to the big western European kingdoms of France, England and Spain – divided into many small- and medium-sized territories, only weakly tied together by the Holy Roman Empire or the Swiss Confederation. Social conflicts usually occurred at this territorial level and did not question the existence of the Empire or the Confederacy as such, even if they were somehow involved. If, and to what extent, petitions and supplications record, so to speak, the voices of the masses or single voices from among the masses will be discussed in the conclusion.

SOCIAL CONFLICTS

The term "social conflict" has become crucial for modern sociology.[12] Yet sociologists cannot agree upon a common theory of conflict in general but have produced endless definitions of particular types and forms of conflict. This essay refers to the widely-known and integrative definition by Lewis A. Coser:

> Social Conflict may be defined as a struggle over values or claims to status, power, and scarce resources, in which the aims of the conflicting parties are not only to gain the desired values but also to neutralize, injure, or eliminate their rivals. Such conflicts may take place between individuals, between collectivities, or between individuals and collectivities. Intergroup as well as intragroup conflicts are perennial features of social life.[13]

Early modern individual, family, and group disputes cover the whole range of social conflicts, and provide most heterogeneous contexts for supplications and petitions: from rival applications for scarce jobs to revolutionary situations, from spontaneous rows to ritualized proceedings, from short disputes between spouses to long-lasting law-suits between lords and communities, from symbolic actions to military interventions.

Social conflicts are historically relevant not just because they happened,

11. For other means of conflict see Andreas Würgler, *Unruhen und Öffentlichkeit. Städtische und ländliche Protestbewegungen im 18. Jahrhundert* (Tübingen, 1995), pp. 169–184.
12. Peter Imbusch, "Konflikt", in *idem et al.* (eds), *Friedens- und Konfliktforschung* (Opladen, 1996), pp. 63–74, and *idem*, "Konflikttheorien", in *ibid.*, pp. 116–148.
13. Lewis A. Coser, "Conflict: Social Aspects", in *International Encyclopedia of the Social Sciences*, 3 (1968), pp. 232–233.

but on the one hand because of the great force of mobilization (events like revolts and civil wars), and on the other because of their high frequency and relative similarity (repeated everyday quarrels with structural character). In the tradition of early modern governments, the older historiography used to interpret social conflicts as disturbance of good order. Recent sociology, anthropology, and history, however, also emphasize positive social effects.

PETITIONS, *GRAVAMINA*, SUPPLICATIONS

The various meanings of the Latin verb *petere* rsp. *petitum/petita, petitio* – go to, demand, desire, claim – hint already at the great variety of ways to articulate interests. The word "petition" obtained different meanings in European languages. While in English, petition became the dominant umbrella term for requests, supplications, demands etc. of all kinds very early, the German, *Petition* became dominant not before 1800, although it may be found occasionally since the fourteenth century. At the turn of the nineteenth century, the term petition was strongly connected with constitutionalism and therefore focused on the political level, whereas the older terms used in German-speaking areas, *gravamina* and supplication, referred to administration and jurisdiction as well as politics.[14]

The Latin word *gravamen*, mostly in the plural form *gravamina*, literally means "load, burden". In the context of early parliamentarism, *gravamina* was the technical term for the written collective grievances the estates submitted to the lord on the occasion of institutionalized representative assemblies. The practice of representation and participation by *gravamina* was spread over the whole of Europe in the late Middle Ages and early modern times. Both contemporary language and modern historiography also used the term in general for any collective voicing of grievances by subjects, whether connected to legal proceedings or revolts. In some ways, therefore, revolts replaced representative assemblies as occasions to voice grievances.

Supplications are far more heterogeneous in terms of their production, content, authors and addressees,[15] which is reflected by the great variety of

---

14. J.H. Kumpf, "Petition", in *Handwörterbuch zur deutschen Rechtsgeschichte*, 5 vols (Berlin, 1971–1998), vol. 3, pp. 1639–1646 [hereafter, *HRG*]; Renate Blickle, "Supplikationen und Demonstrationen", in Werner Rösener (ed.), *Formen der Kommunikation in der ländlichen Gesellschaft* (Göttingen, 2000), pp. 263–317.

15. See Beat Kümin and Andreas Würgler, "Petitions, *Gravamina* and the Early Modern State: Local Influence on Central Legislation in England and Germany (Hesse)", *Parliaments, Estates and Representation*, 17 (1997), pp. 39–60, 43–44.

vernacular terms.[16] The ancient Roman law term *supplicatio* was adopted by the Pope's chancellery and thus arrived at the emerging territorial states in central Europe during the fifteenth century. The latter used *supplicatio* for various traditional forms of requests, demands, and complaints.[17]

Several attempts have been made to classify the various kinds of supplications. The historical auxiliary sciences defined supplications as private writings to the government, and distinguish between mere requests (for material help), formal demands (applications, requests for licences, permits, dispensations etc.) and complaints against the government or law courts.[18] Legal historians distinguished between supplications for favours and supplications for justice, but these terms neither correspond to source terms nor have they been fully adopted by modern researchers. Supplications for favours are said to be requests to higher persons – commonly the prince – for an act of mercy or aid, whereas supplications for justice focus on judicial or administrative matters and are usually directed against an opponent or linked to an extrajudicial procedure or a formalized legal remedy in an ordinary court process. The second case comes close to legal means of redress as the right of appeal or revision.[19]

The congeniality of petitioning and praying – in German, *Bitten und Beten* – points to the religious dimension of petitions calling for mercy. While *gravamina* tried to legitimize themselves with arguments of equity and justice, supplications hoped for acts of grace by the addressees.[20] The rulers' power of grace and mercy echoed God's mercy towards repentant sinners and conferred metaphysical legitimation.[21] As the catholic subjects of the Prince Abbot of Kempten wrote in their supplication: "Your princely grace are somehow our God on earth and know [...] that you get closest to God by your clemency and mercy".[22] The analogy to religious

16. German: *Bitte, Bittschrift, Bittzettel, Klagzettel, Memorial, Gesuch, Ansuchen, Anbringen, Vorstellung, Ansprache* etc; English: besides petition, supplication, request, demand, complaint, appeal, remonstrance, etc; French: *supplication, supplique, requête, remonstrances, representation,* etc.
17. Rosi Fuhrmann, Beat Kümin and Andreas Würgler, "Supplizierende Gemeinden. Aspekte einer vergleichenden Quellenbetrachtung", in Blickle, *Gemeinde und Staat*, pp. 267–323, 287–288, 320–321; Blickle, "Supplikationen", p. 275. The vast number of meanings of *Bitte* are listed in *Deutsches Rechtswörterbuch*, vol. 2 (Weimar, 1932–1935), pp. 351–353.
18. Heinrich Otto Meisner, *Archivalienkunde vom 16. Jahrhundert bis 1918* (Göttingen, 1969), p. 181.
19. See Jürgen Weitzel, "Rechtsmittel", in *HRG*, vol. 4, pp. 315–322; G. Buchda, "Appellation", in *ibid.*, vol. 1, pp. 196–200. The distinction between supplications for grace and justice has already been made by Heinrich Zedler, *Universal-Lexicon*, vol. 31 (Halle [etc.], 1744), pp. 364–365.
20. Cf. the distinction of Johann Jacob Moser, *Von den Teutschen Reichs-Stände Landen [...]* (Frankfurt, 1769, repr. Osnabrück 1967/1968), pp. 1189–1190.
21. H. Krause, "Gnade", in *HRG*, vol. 1, pp. 1714–1719.
22. *Recueil oder Zusammentragung einiger Piecen so die Gravamina der Stifft-Kemptischen Landschafften betreffen* (n.p., 1721), no. 7, pp. 11–14, 12.

practices is underlined by the genuflection with which supplicants stressed both the urgency of the request and their low status vis-à-vis the addressee when handing in their supplications. In order to influence a ruler's clemency, petitioners tended to promise either to pray to God for the ruler's good health and happy government – as mostly during the late Middle Ages and in catholic areas,[23] or to be obedient and improve the observance of orders – as mostly in protestant areas and during the seventeenth and eighteenth centuries.[24]

Petitioning was a general practice. The saying "nobody is forbidden to hand in supplications and appeals"[25] is reflected by the large quantity of supplications from almost anybody to all sorts of recipients surviving in the archives. The mechanism of supplication was independent of social position. Supplications could be addressed to persons who held power-positions themselves or who were, by informal or institutional means, close to power-positions and thus able to do a favour. This ability of course increased in line with the height of the position in the hierarchy. Therefore, most of the supplications were addressed from the bottom to the top, frequently to state or church authorities. But supplicating was possible among equals, as in bureaucratic communication between authorities, or in diplomatic communication between states.[26] Many occasions to supplicate arose even between business partners, members of families, or client networks. The famous composer, Johann Sebastian Bach, for example, supplicated his mentor, Georg Erdmann, to recommend himself for a better job.[27] Even the most formally powerful man could be found writing a supplication. Emperor Rudolf II petitioned the Frankfurt city council to provide skilled gunsmiths for the campaign against the Ottoman Empire. The city council entered this imperial letter in the 1601 volume of the *Ratssupplikationen* (supplications to the council) along with a supplication from a journeyman carpenter, in jail because of bodily injury, pleading for mercy, and the supplication of the bookbinder,

23. Arlette Farge and Michel Foucault, *Familiäre Konflikte. Die "lettres de cachet"* (Frankfurt, 1989), p. 58 (French original: Paris, 1982); Renate Blickle, "Intercessione: Suppliche in favore di altri in terra ed in cielo", in Cecilia Nubola and Andreas Würgler (eds), *Suppliche e gravamina. Politica, amministrazione, giustizia negli Stati Italiani e nel Sacro Romano Impero (secc. 14–18)* (Bologna, 2001) (forthcoming).
24. StAM 5 no. 15580, fos 4r–5v (the reformed city of Kassel, 1722); StAF RS 1601 1, fo. 7, (to the Lutheran city council of Frankfurt). In England however the phrase "your petitioners shall (ever) pray etc." has been in use since the early seventeenth century; David Nicholls, "Addressing God as a Ruler: Prayer and Petition", in *British Journal of Sociology*, 44 (1993), pp. 125–141, 128.
25. Helmut Neuhaus, "Supplikationen als landesgeschichtliche Quellen. Das Beispiel der Landgrafschaft Hessen im 16. Jahrhundert [Teile 1 und 2]", *Hessisches Jahrbuch für Landesgeschichte*, 28/29 (1978/1979), pp. 110–190, and 63–97, 1, 137.
26. H. Zedler, *Universal-Lexicon*, vol. 3 (Leipzig [etc.], 1733), p. 1994.
27. Letter dating from 28 October 1730, in Walther Killy (ed.), *18. Jahrhundert. Texte und Zeugnisse*, vol. 1 (Munich, 1983), pp. 158–159.

Nikolaus Weitz, asking for readmission to the guild, after having been banned because his wife had given birth to their child "too early".[28] In social terms, supplications needed not always be directed from bottom to top. The direction depended on particular power relations in given situations.[29]

According to the decentralized political structure of central Europe, petitions, *gravamina* and supplications can be found in many archives and various contexts. *Gravamina* are usually stored in files regarding specific representative assemblies or revolts. They may contain originals or copies (in full text) of the *gravamina* or just briefly summarized notes. Additionally, the *gravamina*'s contents can be recovered from official registers (protocols) and answers (resolutions), administrative reports, and expert opinions.[30]

As distinguished from *gravamina*, which commonly contain whole lists of articles, supplications often just dealt with one specific matter.[31] Depending on their content, supplications may be found in any file or department. Thus any complete and systematic treatment of supplications must remain illusory. Permanent or selective protocols or registers of supplications do not contain full-text versions, but aggregate great amounts of information about the petitioner, the supplications' contents and sometimes their treatment by the authorities.[32] These protocols could originate from diverse departments of state administration. In the protestant landgraviate of Hesse-Kassel, for example, most supplications were addressed to the central authority which redistributed them to the departments concerned, whereas in the city republic of Bern the petitioners sent their supplications directly to the department concerned.[33]

Some original supplications were stored in separate files in the early

28. StAF RS 1601 2, fos 268r–272v (25 and 30 June).

29. Eberhard Isenmann, "Gravamen", in Gert Ueding (ed.), *Historisches Wörterbuch der Rhetorik*, vol. 3 (Darmstadt, 1996), pp. 1183–1188. For the thesis that supplications were always directed bottom-up see Blickle, "Supplikationen", p. 279.

30. Andreas Schmauder, *Württemberg im Aufstand. Der Arme Konrad 1514* (Leinfelden-Echterdingen, 1998), pp. 83, 147–154.

31. As a rule in Schleswig-Holstein since 1719; Otto Ulbricht, "Supplikationen als Ego-Dokumente. Bittschriften von Leibeigenen aus der ersten Hälfte des 17. Jahrhunderts als Beispiel", in Winfried Schulze (ed.), *Ego-Dokumente: Annäherung an den Menschen in der Geschichte?* (Berlin, 1996), pp. 149–174, 155.

32. For a description of this source see Neuhaus, "Supplikationen", I, pp. 116–121, 141–145. Cf. Würgler, "Suppliche", pp. 517–521; Württemberg protocols (Sekretärsprotokolle des Oberrats, 34 meters) registered every arriving supplication 1579–1777; Landwehr, *Policey*, p. 282. Many archives lack special files or protocols, e.g. for Bavaria; Renate Blickle, "Die Supplikantin und der Landesherr (1629)", in Eva Labouvie (ed.), *Ungleiche Paare* (Munich, 1997), pp. 81–99 and 212–216, 93–97, 214, n. 25.

33. StAM Protokolle 2, Kassel Cc 6, Bd. 2a (1786) und Cc 7, Bd. 2a (1787); Erika Flückiger, "Zwischen Wohlfahrt und Staatsökonomie. Armenfürsorge auf der bernischen Landschaft im 18. Jahrhundert" (Ph.D., University of Bern, 2000), pp. 20–21.

modern period,[34] but often without elaborating on the principles of selection;[35] other such files seem to have been created by nineteenth-century archivists.[36] Many supplications, however, have been destroyed by contemporaries,[37] or in the nineteenth century because they were considered to be worthless.[38]

Protocols and registers with more or less serial data have enjoyed special interest so far.[39] But they probably only document the tip of the iceberg, because local authorities had been advised since the fifteenth century to deal with all supplications at the lowest possible level.[40] And, of course, there were many oral requests which have never been registered at all,[41] and many written supplications have simply disappeared. Nevertheless, the archives of Frankfurt, for example, a city with 20,000 to 30,000 inhabitants during the early modern period, contain about 130,000 supplications to the council from 1600–1810.[42]

Supplications and *gravamina* occasionally got printed by their authors. The revolutionary Twelve Articles of the German peasants in 1525 reached twenty-eight imprints. During the seventeenth and eighteenth centuries most protest movements printed their *gravamina* and supplications with a

---

34. In Frankfurt around 1600.

35. E.g. at Zurich only the supplications for improved salary, privileges for inventions or printing books and for pardon; according to information from Dr Otto Sigg, StAZH, 4 February 1997.

36. Gerd Schwerhoff, "Das Kölner Supplikenwesen in der Frühen Neuzeit", in Georg Mölich and Gerd Schwerhoff (eds), *Köln als Kommunikationszentrum* (Köln, 2000), pp. 473–496, 474–475.

37. In Bavaria since 1566; Renate Blickle, "Laufen gen Hof. Die Beschwerden der Untertanen und die Entstehung des Hofrats in Bayern", in Blickle, *Gemeinde und Staat*, pp. 241–266, 244. At Bern the supplications for alms at least in the eighteenth century; Flückiger, "Armenfürsorge", p. 63.

38. StAM: protocols before 1786; StAF: supplications before 1600.

39. Ludwig Schmugge *et al.*, *Die Supplikenregister der päpstlichen Pönitentiarie aus der Zeit Pius' I (1458–1464)* (Tübingen, 1996); *idem, Kirche, Kinder, Karrieren. Päpstliche Dispense von der unehelichen Geburt im Spätmittelalter* (Zurich, 1995); Filippo Tamburini, *Santi e peccatori. Confessioni e suppliche dai Registri della Penitenzieria dell'Archivio Segreto Vaticano (1451–1586)* (Milan, 1995). Cf. Neuhaus, "Supplikationen"; André Holenstein, "Bittgesuche, Gesetze und Verwaltung: Zur Praxis 'guter Policey' in Gemeinde und Staat des Ancien Régime am Beispiel der Markgrafschaft Baden(-Durlach)", in Blickle, *Gemeinde und Staat*, pp. 325–357.

40. Blickle, "Laufen gen Hof", pp. 263–264 (Bavaria, fifteenth century); Fuhrmann, Kümin and Würgler, "Supplizierende Gemeinden", p. 307 (Hesse, sixteenth century); Landwehr, *Policey*, p. 279 (Württemberg, seventeenth century).

41. Fuhrmann, Kümin and Würgler, "Supplizierende Gemeinden", pp. 306–313; Niklaus Landolt, *Untertanenrevolten und Widerstand auf der Basler Landschaft im 16. und 17. Jahrhundert* (Liestal, 1996), p. 139.

42. Kind information from M. Lauterwald, StAF, 16 April 1996. The number 130,000 is my extrapolation according to StAF, RS 1601, 1 and 2, as well as "Repertorium 559, Rats- und Präfektursupplikationen, Verpackungsprotokoll".

view to governments, (imperial) law-courts and the public sphere.[43] Periodical journals and newspapers might reprint *gravamina* as well as governments' ordinances concerning supplications and other matters.[44]

COLLECTIVE PETITIONS AND CONFLICTS

Collective petitions may be classified according to the social background of their authors, respectively the specific contexts of their production, into: *gravamina* by representative bodies at institutionalized assemblies, rebels' *gravamina* by protest movements, and heterogeneous collective supplications by various corporations and institutions, families and neighbourhoods, or ad-hoc groups.

Gravamina and representative assemblies

In early modern Europe the typical form of institutionalized participation by relevant social groups consisted in representative assemblies. Here the monarch or prince negotiated with the estates – nobles, clergymen, towns, and peasants – about taxes, *gravamina* and other important matters.[45] In central Europe these assemblies or diets mostly worked on a territorial level. The estates' participatory power varied according to the territory and century, from the mere right of being heard to the decisive right of consent. The estates reached the peak of their power in the fifteenth and sixteenth centuries and were then weakened by the emerging absolutist states in the Empire and the expanding city republics within the Swiss Confederation.[46]

Gravamina have been a central source for researchers on representative institutions. By the nineteenth century, historians tried to link liberal political demands, such as the right to assemble and to petition for legislation, with the old custom of collective drafting and signing of

---

43. Blickle, *Revolution von 1525*, pp. 23–24; Würgler, *Unruhen und Öffentlichkeit*, pp. 133–157, 339–345; cf. David Zaret, *Origins of Democratic Culture: Printing, Petitions and the Public Sphere in Early Modern England* (Princeton, NJ, 2000), pp. 81–99, 217–265.
44. Würgler, *Unruhen und Öffentlichkeit*, pp. 202–226; e.g. *Casselische Zeitung/ von Policey, Commercien, und andern dem Publico dienlichen Sachen*, no. LI, 20 December 1734 (ordinance about supplications for oak wood).
45. Peter Blickle, "Conclusions", in *idem* (ed.) *Resistance, Representation, and Community* (Oxford, 1997), pp. 325–338, 333–334; *idem*, *Kommunalismus*, 2 vols (Munich, 2000), vol. 2, pp. 263–285.
46. *Idem*, "Mit den Gemeinden Staat machen", in *idem*, *Gemeinde und Staat*, pp. 1–20, 12–16; Wim Blockmans, "Representation (since the thirteenth century)", in Christopher Allmand (ed.), *The New Cambridge Medieval History*, vol. 7 (Cambridge [etc.], 1998), pp. 29–64; for Switzerland see André Holenstein, "Ständeversammlungen", in *Historisches Lexikon der Schweiz*, www.dhs.ch.

gravamina in assemblies.[47] More recent research underlined this thesis by showing how the *gravamina* of peasants and burghers, for example of the Tyrol in 1525, became the *Landesordnung* (law code) in use until the eighteenth century.[48]

But even during the so-called era of absolutism, the impact of *gravamina* on legislation in a medium-sized German territory was much greater than assumed by older legal and regional histories. In Hesse-Kassel the echo of the estates' – nobles and towns – demands can even be heard in the police ordinances which used to be considered as pure expressions of the princely will. The range of problems raised by *gravamina* covered taxes, disputes about the competence of princely and urban law courts, the concurrence of town guilds and rural crafts, the quartering of soldiers, damage done by game, legislation on luxury, Jews and their economic activities etc. Sometimes the estates urged to improve the schools, to publish the law code, to construct new factories, to take care of wood and forest and so on.[49]

Gravamina allow the study of social, economical, juridical and political conflicts between estates or greater social groups and the state, and the comparison of *gravamina* with state legislation may show the estates' influence on state building.

Gravamina and revolts

Whereas estates had the right to write and hand in *gravamina* at representative assemblies, the protest movements, after the traumatic failure of the Peasants' Revolt in 1525,[50] were increasingly criminalized for drafting demands at communal assemblies. Rebels' *gravamina* have been the main source for research on revolts.[51]

Investigations of the *contents* of rebels' *gravamina* have allowed the answering of crucial questions from the viewpoint of the actors. Thus, older judgements, created by contemporary governments and more or less

---

47. E.g. Burckhard Wilhelm Pfeiffer, *Geschichte der landständischen Verfassung in Kurhessen* (Kassel, 1834).

48. Peter Blickle, *Landschaften im Alten Reich. Die staatliche Funktion des gemeinen Mannes* (Munich, 1973), pp. 200–218.

49. Andreas Würgler, "Desideria und Landesordnungen. Kommunaler und landständischer Einfluß auf die fürstliche Gesetzgebung in Hessen-Kassel 1650–1800", in Blickle, *Gemeinde und Staat*, pp. 149–207, 168–191.

50. Winfried Schulze, *Bäuerlicher Widerstand und feudale Herrschaft in der frühen Neuzeit* (Stuttgart-Bad Cannstadt, 1980), pp. 73–74; Peter Blickle, "The Criminalization of Peasant Resistance in the Holy Roman Empire", *The Journal of Modern History*, 58 (1986), Supplement, pp. S88–S97.

51. See Schulze, *Bäuerlicher Widerstand* (1980); Peter Blickle (ed.), *Aufruhr und Empörung?* (Munich, 1980); idem, *Unruhen in der ständischen Gesellschaft 1300–1800* (Munich, 1988).

repeated by historians, who just blamed "the peoples traditional inclination to rebel", were quickly revised.[52] The *causes* of protest might be summarized by the phrase "novelties create unrest". Such novelties could concern new taxes, labour services, feudal rents, but also religion, state intrusion into communal autonomy, and so on.[53] The study of rebels' *gravamina* thus offers refined statements about the relative importance of the various causes.

The same holds true for the rebels' *goals*. One might distinguish reforming from revolutionary demands. The latter are to be found in the context of peasants' wars (Germany 1525, Upper Austria 1594 and 1626, Switzerland 1653). But usually *gravamina* just aimed to reform the abuses mentioned as causes of revolts; progressive requests were secondary or hidden behind traditional arguments of *legitimation* (the "good old law"), yet they existed: dissolving feudalism, the utopia of the free village, political participation through representative assemblies, a republican government or just "turning Swiss".[54]

The authorities' reaction to *gravamina* was a crucial moment in the *course* of revolts. The government of the city republic of Zurich in 1653, for example, allowed its subjects to voice grievances and handled them with clemency, thus avoiding the military escalation which haunted neighbouring territories.[55] In contrast, the dilatory treatment of the citizens' supplication, with only four articles from 17 June 1612 by the Frankfurt city council, aggravated conflict: by mid-September the citizens and guilds had handed in more than 200 *gravamina*.[56] Comparable processes evolved in territorial states such as the duchy of Württemberg, where local resistance against a new tax grew to a territorial revolt with about 400 regional and local *gravamina*.[57] The authorities' refusal to communicate expanded and radicalized the protest, but split it up too. Some protest movements, however, succeeded in eliminating *gravamina* that were too particular, and handed in only commonly consented lists of general grievances, such as the 115 articles in Zurich in 1713. If the authorities reacted with repression, the protest movements took their

52. Quoted in Würgler, *Unruhen und Öffentlichkeit*, p. 65.
53. Blickle, *Unruhen*, pp. 80–82. For Switzerland see Andreas Würgler, "Soziale Konflikte (Mittelalter und Frühe Neuzeit)", in *Historisches Lexikon der Schweiz*, www.dhs.ch.
54. Thomas A. Brady, Jr, *Turning Swiss: Cities and Empire, 1450–1550* (Cambridge [etc.], 1985), pp. 34–42; Blickle, *Unruhen*, pp. 84–86.
55. *Geschichte des Kantons Zürich*, vol. 2 (Zurich, 1996), p. 316.
56. Partially reprinted in Friedrich Bothe, *Frankfurts wirtschaftlich-soziale Entwicklung vor dem Dreißigjährigen Kriege und der Fettmilchaufstand (1612–1616)* (Frankfurt, 1920). For the revolt in general see Matthias Meyn, *Die Reichsstadt Frankfurt vor dem Bürgeraufstand von 1612 bis 1614* (Frankfurt, 1980).
57. Schmauder, *Württemberg im Aufstand*, pp. 153–154, 287.

gravamina to external powers and/or the imperial law-courts – or turned to conspiracy and went underground, as in Bern in 1749.[58]

The results of comparing *gravamina* from diverse revolts and regions can be classified according to main causes – e.g. tax, food and religious revolts – or according to main targets – antifeudal, antistate, anti-Jewish rebellions. The comparison of the *gravamina's* aims with the conflict's outcome allow us to judge the success of revolts. Whether the outcome had modernizing effects or not is a matter for discussion. At any rate, the definition of human rights has been linked to the tradition of revolts (especially if treated by law courts)[59] as well as the consolidation of notions like property, liberty, and participation.[60] Finally, the thesis was advanced that urban and rural protest movements, with their printed petitions, contributed to the making and politicizing of the public sphere.[61] In general, research on revolts has turned humble subjects into historical actors and changed the topos of the "obedient German". Revolts are now considered to be a structural element of early modern political culture not only in Switzerland, as they have been since the nineteenth century, but also in the Holy Roman Empire.[62]

Supplications and conflicting groups

Notwithstanding their high frequency, revolts have remained extraordinary events. The greater part of daily social conflicts has involved less spectacular, but very complex, clashes between rival groups, corporations, communities, and institutions, between themselves or with the state. The confrontation between communities and states has more often taken the form of verbal supplication than of armed violence. Communities, for example, regularly petitioned for confirmation of their privileges against the expanding central bureaucracy. They handed in countless requests for deferment, reduction, and abolition of taxes, fees and services, for alms and

---

58. Andreas Würgler, "Conspiracy and Denunciation: A Local Affair and its European Publics (Bern, 1749)", in James Melton (ed.), *Constructing Publics: Cultures of Communication in the Early Modern German Lands* (Aldershot, 2001) (forthcoming).
59. Winfried Schulze, "Der bäuerliche Widerstand und die Rechte der Menschheit", in Günter Birtsch (ed.), *Grund- und Freiheitsrechte von der ständischen zur spätbürgerlichen Gesellschaft* (Göttingen, 1987), pp. 42–64.
60. Blickle, *Unruhen*, p. 109, referring to Renate Blickle.
61. Würgler, *Unruhen und Öffentlichkeit*.
62. Peter Blickle, *Deutsche Untertanen. Ein Widerspruch* (Munich, 1981); *idem*, *Unruhen*, pp. 2, 4–5, 97. Most recently te Brake, *Shaping History*, pp. 5–8, 183–188; for Switzerland see Rudolf Braun, *Das ausgehende Anien Régime in der Schweiz* (Göttingen, 1984), pp. 256–313; Andreas Würgler, "Revolution aus Tradition", in Andreas Ernst *et al.* (eds), *Revolution und Innovation* (Zurich, 1998), pp. 79–90.

contributions, and made many complaints against abuses in jurisdiction and administration.[63]

Disputes between (neighbouring) communes about boundaries, the use of pastures, water and forests, the partition of feudal services and state taxes, but also about the village's honour or the marriage market, were abundant. If they could not be settled by ritual forms, or by negotiating with petitions and counterpetitions, they ended up in the law courts. Historical research into conflict has hardly touched upon this sort of quarrel so far.

Group petitions offer insights into the various possible conflict lines within a single community. Frequently, the burghers or citizens attacked their elected organs (burgomaster, councils, juries etc.) for misrule and corruption, and demanded more information about finances and more participation in communal politics.[64] Communities frequently split into two (rarely more) factions.[65] Thereafter, the factions argued about "false supplications",[66] specifically about which of them was empowered to speak in the community's name. On the other hand, communities sometimes banded together against single individuals, as, for example, against the election of a particular individual as burgomaster, or against the confirmation of a residence permit for a Jew; or petitioned for an act of mercy towards a fellow citizen banned from a protestant territory for having married a catholic.[67] But supplications and denunciations of villagers triggered witch-hunting and the expulsion of gypsies and beggars as well.[68] Within the villages, smallholders and freeholders squabbled about access to communal lands or the distribution of tax and service obligations.[69]

Social conflicts generated many ad-hoc groups. These were not linked by institutionalized structures but driven to joint action by a specific constellation of problems and interests, as the examples from Hesse-Kassel show. In 1679, the freshly married husbands of the town of Eschwege petitioned for tax relief in the first year after a wedding; in 1717, the cow farmers of Breitnau petitioned for a licence to keep goats.[70] In 1786, eight

---

63. Fuhrmann, Kümin and Würgler, "Supplizierende Gemeinden", pp. 314–319.

64. Würgler, "Desideria", pp. 165–168; Fuhrmann, Kümin and Würgler, "Supplizierende Gemeinden", pp. 270–272; beyond Hesse, see Würgler, *Unruhen und Öffentlichkeit*, pp. 12–14, 46–52, 61–70, 78–85, 99–115.

65. David Martin Luebke, *His Majesty's Rebels: Communities, Factions, and Rural Revolt in the Black Forest, 1725–1745* (Ithaca, NY [etc.], 1997).

66. StAM 5 no. 14941, fo. 127v (Spangenberg c. 1706).

67. StAM 17e Immenhausen no. 104 (1687); 17e Frankenberg no. 143 (late seventeenth century); 17e Grebendorf no. 5 (1629).

68. Würgler, "Suppliche", p. 538.

69. Friedrich Küch, "Eine Visitation der Obergrafschaft Katzenelnbogen im Jahre 1514", in *Archiv für Hessische Geschichte und Altertumskunde*, N.F. 9 (1914), pp. 145–254, 228–229; Braun, *Das ausgehende Ancien Régime*, pp. 94–100, 148–161; Albert Schnyder-Burghartz, *Alltag und Lebensformen auf der Basler Landschaft um 1700* (Liestal, 1992), pp. 231–254, 387–388.

70. StAM 17e Eschwege no. 81 (1679); StAM 17e, Breitnau no. 2 (1717).

soldiers' widows of Rinteln, fifteen poor of Hersfeld, and in 1575, some fire victims at Felsberg joined forces in drafting supplications for tax reductions.[71] Such groups could gather for spontaneous actions even on a wider regional level as, for example, all the innkeepers of the district of Rodenburg or all the butchers of the districts of Broda and Steinbach in 1786.[72]

Guilds or corporations were engaged in conflicts in many ways. Given their main function to secure an honourable income for their members, they petitioned quite successfully against any plans to install new trades or factories, the formation of other guilds, country journeymen, and confessional refugees.[73] Guilds were not only the authors but also the recipients of supplications about applications for membership, or the waiving of fines or duties.[74] Within a single guild, very often the journeymen sided against the masters. These quarrels were shaped more by rituals than by petitioning, but, nevertheless, journeymen could petition the council as well as their masters.[75]

Family disputes are sometimes documented in supplications. Besides the well-known quarrels about heritage and marriage, they dealt with problems of family relations and education. In early seventeenth-century Frankfurt, the widow Clara Timpel complained about her delinquent son Henry, and supplicated the council to exile him, or send him to jail for at least three years at her cost. The council fulfilled the request. Henry immediately petitioned to be sent on the military campaign against the Ottoman Empire, and promised not to disturb his mother or the city of Frankfurt for three years. The council agreed again.[76] Obviously, the Timpel family made use of state institutions to solve their educational problem. Families petitioned nearly as often to imprison as to release family members.[77] When Arlette Farge and Michel Foucault investigated

71. StAM Protokolle 2, Kassel Cc 6, Bd. 2a, Rinteln, 14 September 1786, no. 53; *ibid.*, no. 91/76, 10 February 1786 (Hersfeld); StAM 17e Felsberg no. 5 (1575).

72. StAM Protokolle 2, Kassel Cc 6, Bd. 2a, Rinteln, 24 September 1786, Nos. 75/679 and 97.

73. Würgler, "Desideria", pp. 201–203. In general see Wehler, *Deutsche Gesellschaftsgeschichte*, vol. 1, pp. 90–94, 110–112.

74. StAF RS 1601 2, fos 252, 256. Similar cases: ebd., fo. 133 (mason Jost Wolff), fo. 176 (goldsmith Sebastian Rese), fo. 268 (bookbinder Nikolaus Weitz).

75. Kocka, *Weder Stand noch Klasse*, pp. 179–185; Katharina Simon-Muscheid, *Basler Handwerkszünfte im Spätmittelalter. Zunftinterne Strukturen und innerstädtische Konflikte* (Bern [etc.], 1988), pp. 247, 294–301.

76. StAF RS 1601 2, fos 172r–173v (9 June), fos 203r–204v (16 June); BMB 1601, fo. 29v (9 June), fo. 35r (16 June).

77. StAF RS 1601 2, fos 29r–v, 96r–97r, 126r–127v, 140. Cf. Hoffmann, "Außergerichtliche Einigungen", pp. 573–575 (Augsburg, sixteenth century); André Holenstein, "Klagen, anzeigen und supplizieren. Kommunikative Praktiken und Konfliktlösungsverfahren in der Markgrafschaft Baden im 18. Jahrhundert", in Magnus Eriksson and Barbara Krug-Richter (eds), *Streitkultur(en)* (Cologne [etc.], 2001), (forthcoming).

this form of state service by imprisonment in Paris, they noticed, with surprise, the great desire of the people for authoritarian resolutions of family conflicts.[78] These empirical findings have stimulated the theoretical turn in Foucault's oeuvre from the concept of "discipline" to the concept of *gouvernementalité*.[79]

Apart from families and authorities, neighbourhoods played an important role in the regulation of social relations and conflicts. While villagers, youth groups, and journeymen sanctioned violations of moral laws with ritual punishments such as rough music (*charivari*),[80] neighbours could write supplications to the authorities, as did some residents of the Arnoldsgasse at Sachsenhausen (near Frankfurt) who complained in c.1600 about the "loose Epicurean house keeping" of Dilman Dietz's wife.[81]

Group supplications and petitions were normally concerned with everyday problems. But in situations of revolt they might utter revolutionary claims. In 1525 peasants from upper Swabia and the guilds of the city of Basle both demanded the reformation of the Church, and in 1798 patriotic clubs in the Pays de Vaud petitioned for the revolutionizing of their country.[82]

INDIVIDUAL PETITIONS AND CONFLICTS

Most of all, supplications seem to have been written or initiated by individuals. Because of the lack of systematic quantifying studies, some evidence has to be taken from various small samples that show individual supplications as constituting from 50 to over 80 per cent of the whole.[83] According to time, region, and context, the women's share lies between 3

78. Farge and Foucault, *Familiäre Konflikte*, p. 273.

79. Thomas Lemke, *Eine Kritik der politischen Vernunft. Foucaults Analyse der modernen Gouvernementalität* (Berlin [etc.], 1997), pp. 126, 143.

80. E.P. Thompson, "'Rough music' oder englische Katzenmusik", in *idem, Plebeische Kultur und moralische Ökonomie* (Frankfurt, 1980), pp. 131–168, 347–361; Albert Hauser, *Was für ein Leben. Alltag in der Schweiz vom 15. bis 18. Jahrhundert* (Zurich, 1987), pp. 216–218.

81. StAF RS 1601 2, fos 199r–201v (Dietz). For religious and disciplinary courts, see Heinrich R. Schmidt, *Dorf und Religion. Reformierte Sittenzucht in Berner Landgemeinden der Frühen Neuzeit* (Stuttgart [etc.], 1995), pp. 291–350.

82. Blickle, *Revolution von 1525*, pp. 23–30; Simon-Muscheid, *Basler Handwerkszünfte*, p. 301; Andreas Würgler, "Abwesender Revolutionär – moderate Revolution: Frédéric-César Laharpe und die Waadt 1789–1798", in: Christian Simon (ed.), *Blicke auf die Helvetik* (Basel, 2000), pp. 139–159.

83. Hessen-Kassel 1594: 62.7 per cent in which N = 543 (Neuhaus, "Supplikationen", vol. 1, p. 126); Baden-Durlach 1798: 84.4 per cent in which N = 148 (Holenstein, "Bittgesuche", p. 336). My samples, A.W.: Hessen, Obergrafschaft Katzenelnbogen, Visitation 1514: 50 per cent in which N = 84 (my analysis of the protocol printed in Küch, "Visitation", pp. 192–218); Frankfurt 1601: 80.8 per cent in which N = 73 (StAF RS 1601 2, June); Hessen-Kassel, Gemeinde Oldendorf 1728: 83.6 per cent in which N = 61 (StAM 17e Oldendorf no. 6,

and 34 per cent.[84] Their great number alone secures the social and historical relevance of individual supplications. They will be discussed first by particular examples, and then from the perspective of their great number, without forgetting the similarities and synergies between individual and collective supplications and *gravamina*.

Singular supplications

Supplications have been drafted on highly varied occasions: in times of catastrophes, about administrative procedures or individual exposure to social problems. Many pleaded for help in situations of need and trouble, such as disasters and accidents, or imprisonment, illness, and death of family members. Margaretha Liechtensteiner, for example, was left a widow eight weeks after having given birth to her child. Her husband left her nothing but debts. In April 1583, she petitioned Zurich city council for a job as teacher. She argued that she needed to improve her situation and that she had learned to write as a girl. The council refused her application, but offered her alms of grain.[85] Countless supplications of that kind have been written, and accepted or rejected by various recipients. The chances of success might depend on sophisticated lobbying, as in sixteenth-century Bern or eighteenth-century Amsterdam.[86] The French philosopher, Voltaire, while prisoner in Frankfurt after his dispute with king Frederick II of Prussia in 1753, wrote several supplications a day, which he sent not only to the city council, but also to the Emperor, the Prussian and French kings etc. – and to newspapers.[87]

The growth of bureaucracy increased the occasions to petition, because petitioning became part of ordinary administrative procedures regarding applications for public positions,[88] membership of a corporation or community, safe conduct of Jews, permits of residence, marriage licences

Supplikenprotokoll); Hessen-Kassel 1786: 62.9 per cent in which N = 89 (StAM Protokolle, Kassel Cc6, Bd. 2a, January–February 1786); Hessen-Kassel, Rinteln 1786: 87.7 per cent in which N = 65 (StAM Protokolle, Kassel Cc6, Bd. 2a, Rinteln 14 September 1786); Hessen-Kassel 1787: 83.6 per cent in which N = 55 (StAM Protokolle, Kassel Cc7, Bd. 2a, January).

84. Samples as above: Hessen 1514: 3 per cent; Hessen-Kassel 1594, 1596, 1787: 13 per cent; Hessen (Oldendorf) 1728: 34 per cent. Schwerhoff, "Kölner Supplikenwesen", p. 482, estimates the women's share at 25 to 33 per cent.

85. StAZH A 92.1 no. 69, (27 April 1583).

86. Simon Teuscher, *Bekannte – Klienten – Verwandte. Sozialität und Politik in der Stadt Bern um 1500* (Cologne [etc.], 1998), pp. 218–234; Henk van Nierop, "Popular participation in politics in the Dutch Republic", in Blickle, *Resistance*, pp. 272– 291, 285.

87. Cf. Voltaire, *Correspondance*, vol. 3, Theodore Besterman (ed.) (Paris, 1975), pp. 967–968, 980–983.

88. E.g. StAF RS 1601 2, fos 5, 10, 19, 187, 211, 231, 234. Cf. Schwerhoff, "Kölner Supplikenwesen", p. 480.

etc.[89] The supplications of enterprises and inventors for patents offer interesting data about economic and technical innovations. Not all of them remained as transitory as the patented wood-saving oven in Zurich (1575), or the planned coffee house at Frankfurt (1712).[90] But one of the important inventions in the history of culture, the printed periodical newspaper, is only documented by the supplication its inventor sent to the city council of Strasbourg in 1605.[91]

Supplications relating to extrajudicial procedures dealt with social conflicts more directly. Normally, individuals or groups were urged by friends and relatives, neighbours, or officials to seek reconciliation before suing each other. There must have been many informal supplications which left scarce evidence or none, unless they reached the level of written procedures. Some governments offered their subjects the opportunity of reconciliation by sending officials out in the country to hear and decide supplications. The community of Hausen in the landgraviate of Hesse thus complained about the village mayor; both sides were heard and then accepted an agreement. Parties were sent to law courts only if no arrangement could be found.[92] These summary proceedings were much cheaper and faster than formal lawsuits. They complemented legal proceedings throughout the early modern period.[93] One of the leading historians of criminal history assumes that not even 50 per cent of all offences and quarrels appeared in law courts in early modern France. More than half of these legal cases did not end with a verdict, but with the parties' agreement[94] – a phenomenon common to diverse levels of jurisdiction in central Europe as well.[95] In addition to the high speed and low price of summary proceedings, they were particularly attractive

89. Fuhrmann, Kümin and Würgler, "Supplizierende Gemeinden", pp. 312–313; Hans Berner, *Gemeinden und Obrigkeit im fürstbischöflichen Birseck. Herrschaftsverhältnisse zwischen Konflikt und Konsens* (Liestal, 1994), pp. 257–309 (membership); Holenstein, "Bittgesuche", pp. 336–346; André Holenstein, "Bitten um den Schutz: Staatliche Judenpolitik und Lebensführung von Juden im Lichte der Schutzsupplikationen aus der Markgrafschaft Baden(-Durlach) im 18. Jahrhundert, in Rolf Kießling und Sabine Ullmann (eds), *Landjudentum im deutschen Südwesten während der Frühen Neuzeit* (Berlin, 1999), pp. 97–153 (permits of residence); David W. Sabean, *Kinship in Neckarhausen, 1700–1870* (Cambridge, 1998), pp. 63–89 (marriage licences).
90. StAZH A 92.1, nos 49–52 (1575–1577); StAF BMB 1712/1713, fo. 12 (31 Mai 1712).
91. Johannes Weber, "'Unterthenige Supplication Johann Caroli / Buchtruckers'. Der Beginn gedruckter politischer Wochenzeitungen im Jahr 1605", *Archiv für Geschichte des Buchwesens*, 38 (1992), 257–265.
92. Küch, "Visitation", p. 206 (1 July 1514) and p. 211 (4 July 1514).
93. Blickle, "Laufen gen Hof", pp. 265–266. Cf. Hoffmann, "Außergerichtliche Verfahren".
94. Garnot, "Justice", pp. 104, 110.
95. Schwerhoff, "Aktenkundig", pp. 89–90; Martin Fimpel, *Reichsjustiz und Territorialstaat. Württemberg als Kommissar von Kaiser und Reich im Schwäbischen Kreis (1648–1806)* (Tübingen, 1999), pp. 56–61, 104–106, 292–295.

because their agreements sought to restore peace after social conflicts, whereas law courts strove for punishment.[96]

Supplications, however, were also an element of legal proceedings. Petitions for grace by murderers or other sentenced delinquents,[97] as well as supplications for legal remedies (known as "appeals" or "revisions" in legal history), have been extensively analysed.[98]

Many similar supplications

Singular supplications can indicate heavy social tensions if they form part of a large body of similar petitions. At the beginning of the seventeenth century, peasants in Schleswig-Holstein adopted an individual strategy to fight the aggravation of serfdom. Instead of organizing revolts, as their fellows in southern Germany had done in the fifteenth and sixteenth centuries, every serf tried to free himself individually by petitioning, because redress by imperial law courts,[99] as sought by many serfs during the seventeenth and eighteenth centuries,[100] was not an option. Seeking a similar individual path to liberty, many protestants reacted to religious tensions by emigration. But reading the numerous supplications (documenting name, family status, profession, confession, origin, course of escape, and so on) for citizenship in places of refuge such as Geneva, the Swiss protestant towns, and Frankfurt, the mass dimension of these individual choices becomes clear. The acceptance of refugees could, on the other hand, cause serious social conflicts in host towns, as, for example, the Frankfurt revolt of 1612–1614.[101]

An example from this revolt shows how the individual and collective aspects of conflict might be interwoven. In 1615 the citizen, Georg Lauburger, petitioned the council for protection, because during the revolt he had been slandered as "obedient thief and traitor", which threatened his honour as a member of the tailors' guild.[102] Defamation in the political

96. Würgler, "Diffamierung", pp. 334–337; Garnot, "Justice", pp. 109–112.

97. Davis, *Gnadengesuche*; Otto Ulbricht, *Kindsmord und Aufklärung in Deutschland* (Munich, 1990), pp. 376–404; Andreas Bauer, *Das Gnadenbitten in der Strafrechtspflege des 15. und 16. Jahrhunderts* (Frankfurt, 1996).

98. Weitzel, "Rechtsmittel", pp. 318–320.

99. Otto Ulbricht, "'Angemaßte Leibeigenschaft'. Supplikationen von schleswigschen Untertanen gegen ihre Gutsherren zu Beginn des 17. Jahrhunderts", *Demokratische Geschichte*, 6 (1991), pp. 11–34.

100. Würgler, *Unruhen und Öffentlichkeit*, pp. 85–99.

101. Meyn, *Reichsstadt Frankfurt*, pp. 173–174, 201–208, 228–233; Liliane Mottu-Weber, "Genève et ses réfugiés (XVIe–XVII siècles), in Hans-Jörg Gilomen *et al.* (eds), *Migration vers les villes* (Zurich, 2000) pp. 157–170.

102. StAF RS 1615 I, fos 174r–v, 179r–v (16.II.1615).

context of collective protest afflicted the craftsman's social and economic existence, because the revolt did not happen outside the realm of honour. When revolts came to an end, the social tensions could shift from collective violence to individual injuries, as might have been the case in Cologne, where historians noticed a massive increase of defamation cases during, and especially after, the revolt from 1608–1610.[103] In order to avoid this problem and quickly restore social peace, the revolts were often followed by amnesties and general pardons (except for ringleaders).[104]

Supplications for alms were endemic in early modern shortage societies – and remarkably successful: from 1594 to 1602 the count of Hohenlohe approved 96 per cent of supplications for firewood and 95 per cent of supplications for grain support.[105] In the city republic of Bern, the alms commission granted 87 per cent of c.1,900 requests in the years 1730–1732, and 99 per cent of c.11,700 in 1780–1782, thus supporting 5 per cent of all the territory's households. Even if one considers that these Bernese supplications had to be approved by local officials, the success rate remains high. Supplications for alms increased during the eighteenth century in absolute figures, as well as in relation to population levels. Thus the modernization of welfare bureaucracy and social politics by the Bernese government appears to have been a mere reaction to growing popular demands.[106]

Granting requests mercifully not only affected state expenses, but also state income. Petitioners paid considerable dispensation fees which could be spent on welfare or education.[107] Needless to say, it was possible to petition for the release of dispensation fees as well.[108] The above mentioned count of Hohenlohe approved no less than 72 per cent of supplications for tax reductions or deferment.[109] Of course, this ratio changed according to economic, social, and political crisis, but it influenced state finances. It would be interesting to know whether the tax bureaucracies calculated these "losses" when fixing taxes.

The lords' clemency policy affected jurisdiction too. Regional studies prove that more than 80 per cent of documented cases ended with a pardon on petition, which could be a complete remission (50 per cent) or just a

---

103. Schwerhoff, "Kölner Supplikenwesen", pp. 321, 448–450.
104. Würgler, "Diffamierung", pp. 334–337.
105. Thomas Robisheaux, *Rural Society and the Search for Order in Early Modern Germany* (Cambridge, 1989), pp. 172–173.
106. Flückiger, "Armenfürsorge", pp. 63–68, 407–416.
107. Klaus Becker, *Die behördliche Erlaubnis des absolutistischen Fürstenstaates* (Marburg, 1970), pp. 401–407.
108. Johann Jacob Moser, *Von der Landeshoheit in Gnadensachen* (Frankfurt [etc.], 1773), ch. 8, § 11, p. 36; Becker, *Erlaubnis*, p. 412.
109. District of Langenburg, 1594–1602; Robisheaux, *Rural Society*, pp. 172–173. For Hesse-Kassel, see StAM, "Repertorium zu Bestand 5", s.v. "Suppliken, Einzelpersonen", pp. 123–129.

reduction of the punishment (40 per cent).[110] The right to pardon was esteemed to be one of the ruler's most distinguished rights and a main source of princely authority.[111] Whether it was simply a case of arbitrary princely action interfering with a rational juridical apparatus, or, on the contrary, a princely instrument to correct sentences based on social prejudice, has been discussed ever since the eighteenth century.[112]

Even politics was influenced by supplications. Legislative power, considered to be an exclusively princely prerogative in absolutist doctrine, appears to have been strongly influenced by the common practice of petitioning. The preambles of many laws and ordinances mention that the legislation responded to popular complaints, suggestions, and demands, and these claims were not just rhetorical. Urged by large numbers of individual and collective petitions, the Hesse-Kassel government, for example, issued, revised, or abolished ordinances concerning Jews, emigration, domestic servants, quartering etc. Although the government finally decided whether, and when, to issue or revise a law, the legislation process was surely more influenced by subjects than early modern political theory and modern historiography on legislation have so far assumed.[113]

The competence to allow exceptions from general laws in particular circumstances nevertheless belonged exclusively to the ruler (who could delegate it to lower levels of authority).[114] Supplications for dispensation concerned almost all matters regulated by the state (or church). As soon as there existed a law about the number of guests admitted to a wedding,[115] a fire regulation against straw roofs,[116] a guild regulation about journeymen's travels etc., people would petition for dispensation as a matter of course, because they wanted to invite all their relatives to a wedding party, because they could not afford a tiled roof, or because they were unable to travel. The excessive granting of dispensations, i.e. exceptions from the rule, caused difficulties with the general implementation of ordinances.[117]

Since the late fifteenth century, governments had tried to restrain the masses of supplications by ordinances. Despite some restrictive regulations, these ordinances testify to the fact that petitioning remained, in

---

110. Bauer, *Gnadenbitten*, pp. 203, 207. Davis, *Gnadengesuche*, p. 75 gives success-ratios of 93.5 per cent.
111. Davis, *Gnadengesuche*, pp. 26–28; Bauer, *Gnadenbitten*, p. 204.
112. David Martin Luebke, "Frederick the Great and the Celebrated Case of the Millers Arnold (1770–1779): A Reappraisal", *Central European History*, 32 (1999), pp. 379–408, 385–402; Martin Dinges, "Justiznutzungen als soziale Kontrolle in der Frühen Neuzeit", in Blauert and Schwerhoff, *Kriminalitätsgeschichte*, pp. 503–544, 525–532.
113. Würgler, "Desideria", pp. 196–203.
114. Becker, *Erlaubnis*, pp. 17–43; Holenstein, "Umstände", pp. 10–18.
115. StAM 17e Bischhausen no. 66 (1666).
116. StAM 17e Elnhausen no. 38 (1781) and no. 28 (1784).
117. Kümin and Würgler, "Petitions", p. 55.

practice, an unquestionable custom despite the lack of a positive right to petition.[118] Complementary to the ordinances, new institutions, such as the "Supplication-Committee" at the level of the Holy Roman Empire[119] or territorial committees, were installed or planned.[120] Even the coming into existence of central authorities, such as the Duke of Bavaria's "Hofrat" (the court council) in the fifteenth century, has been traced back to the increasing number of supplications.[121] Conversely, supplications also triggered the abolition of institutions such as the "Landrat" in Hesse-Kassel in 1798.[122]

Similarities and synergies

Supplications and *gravamina* were frequently interwoven. Often, *gravamina* also included a petition: after complaining about this or that, texts usually end with a petition to abolish the causes of the *gravamina*. In contrast, many social conflicts started with humble supplications and ended with rebels' *gravamina*. Numerous individual supplications might be gathered and condensed into collective supplications, or even *gravamina*. Denied *gravamina* could be handed in again as humble supplications.[123] Ordinary people could pursue their interests in various ways and make strategic choices between supplications and *gravamina* (as well as other means). By supplications, *gravamina*, and petitions, ordinary people forced their rulers to react to specific problems. They thus played a part in the setting of political agendas.[124]

A common feature of social conflicts on all levels is the need for mediation. On the one hand, the emerging territorial state *sought* the role of mediator by expanding into formerly autonomous local or corporate spheres. But, on the other hand, the state *was sought* by individuals and collectives who trusted in its mediating capacities. By confidently petitioning (and complaining) to the ruler, the subjects triggered expand-

---

118. Neuhaus, "Supplikationen", vol. 1, pp. 115–116; Fuhrmann, Kümin and Würgler, "Supplizierende Gemeinden", pp. 293–296 (Württemberg), pp. 304–313 (Hesse-Kassel); Holenstein, "Bittgesuche", pp. 346–347 (Baden-Durlach); Landolt, *Untertanenrevolten*, p. 137 (Canton of Basle); Van Nierop, "Popular Participation", p. 284 (Amsterdam).
119. Helmut Neuhaus, *Reichstag und Supplikationsausschuß. Ein Beitrag zur Reichsverfassungsgeschichte der ersten Hälfte des 16. Jahrhunderts* (Berlin, 1975).
120. Schwerhoff, "Kölner Supplikenwesen", pp. 485–488.
121. Blickle, "Laufen gen Hof", pp. 259–266. For the coming into existence of the Pope's penitentiary see Schmugge, *Supplikenregister*, pp. 22, 57, 238.
122. Würgler, "Desideria", pp. 197–198.
123. E.g. the request of Gudensberg in Hesse to remove the gunpowder depot: the *gravamina* in StAM 73 no. 140, Bd. 2, no. 26a. (18 October 1785); the supplication in StAM Protokolle 2, Kassel Cc 6 Bd. 2a, no. 73/150 (17 March 1786).
124. Würgler, "Desideria", p. 171.

ing state action. The numbers, recipients, contents, and resolutions of supplications may reveal channels of power. After all, the early modern state was *partly* the result of government reaction to popular petitions.[125] Institutions are nothing else but permanently repeated actions – where many people tread repeatedly, paths come into existence.[126]

VOICES FROM AMONG THE MASSES? CONCLUSIONS

The specific quality of petitions as sources lies in the combination of a large social spectrum of authors with highly spontaneous and voluntary production. And, despite their humble, if submissive, rhetoric, petitions were neither nonpolitical nor politically without consequences. In spite of the quantity of petitions, one should not forget that only written or registered supplications were documented. Many exchanges took place orally on the occasion of audiences. This problem is not specific to petitioning, but has to be recalled when interpreting quantifying results.

Petitions, even if preserved as full-text originals, were not pure "ego-documents". First, they were embedded in a functional context (they wanted to reach a specific goal), and they had to follow formal rules (defined by ordinances). Secondly, the content of a petition was usually translated from oral dialect to written and formalized language by a scribe. Professional scribes combined textbook advice on how to write a petition[127] with the recipients' horizon of norms and values. The influence of a lawyer, priest, teacher, or petition writer could therefore severely alter the arguments: from legitimization by justice and equity to repentance and obedience, in the case of a Bavarian woman supplicating to the duke in 1620, or from radical biblicism to conventional good old rights in peasants' *gravamina* in 1790.[128]

Petitions illuminate many aspects of reality hardly documented in other (state) sources: for example, they show that the above mentioned widow asking for a job as a teacher had been supported by friends and "other good people" for more than three years before she addressed the Zurich city

---

125. Heinrich Richard Schmidt, "Sozialdisziplinierung? Ein Plädoyer für das Ende des Etatismus in der Konfessionalisierungsforschung", *Historische Zeitschrift*, 265 (1997), pp. 639–682, 680.
126. Gerhard Göhler, "Wie verändern sich Institutionen? Revolutionärer und schleichender Institutionenwandel", *Leviathan: Sonderheft*, 16 (1997), pp. 21–56, 28. Cf. Sabean, *Kinship in Neckarhausen*, p. xxv.
127. E.g. Fabian Frangk, *Ein Cantzley und Titel buechlin* (Wittenberg, 1531) (repr. Hildesheim 1979).
128. Blickle, "Supplikantin", pp. 93–99 (1620); Claudia Ulbrich, "Rheingrenze, Revolten und Französische Revolution", in Volker Rödel (ed.), *Die Französische Revolution und die Oberrheinlande, 1789–1798* (Sigmaringen, 1991), pp. 223–244, 238.

council. She even mentioned her feelings when writing the request: her hands were shaking for fear, as if she had a feverish cold, and therefore she was not able to write proper letters.[129]

Whether such utterances were true, or just rhetorical skill, is subject to dispute. Scholarly positions depend on the type of petition and procedure under consideration. Some underline the fictional qualities of the "stories" told by murderers who tried to get pardoned,[130] others emphasize that the claims of a request had to be attested by local authorities and eventually examined by higher authorities.[131] The warning of some Bavarian peasants that a refusal of firewood requests would make "babies freeze in their mothers' wombs" was straightforward, but the matter of dispute was not firewood, but the timber trade.[132]

Although petitions were increasingly drafted in writing, it is remarkable that petitioners tried again and again to hand them in personally. In spite of interdictions, they travelled long distances – from Kassel to Stockholm, from Frankfurt to Vienna[133] – to wait for the recipient after a mass or dinner, on a hunting trip or a journey to a watering place, in front of the town hall or the office.[134] Greater groups, corporations, or communes sometimes staged proper demonstrations when handing in petitions. The modern culture of political demonstrations, as well as the collecting of signatures for common petitions, obviously has far-reaching traditions in the early modern culture of social protest,[135] and cannot be termed an innovation of the French Revolution.[136] Liberals and radicals knew about that when they styled their rallies at Fribourg in 1830, or at Geneva in the 1840s, explicitly in the eighteenth-century tradition.[137]

Altogether petitions, *gravamina* and supplications are among the most important sources not generated but dealt with by the state, offering the

129. StAZH A 92.1 no. 69, (27 April 1583).
130. Davis, *Gnadengesuche*, pp. 17–19, 139–141; Ulbricht, *Kindsmord und Aufklärung*, pp. 380–381. Cf. Schnyder-Burghartz, *Alltag*, pp. 240–241.
131. Fuhrmann, Kümin and Würgler, "Supplizierende Gemeinden", pp. 307, 313–314; Ulbricht, "Supplikationen", pp. 154–155; Holenstein, "Bitten", pp. 108–109.
132. Stefan von Below and Stefan Breit, *Wald – Von der Gottesgabe zum Privateigentum. Gerichtliche Konflikte zwischen Landesherren und Untertanen um den Wald in der frühen Neuzeit* (Stuttgart, 1998), pp. 123–128, quotation p. 123.
133. Stockholm: *Casselische Zeitung*, no. 39, 28 September 1733, pp. 305–306; Vienna: Werner Troßbach, *Soziale Bewegung und politische Erfahrung. Bäuerlicher Protest in hessischen Territorien 1648–1806* (Weingarten, 1987), pp. 212–214.
134. Examples listed in Luebke, "Frederick", pp. 402, 406, and Blickle, "Supplikationen", pp. 294–296.
135. Würgler, *Unruhen und Öffentlichkeit*, pp. 15, 161; Luebke, *Rebels*, pp. 189–190; Blickle, "Supplikationen", pp. 316–317.
136. Charles Tilly, *Die europäischen Revolutionen* (Munich, 1999), pp. 73–75.
137. Würgler, *Unruhen und Öffentlichkeit*, p. 322.

widest social spectrum of authors or initiators, voicing an almost unlimited variety of issues in large quantities. Therefore, many historical disciplines have used them occasionally (but not systematically) for specific purposes. Petitions are open to various approaches, such as close reading in the hermeneutic tradition, serial analysis of petitioners, contents, and addresses, prosopographical or microhistorical reconstructions and linkings, and so on. With respect to social conflict, petitions are useful for analysing the causes, motives, and aims, the rhetoric, language, and legitimation, the course, escalation, and radicalization, the intention, success, and failure of conflicts on all levels. It may be true that actions speak louder than words. But the texts of petitions are easier to read and understand than ritualized actions, and they are more complex and precise in their statements than symbolic events. Finally, petitions are not dependent on a reporter's words, but they voice (ordinary) peoples' interests and experiences by documenting their actions.

IRSH 46 (2001), Supplement, pp. 35–56 DOI: 10.1017/S0020859001000323
© 2001 Internationaal Instituut voor Sociale Geschiedenis

Supplications between Politics and Justice: The Northern and Central Italian States in the Early Modern Age*

Cecilia Nubola

"Those who think to do away with petitions would overthrow the entire system of the State". This remark – taken from an anonymous eighteenth-century account of the political organization of the Duchy of Parma and Piacenza – describes well the importance attributed to complaints in the organization of the state.[1] Through complaints, or petitions, it is generally possible to verify a number of fundamental forms and modes of communication between society and the institutions of the *ancien regime*, and to reconstruct the procedures of mediation, repression, acceptance, and agreement adopted by princes, sovereigns, or magistracies in response to social demands.

Petitions are potentially very flexible instruments and pervade every aspect of social, institutional, administrative, and judiciary life. "Petitioning" refers to different concepts of authority and sovereignty as well as to specific power relations between rulers and those ruled. For this reason, it becomes necessary to take a close look at the relations and differences between various uses of petitions – both from the point of view of the petitioners and from the point of view of the answers provided by the institutions. On the other hand, the term "supplication" will be used in its most general meaning with reference to letters (or documentation) which single citizens, or organized and recognized groups, sent to the state authorities requesting grace, favours, privileges, or calling attention to injustices and abuses. These documents gave rise to legal proceedings,

* The research reported in this paper is part of the project "Petitions and Supplications in Early Modern Europe: Fifteenth–Eighteenth century" currently under development at the Istituto storico italo-germanico di Trento. The project is coordinated by Andreas Würgler and the author. Many thanks to Friederike Oursin for the translation into English.

1. The "Sistema politico universale delli Ducati di Parma e Piacenza" is an anonymous report ascribed to a government official and expert in administrative matters; it was presumably compiled between 1737 and 1738, and describes the juridical and administrative procedures of the duchies in the Po valley as they developed during the period of the Farnese dynasty. See Sergio Di Noto (ed.), *Le istituzioni dei Ducati parmensi nella prima metà del Settecento* (Parma, 1980), p. 109; Paola Repetti, "Scrivere ai potenti: Suppliche e memoriali a Parma (secoli XVI–XVIII)", *Sogittura e civiltà*, 24 (2000), pp. 295–358.

administrative acts that led to proceedings in tribunals, magistracies, and chancelleries.[2]

In the central and northern Italian states of the early modern period, just as in the rest of Europe, the use of petitions and supplications – the quest for a direct relationship with the authorities – was one of the main approaches to the relation of power, of communication between the rulers and those ruled.[3] As a result, special agreements with individuals or groups came about; respect for statutes, habits, and local or class privileges was established; grace was conceded *ad personam*; remissions of punishments, subsidies, extensions of payments due, and the execution of laws were granted. Given the relatively small size of the Italian states, managing power in a paternalistic and personal fashion could persuade subjects to opt for a form of agreement or mediation, for a compromise solution rather than a resort to more violent forms of opposition and rebellion, which did occur but hardly ever extended beyond local or civic level.[4]

THE SOVEREIGN PRINCE AS THE FATHER AND FOUNDATION OF JUSTICE AND GRACE

In order to understand the development of supplications as a privileged form of communication between subject and authority, it is useful to look at the idea of regality, the prerogatives, the myth, and its representations in philosophical political literature, in social behaviour, and in government practice. The sovereign is in turn father, judge, legislator, and reference point of justice and of fairness, to whom subjects can turn. These are ideas,

2. For general historiographic indications see Andreas Würgler, "'Voices from the Silent Masses': Humble Petitions and Social Conflicts In Early Modern Central Europe" in this issue, pp. 11–34; Beat Kümin and Andreas Würgler, "Petitions, Gravamina and the Early Modern State: Local Influence on Central Legislation in England and Germany (Hesse)", *Parliaments, Estates & Representation*, 17 (1997), pp. 39–60; Andreas Würgler, "Suppliken und Gravamina: Formen und Wirkungen der Interessenartikulation von Untertanen in Hessen-Kassel 1650–1800", *Geschichte als Argument. Skriptenheft II. IV Frühe Neuzeit. V. 19. und 20 Jahrhundert* (Munich, 1996), pp. 9–10; the essays by Renate Blickle, Rosi Fuhrmann, Beat Kümin, Andreas Würgler, André Holenstein in Peter Blickle (ed.), *Gemeinde und Staat im Alten Europa* (Munich, 1997), pp. 241–357; Andreas Würgler, "Suppliche e "gravamina" nella prima età moderna", *Annali dell'Istituto storico italo-germanico in Trento/Jahrbuch des italienisch-deutschen historischen Instituts in Trient*, 25 (1999), pp. 515–546.

3. The central and northern Italian states of the early modern period had relatively small territories: the Savoy state (Turin), the state of Milan, the ecclesiastical principality of Trent, the Este state of Modena and Piacenza, the Grand Duchy of Tuscany, the Republic of Venice, and the Republic of Genoa. For an introduction and a general bibliography see Giorgio Chittolini, Anthony Molho and Pierangelo Schiera (eds), *The Origins of the State in Italy, 1300–1600*, in *The Journal of Modern History*, 67, Supplement (1995).

4. For the Italian states, specific research on petitions and supplications is still in short supply in spite of the full archives. Here, I only wish to present some lines of research and outline the problem in a general fashion.

myths, that cannot refer to an anonymous or generic institution but need to be embodied in a physical person, the leader, the supreme representative of a community, a collective identity, a state.[5] From here stems the fact that supplications are preferably addressed directly to the supreme authority, even if the supplicants themselves know that their demands will be subject to filters and procedures, and that minor officials and expressly delegated magistracies will evaluate them.

In any case, the prince should not be confused with the body of tribunals, parliaments, and magistracies of any degree. This may partially explain why, in the petitions and supplications, also in moments of serious conflict (e.g. in cases of revolt or rebellion), it is excluded outright that the prince be held directly responsible for the injustices that are the cause of the rebellion. All the responsibility must fall upon persons and positions of lower standing (corrupt officials), while the relationship of trust and of filial obedience with the prince is to be preserved and confirmed. Laws, regulations, and officials can be unjust and corrupt – never the prince. Countless examples could be given here. Supplicants had to respect and comply with certain rules of conduct, which were both symbolic as well as eminently strategic and practical, whether they were addressing supplications to the highest authorities in an ultimate and extreme attempt to obtain justice, or whether a revolt was already under way. A remarkable example is the interpretation – or the many possible interpretations – of the people's "political loyalty" during the most important Italian revolt of the seventeenth century – in Naples from 1647–1648.[6]

In July 1647, during the early stages of the revolt led by Masaniello, the attitude of the Neapolitan people towards the authorities was the object of concern, and of contradictory interpretations. This emerges from the accounts sent to the King of Spain on behalf of the Duke d'Arcos, the viceroy of Naples:

> The origin of all this lies in the mortal hatred that the innumerable people of Naples and the Kingdom harbour against the Nobility, justly accumulated because of the violence it has already inflicted and because of the oppression of the taxes which it cannot sustain alone. And thus, as a feeling cradled in the hearts

5. For some examples of how this idea – espoused by the population – is still alive and well in Western societies, see the letters to the President of the French Republic in the 1970s, in Yves-Marie Bercé, *Le roi caché. Sauveurs et imposteurs: Mythes politiques populaires dans l'Europe moderne* (Paris, 1990), pp. 412–415; for Italy, Camillo Zadra and Gianluigi Fait (eds), *Deferenza rivendicazione supplica: Le lettere ai potenti* (Treviso, 1991). For one of the forms of supplication in contemporary society, see Didier Fassin, "La supplique: Stratégies rhétoriques et constructions identitaires dans les demandes d'aide d'urgence", *Annales. Histoire, Sciences Sociales*, 55 (2000), pp. 955–981.
6. On the Neapolitan revolt from 1647 to 1648, see especially Francesco Benigno, *Specchi della rivoluzione: Conflitto e identità politica nell'Europa moderna* (Rome, 1999), pp. 199–285. The Kingdom of Naples was under the Spanish monarchy from 1503 onwards.

for a long time, the hate has violently exploded at the first blow. But the people have in truth shown strong loyalty and love for Your Majesty. They bowed their flags to Your Majesty's portraits, the ones taken from the very houses they had burned, and always said "viva il Re" and "viva la Spagna". In addition, towards me they have shown no hate because at the same time they kept repeating "viva il duca d'Arcos". Of course, one remains in visible danger and the service of your Majesty is in the hands of a furious people who obey an uncultured man, without good sense and reason [Masaniello].[7]

The Neapolitan people's symbolic gestures of loyalty to the sovereign were indisputably ambiguous, but they reflect the attempt – even in open rebellion – to keep a certain distance, or to avoid the accusation of rebellion, of high treason.[8] The people did not act against the King of Spain, therefore, but rather to re-establish a justice denied in his name. Even diverse and contradictory forces and aspirations – different goals worth fighting for – could crystallize around the principle of loyalty to the supreme authority. During the course of the revolt in reality, as its political objectives became clearer and more radical, this principle was overturned. The political models aspired to were no longer sovereignty and the monarchy, but rather the republics: firstly the myth of republican Rome, but also, much more concretely, analogous contemporary European phenomena, namely the liberty and patriotism of the Swiss, as well as the Dutch and Portuguese revolts. In the same manner, the principle of "loyalty" to the monarchy was exposed as a "cruel burden leading to extreme poverty", to which the political form of the republic opposed itself – freedom in place of tyranny.[9]

The principle of loyalty referred to here was part of a widespread "political culture". In literature dedicated to the "good prince", "good government", "government of the home" (*oeconomica*) – topics that were widely discussed throughout the early modern period in Italy – the prince is represented as the father of that group of families which makes up the state. His qualities must correspond to those of a good *paterfamilias*. Above all, he needs to be just and mindful of the wellbeing of those

7. Letter from the Duke d'Arcos, Viceroy of Naples, to the King of Spain, Naples, 15 July 1647, printed in the appendix to Rosario Villari, *Per il re o per la Patria: La fedeltà nel Seicento* (Rome [etc.], 1994), pp. 150–151.
8. On the juridical construction of the offence of high treason and on its political use, see Mario Sbriccoli, *Crimen laesae maiestatis: Il problema del reato politico alle soglie della scienza penalistica moderna* (Milan, 1974).
9. These ideas are expressed in a pamphlet with the title "Ragionamento di Tomaso Aniello [Masaniello] Generalissimo per eccitare il suo Popolo napoletano alla libertà", published in an appendix to Villari, *Per il re o per la Patria*, pp. 67–72, 69. On the great number of writings regarding the analysis of European revolutions in the 1640s, many of which are written in Italian, see Peter Burke, "Some Seventeenth-Century Anatomists of Revolution", *Storia della Storiografia*, 22 (1992), pp. 23–35.

entrusted to his care in respect of "natural" and given roles and hierarchies. But the prince is also identified as supreme judge, peacekeeper, source of arbitration, distributor of justice, and dispenser of grace, to whom one may turn in order to seek favours and privileges, derogations to laws and norms, exceptions, deferment, right up to the ultimate entreaty, i.e. that of grace capable of revoking a death sentence.[10]

Cosimo I De Medici, Grand Duke of Tuscany (1519–1574), can be seen as the example of an Italian prince whose politics were characterized by the wish to intervene directly and personally in criminal and civil justice, as well as by the pursuit of a direct and personal relationship with his subjects. In a letter of 1568, addressed to the Magistrato supremo, the highest court and political organ of the state (written when Cosimo I had already handed over government functions to his son, Francesco), the duke clearly states those rules of good conduct which, according to him, ought to govern all relations with subjects. It is the prince's duty to build and maintain a trusting relationship with his citizens and subjects, a relationship whose validity is warranted by the easiness and freedom with which the latter can turn to their prince and manifest their needs. In addition, the supplication – the letter personally addressed to the prince – is identified as the "quickest", "most secure", and "most secret" means to achieve the "public and private benefit", the "common and individual good":

When we [Cosimo I] left the government of our States – and some years have already passed since – we had established a good custom, which was highly appreciated by our citizens and by all of our subjects. The [custom] was that any kind of person, for comfort and facility in negotiating, could write to us and have the letter arrive in our hands. From this many good results ensued. Everyone could always reach us and they could be certain, that no one would ever come to know that which was written and in this way we could come to know what was communicated and they [the citizens and subjects] could speak their mind without anyone else, except for us, knowing it [...]. From this it followed that, once we understood what was necessary, we provided as we thought best for the common and individual good of those who wrote to us.

[...] For this reason, with this [letter] of ours we [...] wanted to make you see that we [Cosimo] and the prince [Francesco] will always be very happy to see these letters and that no one else will see them and that we shall then see to the needs, public or private as they might be, with that love that you have come to

10. Daniela Frigo, "La dimensione amministrativa nella riflessione politica (secoli XVI–XVIII)", in Istituto per la scienza dell'amministrazione pubblica, *L'amministrazione nella storia moderna*, 2 vols (Milan, 1985), vol. 1, pp. 21–94; António Manuel Hespanha, "Justiça e administração entre o antigo regime e a Revolução", in Bartolomé Clavero, Paolo Grossi and Francisco Tomas y Valiente (eds), *Hispania entre derechos propios y derechos nacionales*, 2 vols (Milan, 1990), vol. 1, pp. 135–204.

know from the results [obtained] in the many years we have governed you. And
the prince shall do the very same [...].[11]

Arguably, the idea of a sovereign who is protective, and acts as an
attentive father to the vast family that makes up the state, reaches its most
complete expression in enlightened absolutism. In this very period –
around the middle of the eighteenth century – an immense effort of
indoctrination was under way, affecting all the people, through traditional
instruments such as catechesis and preaching, but also (much more than in
the past) through schools and primary education, now open to social
classes that had been excluded from instruction before. The following is
but one indicative example, taken from a reader for school children in the
northern Italian territories of the Habsburg monarchy. The chapter
dedicated to patriotism and to the love of one's country contains all the
topoi of the mythology of the sovereign taking special interest in the
problems his subjects place before him "orally or in writing":

> In the State, the monarch directs and arranges all things for the highest good. He
> ensures that order, abundance, and comfort reign everywhere. [...] He is the
> loving father of that great family, which makes up the State. He perceives the
> miseries and the afflictions of the subjects and he does not shun the fatigue of
> having them made known to him, be it orally, or in writing. He leaves no one
> without help or succour, the examination and the circumstances allowing. He
> forgoes rest, happiness, and comfort in order to attain peace and comfort for his
> subjects.[12]

SUPPLICATIONS TO THE "PAPAL PRINCE" AND THE ROMAN CURIA

The Pope, the *sovrano pontefice*, was a special kind of Italian prince. His
double nature as spiritual leader of the Catholic Church and secular prince
of the papal state made him the religious authority, but it also allowed him
to exert social and political influence in the Italian states. It is in the person
of the Pope that one can see most clearly the dissolution of the boundary
between justice and grace – i.e. the boundary between crime, understood
as disobedience to civil and political law, and sin, understood as
disobedience to moral or religious law. Even though the two realms
remained separate, at least theoretically, by the end of the Middle Ages any

11. The letter of Cosimo I is transcribed in Elena Fasano Guarini, "Considerazioni su giustizia
stato e società nel Ducato di Toscana del Cinquecento", in Sergio Bertelli, Nicolai Rubinstein,
and Craig Hugh Smyth (eds), *Florence and Venice: Comparisons and Relations*, vol. 2,
Cinquecento (Florence, 1980), pp. 135–168, 143–144.
12. *Libro di lettura per gli scolari delle scuole italiane nelle città, borghi terre e più grandi villaggi
degl' imp. reg. dominii. Tomo secondo, Consistente nell'introduzione alla probità e rettitudine.
Tradotto dal tedesco dal sacerdote Giovanni Marchetti* (Rovereto, 1795), p. 101.

difference between spiritual power and secular power, between jurisdiction and grace, tends to disappear in the highest supreme acts executed personally by the Pope. In the same manner, the distinction between the tribunal of conscience, of moral and religious sins/crimes (from which absolution is obtained by way of oral or written confession) and the judicial tribunal becomes less pronounced.[13]

If we take a look at the organization of the Roman Curia, it is not easy (if at all possible, given the current state of research) to reconstruct the complex multitude of tribunals and congregations, to distinguish those of the papal state and the city of Rome from those directed at "Christianity", and to account for their complicatedly intertwined competences.[14] Generally, it can be said that almost every proceeding, every decision, every sentence or concession of grace had its origin in a supplication. The convoluted machinery of the curial offices can be taken as an example of a precocious and generalized organization of the "supplicational system", if one bears in mind that 7,365 volumes of the series *Registra supplicationum* are kept in the Archivio Segreto Vaticano, relative to the period dating from 1342 until 1899.[15] Another systematic and impressive series of registers of supplications is kept in the Archives of the Sacra Penitenzieria Apostolica.[16]

Especially after the Council of Trent (1545–1563), following the amplification of Roman centralization to the detriment of the powers and prerogatives of bishops and local tribunals, a growing number of followers and subjects had to turn to Rome. One had to do so in order to obtain absolutions, dispensations, sentences, and graces for transgressions of a sexual and matrimonial nature (abortion and infanticide, incest, rape, sodomy, marriage between blood relations); for questions pertaining to

13. Overall, on the development of the papal state and the papal Curia in the first centuries of the modern period see Paolo Prodi, *The Papal Prince: One Body and Two Souls: The Papal monarchy in Early Modern Europe* (Cambridge, 1987). On sins/crimes see Elena Brambilla, *Alle origini del Sant'Uffizio: Penitenza, confessione e giustizia spirituale dal medioevo al XVI secolo* (Bologna, 2000); Paolo Prodi, *Una storia della giustizia: Dal pluralismo dei fori al moderno dualismo tra coscienza e diritto* (Bologna, 2000).

14. On the organization of justice in the city of Rome see, in particular, Peter Blastenbrei, *Kriminalität in Rom 1560–1585* (Tübingen, 1995); on the supplications to the Roman Curia see Irene Fosi, "Sovranità, patronage, e giustizia: suppliche e lettere alla corte romana nel primo Seicento", in Gianvittorio Signorotto and Maria Antonietta Visceglia (eds), *La corte di Roma tra Cinque e Seicento "teatro" della politica europea* (Rome, 1998), pp. 207–241.

15. Bruno Katterbach, *Inventario dei registri delle suppliche* (Vatican City, 1932).

16. On the Sacra Penitenzieria see Ludwig Schmugge, Patrick Hersperger and Béatrice Wiggenhauser, *Die Supplikenregister der päpstlichen Pönitentiarie aus der Zeit Pius' II (1458–1464)* (Tübingen, 1996); many transcriptions of supplications to the Penitentiary can be found in Filippo Tamburini, *Santi e peccatori: Confessioni e suppliche dai Registri della Penitenzieria dell'Archivio Segreto Vaticano (1451–1586)* (Milan, 1995), and in Filippo Tamburini and Ludwig Schmugge (eds), *Häresie und Luthertum: Quellen aus dem Archiv der Pönitentiarie in Rom (15. und 16. Jahrhundert)* (Paderborn [etc.], 2000).

ecclesiastical organization and discipline (benefices, pensions, establishing monasteries or new churches, entering into a monastery, becoming a cleric); and for questions of a moral-economic nature, such as usury. The list could be continued to include almost every aspect of the religious and social life of the clergy, lay people, and ecclesiastical institutions. All this necessarily led to Rome, to the central authorities of the Catholic Church where the knowledge of sins and crimes, the judgment of guilt, the possibility of intervening, regulating, punishing, and absolving were centralized.

The courts and the congregations called to deal with the examination of the supplications were primarily the Signatura of Justice, the Signatura of Grace, and the Dataria apostolica, which becomes more and more important by the end of the seventeenth century.[17] The reforms of Sixtus V (1585–1590), however, extended the handling of supplications to other major congregations of cardinals that could deliberate freely or propose their acceptance.[18]

Normally, supplications were letters or documents standardized according to the style of the Roman Curia, and the course of the documentation – from the presentation of the supplication to the papal decision – was long, complex, and expensive.[19] A completely different outcome was reserved for those supplications that could count on influential sponsors at court – members of the Pope's family; cardinals, and prefects of the congregations; members of the aristocracy, or of the feudality of the Catholic states; members of the Roman patriciate, or influential figures of the curial or financial oligarchies. All those who could pride themselves on relations of familiarity, service, direct or indirect acquaintance with cardinals, or with the Pope's family – in other words, with those who were inside the net of patronage or clientele of the papal court – could place their hopes in a system of justice that, in many cases,

17. Niccolò Del Re, *La Curia romana: Lineamenti storico-giuridici* (Vatican City, 1998), pp. 212–225, 447–454.

18. Thomas Frenz (ed.), *I documenti pontifici nel Medioevo e nell'età moderna* (Vatican City, 1989), p. 75, or *idem, Papsturkunden des Mittelalters und der Neuzeit* (Stuttgart, 1986).

19. By the beginning of the thirteenth century, supplications began to be presented not only orally but also in writing, and very soon forms were introduced to facilitate their examination as well as the verdict, such as, e.g., Cardinal Guala Bicchieri's *Libellum de formis petitionum secundum cursum Romanae Curia*. In 1331, the constitution *Paterfamilias* specified fifty-three types of requests that could be received by the papal Chancellery: see Jacques Verger, "Que peut-on attendre d'un traitement automatique des suppliques?", in Lucie Fossier, André Vauchez and Cinzio Violante (eds), *Informatique et histoire médieévale* (Rome, 1977), pp. 73–78, 73; Bernard Guillemain, "Une opération en cours: le traitement informatique des suppliques d'Urbain V", in Paolo Vian (ed.), *L'Archivio Segreto Vaticano e le ricerche storiche* (Rome, 1983), pp. 193–205, 199.

could prove to be solicitous, efficient, and quick.[20] One example: when on 31 August 1623 the Bolognese noblewoman, Artemisia Duglioli Ghisilieri, wrote to the newly-elected Pope, Maffeo Barberini (Urbano VIII), who was a relative of hers as well as a long-standing friend, asking for justice in favour of her nephew Cesare Ghisilieri ("well-known at the Roman court for having served Cardinal Farnese for fifteen years") who had been assassinated by a priest, the answer was not long in coming: on 14 September, Artemisia could thank the Pope for "having given the order to begin the trial against the imprisoned delinquent and for having the proceedings sent to Rome".[21]

A SPECIAL KIND OF SUPPLICATION: THE ANONYMOUS DENUNCIATION

Openness and secrecy, public moments and private moments, speech and writing – these, then, were among the essential expressions of the relationship between subjects and sovereign which passed through the *via supplicationis*. It should not be forgotten, however, that in the centuries of the early modern era, along with the written supplication, the ceremony of the audience survived, i.e. the possibility of personally appearing before the prince to present individual or collective requests.[22]

In contrast, a right that could not be waived was the "most secret way" – to use an expression of Cosimo I – that is, the guaranteed rights to inform the prince about personal or family needs, to voice complaints, to denounce injustices or abuse, to ask for or to propose special interventions, in private form, without "publicity". A letter's private nature protected the supplicants from the (not so remote) possibility of becoming the object of an investigation, of running personal risks, of exposing themselves to threats, intimidation, and vendettas. From the position of power,

20. This also depended on the unique character of the papal "monarchy", the discontinuity between one papacy and the next: each change of pope brought with it not only a change in the goals of a religious nature, but also a whole new series of political ties and allegiances, a change in clientele, new career possibilities at the Roman court, in the papal state, and in the ecclesiastical structure of the Catholic world; Renata Ago, *Carriere e clientele nella Roma barocca* (Rome [etc.], 1990).

21. Fosi, "Sovranità, *patronage*, e giustizia", p. 220. In particular, she points to the mediation role of noble and patrician women in defence of the family honour.

22. On the public manner of administrating justice on behalf of the French sovereign, see Sarah Hanley, *The Lit de justice of the Kings of France: Constitutional Ideology in Legend, Ritual, and Discourse* (Princeton, NJ, 1983). In the papal state the restoration of the public audience from 1691 to 1695 by Pope Innocent XII (1691–1700) created great expectations but scarce practical results in the administration of justice, and did not last long; see Claudio Donati, " 'Ad radicitus submovendum': Materiali per una storia dei progetti di riforma giudiziaria durante il pontificato di Innocenzo XII", in Bruno Pellegrino (ed.), *Riforme, religione e politica durante il pontificato di Innocenzo XII (1691–1700)* (Galatina, 1999), pp. 159–178, 163–164.

guaranteeing secrecy not only promised a more direct perception of social
and territorial problems, but it also made it easier to control the
population's ideas, moods, and feelings with regards to the authorities.
From this point of view, it is not so strange that anonymous letters – and
especially denunciations – received almost the same treatment as signed
supplications.

Supplications and anonymous letters were two pillars of the government
system and the relationship between ruled and ruler throughout the entire
ancien regime in the republic of Venice, and the importance of anonymous
letters is on a par with that of supplications. The system of secret
denunciations was praised as a truly unique instrument for determining the
truth and for protecting the republic's safety. The system of denunciations
made it easy for the authorities to acquire "the universal cognition of the
important things and the happiness of the State".[23]

In the republic of Genoa, around the middle of the seventeenth century,
the use of *lettere orbe* – anonymous letters of denunciation – increased
dramatically. This is to be attributed to a strengthening of their official
political reception, so much so that 60 per cent of the letters from Genoa
and 80 per cent of those from the rest of the territory led to administrative
or judicial action.[24] The anonymous letter-writers also requested more
attention from the authorities for their kind of document. They demanded
that the form of communication represented by the anonymous letters be
taken into account by the authorities in exactly the same way as
supplications written by lawyers, or as those events that reflected
vendettas or private forms of justice, such as throwing stones or dung at
houses and front doors.[25] The two most common reasons given for writing
anonymous letters were closely connected: on the one hand, there was the
desire to denounce a crime for "obligation of conscience" so that justice
may be done; on the other hand, there was the desire to avoid "attracting
hate and living in anxiety".[26] Faced with an impotent or conniving justice,
the anonymous supplication became, at times, the only possible form of
denunciation for crimes, private forms of violence, arbitrary or deviant
behaviour, which so often remained secret or went unpunished due to the
social rank or protection of the accused.

23. This is asserted in the eighteenth century by Marco Foscarini (1696–1763) nobleman, official
historiographer and Doge of Venice (1762–1763); Paolo Preto, *I servizi segreti di Venezia*
(Milan, 1994), pp. 170–171. More generally, on the system of denunciations, the *bocche di leone*,
made of stone and located inside the *palazzi* of the magistracies, and the governing organs in
Venice and the territory designated expressly for receiving anonymous letters, see *ibid.*, pp. 168–
177.
24. Not only did the majority of anonymous letters have consequences, moreover, the "voices",
the information orally compiled, could suffice for undertaking administrative or legal action;
Edoardo Grendi, *Lettere orbe* (Palermo, 1989), p. 84.
25. Anonymous letter sent 1607; Grendi, *Lettere orbe*, p. 12.
26. *Ibid.*, p. 13.

Still in Genoa, beginning with the year 1607 with the *legge dei biglietti* ("law of the notes"), the principle of anonymity received a kind of political legitimacy and specific regulation. The task of evaluating the anonymous denunciations was delegated to the Consiglio Minore, an organism composed of 100 aristocrats. It was to deliberate and check the denunciations for a growing number of crimes such as bearing arms, protecting bandits, insolence, and fiscal fraud. The same procedure was extended to a series of typically aristocratic crimes such as occult crimes to verify public opinion (1612), fighting duels (1641), games and betting, or other manoeuvres for electing the Doge (1642).[27]

THE WAYS OF SUPPLICATION

If this was the understanding and positive evaluation reserved for anonymous letters, supplications were given even greater consideration. To follow the institutional itinerary of a supplication – from the draft to the *rescritto*[28] – is no simple task, because the norms and regulations are not organically collected but need to be followed in decrees, chancellery manuals, and collections of answers to supplications (*rescritti*) often compiled for internal office use.[29]

The supplications to the highest authorities of the state were distributed to various magistracies and offices; and, for every supplication, sometimes lengthy and complex procedures were begun. In Venice, the Consiglio dei Dieci (The Council of Ten – the republic's most important political-judicial organ) also had the task of "filtering" the correspondence that came from the authorities of the territory and from subjects, on the one hand, and from other supreme institutions, such as the Collegio, the Signoria, and the Consiglieri, on the other.[30] The Collegio, especially, was

27. *Ibid.*, pp. 15–16.

28. *Rescritto*: the prince's written answer to a subject's request. If, in old canon law, the term was uniquely used for the Pope's written answers, beginning with the Middle Ages its use was expanded, insofar as the answers written by those who had legislative or jurisdictional power were also called *rescritti*.

29. A number of very interesting topics that cannot be addressed here are those connected with the first fundamental passage of the supplication: the mechanisms of writing, the linguistic aspects, the strategies of the discourse, the material compiler of these documents, the mechanisms of transmission to the rulers. For these aspects, as well as for an analysis of the supplications' contents, specific archival research is necessary. On the linguistic and formal aspects of the supplications see Paola Repetti, "Scrivere ai potenti"; Maria Nadia Covini, "Vigevano nelle carte dell'auditore: Aspetti dell'intervento ducale nell'amministrazione della giustizia", in Giorgio Chittolini (ed.), *Vigevano e i territori circostanti alla fine del Medioevo* (Milan, 1997), pp. 303–324, 307–308.

30. Claudio Povolo, "Nella spirale della violenza: Cronologia, intensità e diffusione del banditismo nella terraferma veneta (1550–1610)", in Gherardo Ortalli (ed.), *Bande armate, banditi, banditismo e repressione di giustizia negli stati europei di antico regime* (Rome, 1986), pp. 21–51, pp. 43–44.

a regulated body entrusted with, among other things, dealing initially with a large number of supplications, instituting the documentation, and dividing it among the various offices for evaluation. Accordingly, the supreme magistracies sorted the supplications and passed them on to the lower magistracies, especially bearing in mind the types of requests, contents, place of origin, the different offices' competences, but also the more strictly political priorities or appropriateness.

In the republic of Venice, for example, a supplication from German merchants reached the Consiglio dei Dieci in 1604, requesting permission to carry arms in order to defend themselves against brigands, and it was passed to the Cinque Savi alla Mercanzia for evaluation. Some years later, a similar supplication from a group of Flemish merchants was passed from the Consiglio dei Dieci to the Podestà of Rovigo, in whose territory the merchants had been robbed. The case was entrusted to him, along with broad powers, such as the authority to proceed against the delinquents with inquisitorial process, and the possibility of offering immunity to those who denounced themselves for the crime.[31]

The chancelleries of the various magistracies collected the documentation pertaining to the supplications, and much of this material, especially the *rescritti sovrani*, was judged to have value as a precedent (as in the case of judicial pronouncements) in guiding decisions in similar cases. In this way, collections of rules, manuals, and real treatises based on routine procedure were constructed, which became a *corpus* that we can define as normative, capable of making up for flaws in the legislation.[32] One example is the *Rituale*, a text containing the collection of *rescritti* used by the magistracies in the Duchies of Parma and Piacenza, which presumably was compiled during the years of government of Ranuccio I Farnese (1592–1622) and subsequently expanded in the first half of the eighteenth century.[33] The *Rituale* was a book that contained the formulae of the *rescritti* for criminal and civil cases, and had been compiled with the Prince's approval. Naturally, the presence of a formula in the *Rituale* suitable for the *rescritto* pertaining to a particular type of supplication did not entail its automatic application. Every supplication or *memoriale* was evaluated individually, and the *rescritto* was prepared only

> [...] for those cases that will be held worthy of it and with the Prince's consent. Thus, there is a *rescritto* for any kind of homicide, but from this it does not follow that a supplication can be presented for all homicides, all thefts, and all capital offences; the *rescritto* will be used exclusively for those cases worthy of it.[34]

31. Povolo, "Nella spirale della violenza", pp. 21–23.
32. Luca Mannori, *Il sovrano tutore: Pluralismo istituzionale e accentramento amministrativo nel principato dei Medici (Secc. XVI–XVIII)* (Milan, 1994), pp. 8–10, 412–413.
33. Repetti, "Scrivere ai potenti", pp. 297–298; Di Noto, *Le istituzioni dei Ducati parmensi*, pp. 26–27, 74.
34. Di Noto, *Le istituzioni dei Ducati parmensi*, p. 74.

In the second half of the sixteenth century, voices against the indiscriminate and generalized use of supplications were beginning to be heard. Furthermore, in the Duchies of Parma and Piacenza, for example, in the second half of the eighteenth century, writing *memoriali*, appeals, petitions, supplications, or letters addressed to "His Royal Highness" asking for justice or any other measure, had become such a widespread practice that it has been labelled an "intolerable abuse". Thus, a decree was proposed to take action by forbidding "anyone to present or pass on *memoriali*" to His Royal Highness, "regarding the affairs for which one can implore justice from judges and tribunals, and not even in those cases in which one can turn to the Dettatura, or the Congregation of Ministers".[35] In the general climate of institutional and juridical reform, only the abuses were considered for reform – not the overall system of supplications.

By way of supplications, the rulers were informed about the needs and the necessities of a substantial part of the population. They felt a kind of "institutionalized obligation" to answer those social needs, to intervene in the private sector, and to take upon themselves the necessities of single subjects, of informal or institutionalized family groups, or organized groups such as the estates, religious associations, guilds, and communities. This form of communication – even in an ambiguous and subordinated fashion, not covered by a ruling or any form of certainty – allowed the supplicants not only to "humbly supplicate" but also to "come to terms" with the rulers. It gave them the chance to propose a strategy for the resolution of problems, to negotiate a reduction or modification of a sentence, by offering a "favour" or a service, a token of their working professionalism in exchange for a positive answer.

From the prisons of Venice, for example, hundreds of supplications reached the magistracies in which the supplicants and their families and protectors contrived reasonable exchanges or offered compensation worthy of being taken into consideration. In this manner, a former guard of the Venetian prison, himself jailed for homicide, offered to work as a guard for half the regular pay in exchange for his release. Others offered to reveal the names of thieves or to disclose escape plans or conspiracies in exchange for freedom. Prisoners sentenced to death obtained grace by offering themselves as executioners.[36]

Of course, those with trades essential to the state's economy, or whose occupations were not easily replaced, had higher contracting stakes. One

---

35. Daniele Marchesini, *Il bisogno di scrivere: Usi della scrittura nell'Italia moderna* (Rome [etc.], 1992), pp. 39–40.
36. Giovanni Scarabello, *Carcerati e carceri a Venezia nell'età moderna* (Rome, 1979), p. 37–38. For many examples of the most common requests sent to the Venetian magistracies by prisoners, see pp. 34–41.

famous case is that of the Florentine Benvenuto Cellini (1500–1571), goldsmith, sculptor, architect, thief, sodomite, and murderer, whose artistic and criminal careers were punctuated with requests for grace and privileged treatment obtained from princes and popes, not for the wealth or nobility of his person but for his talent and artistic ability.[37] However, this is not the only case of a man whose genius placed him above the law.[38] In Venice, workers at the shipyards, condemned to one year in prison in 1594, managed to obtain a swift release after having simply endured a scolding. And a master of the mint was allowed to go to work in the daytime and return to prison only for the night.[39]

"EXERCISING SEVERITY AND CLEMENCY"

The medieval prince's prerogative as guarantor of the highest justice remains operative in the modern period while the other attribute of sovereignty – legislative power – has difficulties imposing itself. In fact, the juridical order is considered as *given*, already existing. The laws are not created *ex novo* but go back to tradition and custom, and they must be adapted in order to make them responsive to changed political situations in the government of territories, as well as in individual cases. Moreover, respect of custom is the best guarantee for peace and order. Starting with these principles, I think the characteristic of *ancien-regime* political systems based largely on supplications can be better understood: the rulers do not intervene in a "directive" sense but only in order to "correct", when their intervention is required.[40]

The princes of the Italian states administered "extraordinary justice" by way of the supreme magistracies. In fact, not only cases pertaining to matters in some way connected to the prerogatives of sovereignty (feudal questions, taxes, privileges, etc.) were instituted and discussed in these

37. Paolo L. Rossi, "The Writer and the Man: Real Crimes And Mitigating Circumstances: *Il caso Cellini*", in Trevor Dean and K.J.P. Lowe (eds), *Crime, Society and the Law in Renaissance Italy* (Cambridge, 1994), pp. 157–183. See also *The Autobiography of Benvenuto Cellini*, George Bull (transl.) (Harmondsworth, 1973).
38. Pope Paul III writes in reference to Cellini: "You do not understand these things as well as I do. You should realize that men like Benvenuto, unique in their profession, must not be subject to the law"; Rossi, "The Writer and the Man", p. 183.
39. Scarabello, *Carcerati e carceri*, pp. 37–38.
40. On these topics see Paolo Grossi, "Un diritto senza stato (la nozione di autonomia come fondamento della costituzione giuridica medievale)", in Paolo Grossi, *Assolutismo giuridico e diritto privato* (Milan, 1998), pp. 275–292; Luca Mannori, "Introduzione", in Luca Mannori (ed.), *Comunità e poteri centrali negli antichi Stati italiani* (Naples, 1997), pp. 7–42; Mannori, *Il sovrano tutore*; Angela De Benedictis, "Giustizia, società, e corpi in età moderna: alcuni spunti di riflessione", in Angela De Benedictis and Ivo Mattozzi (eds), *Giustizia, potere e corpo sociale* (Bologna, 1994) pp. 11–22; Angela De Benedictis, *Repubblica per contratto: Bologna: una città europea nello Stato della Chiesa* (Bologna, 1995), pp. 21–105.

institutions, but, more generally, petitions and supplications that required the prince's intervention.[41] Especially, cases regarding the lower social classes were to receive particular attention and protection (removing them from the competent magistracies if necessary) in accordance with the principle of "rendering justice to the poor" which – for example – had been clearly stated in the reform of the Tuscan juridical order of the end of the seventeenth century.[42] For this reason, the same reform law set forth that in the treatment of cases before the supreme magistracy a precise order of precedence was to be respected: first came the procurator of the poor for the cases of the poor, then the women, then followed those "who were waiting", and last to be admitted were the foreigners.[43] Just as the Este duchies of Modena and Piacenza had the Procuratore dei Poveri, a court appointed a defending counsel who – once the trial was over – had the *duty* of presenting to the prince a supplication for grace, or the reduction of the sentence in favour of the defendants.[44]

In all cases, exercising clemency, interpreting, and adapting the law to situations and persons is a prerogative reserved for the prince or the highest magistracies of the republic. For this, Grand Duke Cosimo I repeatedly accused the Nove Conservatori del Dominio e della Giurisdizione of Florence – the central magistracy responsible to the government of the territory – of excessive indulgence. He urged them to the strict application of the law, "wanting the graces to come from his majesty and not from the Magistrate, and that anyone be punished according to the infractions and without privilege".[45]

The prince's presence could be judged by interpreting it positively or negatively in turn. In comparison with ordinary proceedings, which were slow, confused, and expensive, the supplication could be a short cut to justice, to obtain by way of grace that which could not be obtained by way of justice, or a means of filling in the gaps in the law.[46] On the other hand, according to a high state official, the disorder in justice was to be attributed to a lack of specific laws. The primary responsibility for this lay with the

41. Guarini, "Considerazioni su giustizia stato e società", p. 142.
42. *Riforma generale e rinnovazione di leggi per tutti i magistrati e iusdicenti* promulgated by Cosimo III in 1678; Giuseppe Pansini, "Il Magistrato supremo e l'amministrazione della giustizia civile durante il principato mediceo", *Studi senesi*, 85 (1973), pp. 283–315, 299.
43. Pansini, "Il Magistrato supremo", p. 304.
44. Carmelo Elio Tavilla, *Riforme e giustizia nel Settecento estense: Il supremo consiglio di giustizia (1761–1796)* (Milan, 2000), p. 80.
45. Fasano Guarini, "Considerazioni su giustizia stato e società", p. 141; Elena Fasano Guarini, "Potere centrale comunità soggette nel ducato di Cosimo I", *Rivista storica italiana*, 89 (1977), pp. 490–538, 494–495.
46. Pansini, "Il Magistrato supremo", p. 291–292; Covini, "Vigevano nelle carte dell'auditore", p. 306; John K. Brackett, *Criminal Justice and Crime in Late Renaissance Florence 1537–1609* (Cambridge, 1992), p. 71.

princes because they elected to detain "the absolute power of exercising severity and clemency".[47]

Turning to the supplication, especially in judicial matters, is justified by the conception and practice of a form of justice where the *arbitrium* and the principle of negotiation play an elemental role. Sentences and penalties must consider the quality, role, and place taken in the social hierarchy by the accused – in a word, the individual's *status*. The supplication was an efficient instrument insofar as it allowed the modification, annulment, and reconsideration of sentences and punishment, evaluating both specific cases and the social hierarchy. This is explicitly declared, for instance, in the *Sistema politico universale delli Ducati di Parma e Piacenza*:

> [By way of the system of supplications] when inflicting a certain punishment it is easier to find the best proportioned one not only for the case but also for the person. In fact, a penalty that is heavy for a common person can be minimal for a nobleman. In this way, after having inflicted a most severe punishment one has the possibility of reducing it according to the case under examination.[48]

Petitions and supplications, therefore, modified the course of justice deeply in every phase: trial, verdict, and conviction. Following the presentation of a request for grace, the conviction could be substantially reduced or – in fewer cases – a complete remission of the penalty could be granted.

Even for serious crimes such as wounding or homicide, grace (i.e. a decrease of a fine, detention, or banishment, remission from capital punishment) could be obtained rather easily if the condemned stuck to a certain codified *iter*. The essential and unavoidable condition was obtaining *la pace*, that is to say, a notary deed – the *Charta remissionis et pacis* (letter of remission and peace) – with which the wounded or the family of the victim conceded pardon and reconciliation to the condemned.

Pace followed traditional procedures and rituals, which were more or less similar in different parts of Europe and which had a certain continuity throughout the whole *ancien regime*. In 1748, in a valley of the Episcopal Principality of Trent, Pietro Torneri killed Salvatore Filosi. The latter had led a group of men to besiege Pietro's house, threatening to plunder it and kidnap his daughter. Torneri was condemned for homicide in a first trial. He then requested a revision and presented the notary document of peace (drafted as follows) to the court. Filosi's complete family, including women and children (all those present are mentioned in the notary deed) had been at the ceremony.

The closest relatives, then,

---

47. Di Noto, *Le istituzioni dei Ducati parmensi* , pp. 95–96.
48. *Ibid.*, p. 109.

[...] in their own name and in the name of the other blood-relations, on account of the prayers of Torneri, following the intervention of common friends and wanting to live according to the precepts of the religion, spontaneously, with cheerful spirit and pleased faces, after having drunk wine together, wishing each other health, declare a stable and irrevocable peace with Torneri, they forgive him that homicide and all the other offences received, promising not to damage him in any way and not to pursue the lawsuit brought forth against him with the criminal authority, which they beseech, on the other hand, to be benign in the sentence taking into consideration the motivations leading to the crime. And then, as a kind of compensation for that homicide (as had been arranged by the intermediaries) Torneri pays the Filosi 330 liras in silver, with which they declare themselves to be satisfied, plus a certain amount of grain, already entrusted to the widow.[49]

Here we have all of the essential elements pertaining to documents of reconciliation and remission: the presence of everyone bound by blood ties to the dead victim, being his heirs; the friends or neighbours as witnesses and mediators of the agreement; the ceremony of drinking wine together; the declaration of the act's spontaneous nature; the setting of the amount of the damages.[50]

As peace was necessary for requesting grace, these documents could be subject to extortions, threats, or negotiations, and could be bought. In fact, some statutes, such as those of a number of towns in the Episcopal Principality of Trent, explicitly mentioned the "price of the peace" in proportion to the crime and to the reduction of the sentence, which could be obtained by presenting these documents.[51]

The requests for grace conveyed to the magistracies or the prince according to the importance or nature of the infraction were generally drawn up by a lawyer, according to a precise scheme. Here, following the elements of a linguistic and structural nature, the references to the nature of the crime and the magistracy which had handled the trial, there was the story of the crime itself, the declarations of possible penal precedents, the circumstances that might favour the reception of grace (errors or lacunae in the trial proceedings, repentance, poverty, banishment or prison suffered for a number of years, and so forth). Attached were the document of peace

---

49. The notary document's transcription and translation from Latin is taken from Giuseppe Papaleoni, *Una composizione per omicidio nel 1749* (Trento, 1887), pp. 11–12.
50. Though the rituals of reconciliation always took place in the presence of a notary, they were not necessarily put in writing (and in this case it becomes more difficult to find traces in the archives or in the trial records). The ritual gestures – eating together, touching of hands, hugging or kissing in public – could be compared to the form of the public instrument; Ottavia Niccoli, "Rinuncia, pace, perdono. Rituali di pacificazione della prima età moderna", *Studi Storici*, 40 (1999), pp. 219–261, 235–236.
51. Giorgio Politi, *Aristocrazia e potere politico nella Cremona di Filippo II* (Milan, 1976), p. 377; Papaleoni, *Una composizione per omicidio*, p. 9.

and possibly the certificate of poverty, usually drawn up by the parish priest or a local official.[52]

It was not possible to request grace for every crime. Laws and statutes listed a wide range of crimes defined *atroci* (lese-majesty, heresy, sacrilege, blasphemy, sodomy, murder, parricide, robbery, counterfeiting money, etc.) for which it was not possible to request grace or any such request could have been considered only by the sovereign.[53] Considering that only a little work has been done in this field for the Italian states, and that the judicial practices and laws partially differed from state to state, it becomes clear that the supplications for grace were actually quite common, but also extended to those crimes defined as *atrociora* which – because of their nature – seemed necessarily to lead to capital punishment.

Here are only two examples from politically different territories – Siena (a town subject to the Grand Duchy of Tuscany), and Bozen (part of Habsburg Austria). In both cases, the crime is "atrocious" – infanticide. In 1765 in the territory of Siena, only one death sentence (by hanging from the gallows) was pronounced for infanticide but it was commuted to five years of prison by grace.[54] One century earlier (1675), in Bozen, a woman was initially given the death penalty by the judge of Bozen, but obtained the conversion of the sentence to perpetual banishment from the court in Innsbruck. In any case, the sentence was extremely severe: in the seventeenth century, losing one's honour and being expelled from one's town was not all that different from death, but at least the women were not subjected to torture as provided for that crime by the *Landesordnung* (territorial law-code) of the Tyrol.[55]

It is very hard to grasp the motivations for the concession or denial of grace by referring exclusively to laws and regulations. Customs, choices, and conveniences of a political, economic, and social nature must also be taken into account. Their weight can only be assessed with difficulty on a case-by-case basis; but they surely are quite relevant.

52. Politi, *Aristocrazia e potere politico*, pp. 377–378; Giovanni Liva, "Criminalità e giustizia nel Ducato di Milano tra Cinque e Seicento (1570–1630)", in Archivio di Stato di Milano (ed.), *Aspetti della società lombarda in età spagnola*, 2 vols (Como, 1985), vol. 1, especially the documents on pp. 29–31.

53. On the juridical aspects of the *crimina atrociora* see Luigi Lacché, "'Ordo non servatus': Anomalie processuali, giustizia militare e 'specialia' in antico regime", *Studi storici*, 29 (1988), pp. 361–384; Politi, *Aristocrazia e potere politico*, pp. 379–380.

54. Laura Carli Sardi, "Analisi statistica sulla criminalità nel 1700 (reati e pene) con riguardo allo stato senese", in Luigi Berlinguer and Floriana Colao (eds), *Criminalità e società in età moderna* (Milan, 1991), vol. 12, pp. 327–475, 373.

55. The territorial law code of Tyrol in the sixteenth century, which was in force until the second half of the eighteenth century, decreed that women guilty of infanticide be buried alive and, upon death, impaled with an iron stake through the heart; Heinz Moser, *Die Scharfrichter von Tirol: Ein Beitrag zur Geschichte des Strafvollzuges in Tirol von 1497–1787* (Innsbruck 1982), p. 102; Siglinde Clementi and Martha Verdorfer, *Storie di cittadine: Bolzano/Bozen dal Medioevo ad oggi* (Vienna [etc.], 2000), pp. 91–94.

TOWARDS THE MYTH OF THE STATE *SUPER PARTES*

In these complex processes of communication between rulers and ruled, which runs along the *via supplicationis*, one can essentially locate the passage from the "myth" of the prince, as the supreme authority vouching for justice, to the "myth" of the state *super partes*. In ancien-regime societies, which were characterized by violence, feuds, and local conflicts, the prince, the sovereign, or the most important institutions of the republics embody a superior form of justice. An abstract entity, the state, with its offices, courts, and magistracies tends to become – or, if we prefer, to be represented and "justified" as – superior and equidistant with respect to the "parts": community and estate ties, families, relatives, clans, and factions. This holds true also in horizontal and vertical conflict situations or violence, which cannot be resolved from within, i.e., from inside the families or communities.

Communities often called on the central authorities to intervene against feudatories and local lords when their crimes or arbitrary acts remained unpunished and the communities turned out to be impotent. In 1629, for example, "the poor and afflicted subjects", the men of Masone, a community of the Ligurian territory, sent a supplication to the Senate of the Republic of Genoa to expound the continuous vexations they are subjected to by Paolo Agostino Spinola, the feudal lord, defined as "a gentleman, otherwise of good mind, but in these circumstances perverted by passion".[56] Involving the centre of power represented the ultimate and extreme possibility of obtaining an improvement of their conditions, but they had to complain in writing as they could not personally go to Genoa to sustain their arguments "because if they would have gone, they would have been tried for lese-majesty". This had been Spinola's threat, if only they had dared tackle the question. A meeting of the community to discuss the situation, in fact, ran the risk of being considered a "secret meeting and rebellion". Thus, the community's letter intended to anticipate possible actions in this direction. The men wanted to avoid the feudal lord turning to the central authorities first and asking for the intervention "of the regal arm and the supreme authority" for the repression of "rebels". The community itself also requested an external intervention, an envoy "as rigorous as possible, who can prosecute and punish as he sees just", however "independently", and who "must upon his return account to

---

56. This supplication is transcribed in Grendi, *Lettere orbe*, pp. 106–108. The men of the community accuse the feudal lord of forbidding them to extract their copper on penalty of imprisonment, of paying too little for coal, of inflicting new restrictions every day, such as, for example, not being able to sleep outside his jurisdiction for more than one night, not being able to leave the village without a special permit, not being allowed to buy even bread outside his jurisdiction.

Your Most Serene Highnesses for the manner and form in which they are governed".[57]

The urban and rural communities, on the other hand, or the organisms representing rural communities, which had developed particularly in the northern Italian territories and states between the fifteenth and the sixteenth centuries, were often used by the central authorities in an antifeudal way. They could act as counterparts, as "interlocutors" in numerous and divergent cases – e.g. to intervene or regulate in local political and social competition, to mediate in conflicts (or also cause them to break out), to find adequate referents to whom the execution of laws and regulations, the collection of taxes, and so forth could be entrusted.[58]

In any case, this was not a progressive or inevitable organization of the territory, of the "peripheries" on behalf of the centre, but a complex political dialectic "fought with memorials, supplications, and protests".[59] The rural territorial organisms and the urban communities could refer to the *capitoli di dedizione* when they acted as interlocutors to the central authorities. In these documents, the communities and territories swore loyalty to the prince (or the republic) in exchange for the confirmation of certain autonomies, respect of statutes, customs and privileges.[60] On the basis of this political understanding of a pact-based and contractual nature, petitions and supplications of a more political nature (against the actions of representatives of the central power, for example), or fiscal (against a tax increase), appealed to the respect of the *capitoli di dedizione*. In the same manner, the communities also appealed to the *capitoli di dedizione* to substantiate the correctness of the "right to resist": should the prince violate the agreements, the subjects are authorized to disobey and rebel.[61]

---

57. Grendi, *Lettere orbe*, pp. 106–108.
58. For territorial representation of the rural communities see Giorgio Chittolini, *Città, Comunità e feudi negli stati dell'Italia centro-settentrionale (secoli XIV–XVI)* (Milan, 1996), especially ch. 7, "Principe e comunità alpine", pp. 127–144, and ch. 11, "L'affermazione di Contadi e Territori", pp. 211–226. For the feuds among factions and the relationships between these and the central authorities of the states, see Edward Muir, *Mad Blood Stirring: Vendetta and Factions in Friuli during the Renaissance* (Baltimore, MD, [etc.] 1993); Furio Bianco, "Mihi Vindictam: Aristocratic Clans and Rural Communities in a Feud in Friuli in the Late Fifteenth and Early Sixteenth Centuries", in Dean and Lowe, *Crime, Society and the Law in Renaissance Italy*, pp. 249–273; Angelo Torre, "Faide, fazioni e partiti, ovvero la ridefinizione della politica nei feudi imperiali delle Langhe tra Sei e Settecento", *Quaderni storici*, 21 (1986), pp. 775–810.
59. Chittolini, "L'affermazione di Contadi e Territori", p. 217.
60. Giorgio Chittolini, "I capitoli di dedizione delle comunità lombarde a Francesco Sforza", in idem, *Città, Comunità e feudi negli stati dell'Italia centro-settentrionale (secoli XIV–XVI)*, pp. 39–60; more generally see Angela De Benedictis, "I contratti di potere come ragioni dello stato", in Pierangelo Schiera (ed.), *Ragion di Stato e ragioni dello Stato (secoli XV–XVII)* (Naples, 1996), pp. 67–93.
61. The relationships among *patti di dedizione*, petitions, and revolts need to be further investigated; see Giorgio Politi, "Rivolte contadine e movimenti comunali: Una tesi", in Stefano

Requests for intervention "from the bottom" consolidated the centre's power to intervene in the "peripheries". The state's growing invasive and bureaucratic presence accelerated the process of centralization, which had as long-term consequences the loss of "freedom" and the autonomies and traditional rights of communities.[62] Not only the supplications of communities and groups called for a "weightier" presence of the state. Single persons turned to princes and magistracies in the hope that these might take on their personal problems – that, for example, they might intervene in favour of women, children, and weaker social classes against the power of family or social privileges. In other cases, the request for intervention was an implicit declaration of an impotence to resolve family conflicts "from inside".[63]

In this context the supplications of widows in early modern Tuscany to the Magistrato sopra i pupilli are significant.[64] This magistracy was essentially responsible for administrating the patrimony of orphans, whose fathers had not left a will or appointed a guardian. But it also administrated the patrimony of persons considered physically or mentally unfit to administer the family estate responsibly. The system of transmission of the patrimony and the rights of tutelage of underage children provided that at the father's death, if no will had been made, the children were often removed from the mother and entrusted to the care of relatives of the father's. The procedure was the norm if the widow remarried. In order to keep their children with them and to obtain custody and the usufruct of their late husbands' patrimony, many widows appealed to the state

---

Gasparri, Giovanni Levi and Pierandrea Moro (eds), *Venezia: Itinerari per la storia della città* (Bologna, 1997), pp. 159–191; Giorgio Lombardi, *La Guerra del sale: Caleidoscopio di una Historia*, in *idem* (ed.), *La guerra del sale (1680–1699): Rivolte e frontiere del Piemonte barocco*, 3 vols (Milan, 1986) vol. 1, pp. 39–178, especially pp. 95–96, 118–122; De Benedictis, *Repubblica per contratto*.

62. Costanza D'Elia, "Supplicanti e vandali. testi scritti, testi non scritti, testi scritti dagli storici", *Quaderni storici*, 31 (1996), pp. 459–485 presents the supplications sent, in the first half of the nineteenth century, from certain communities in the province of Salerno (southern Italy) against land reclamation projects and, more generally, against the state's invasive presence in the local economy.

63. *Le désordre des familles: Lettres de cachet des Archives de la Bastille* présenté par Arlette Farge et Michel Foucault (Paris, 1982). On the supplication as a "tale" of individuality see Otto Ulbricht, "Supplikationen als Ego-Dokumente: Bittschriften von Leibeigenen aus der ersten Hälfte des 17. Jahrhunderts als Beispiel", in Winfried Schulze (ed.), *Ego-Dokumente: Annaherung an den Menschen in der Geschichte* (Berlin, 1996), pp. 149–174.

64. The Magistrato sopra i pupilli was a magistracy instituted already at the end of the fourteenth century, completely reformed a century later, and again in 1565. It remained operative until the beginning of the nineteenth century; Giulia Calvi, "Dal margine al centro: Soggettività femminile, famiglia, Stato moderno in Toscana (XVI–XVIII secc.)", in Società italiana delle storiche, *Discutendo di storia: Soggettività, ricerca, biografia* (Turin, 1990), pp. 103–118; Giulia Calvi, *Il contratto morale: Madri e figli nella Toscana moderna* (Rome [etc.], 1994).

magistracies to defend themselves against the sometimes violent actions of their husbands' relatives. It is, therefore, the state "which legitimizes these women as interlocutors in family conflict matters, and begins granting the widows the right to take the word".[65] Requests and negotiations were accepted as long as they conformed both to a code of behaviour and expression commonly accepted, and to the laws and regulations produced by the same magistracy (even if the prince could ask to have the last word and the final decision), which could differ from the family tradition, just as they could differ from the local and communal laws and statutes. But not only widows were involved in this kind of dealing. Over the course of time, stories emerge from the archives of the magistracies of women who matured into self-consciousness and acquired insight into their own needs and then tried to obtain their acknowledgement.

In 1741 Caterina Guardi, a "poor girl and orphan" wrote to the Florentine magistrate. The girl was living in her father's house where she remained alone after the death of her father and her brothers, "not having wanted to get married or become a nun". Not being on good terms with her brother-in-law, who was trying to steal "some personal belongings she is fond of", she supplicated the magistrate to be left in "the free possession of the paternal goods, which are her maintenance, and of the increases, which she has managed to obtain".[66]

We do not know the outcome of the supplication. Perhaps a positive outcome for Caterina is inconceivable. But certainly, the request to be able freely to dispose of paternal patrimony, the refusal of the obligatory choice between becoming a nun or becoming a wife, is alone a sign of change. It is surely not – not yet – an inconceivable assertion of rights. But is a quest – through a humble supplication addressed to the functionaries of the Florentine state – for a solution which ought to take into account and evaluate personal needs, individual and unique life stories. This goes against forms of behaviour, mentalities, traditions, and certainly laws and regulations considered (and often concretely applied as) objective and unchangeable entities.

65. Calvi, "Dal margine al centro", pp. 105–106.
66. *Idem, Il contratto morale*, pp. 210–211.

IRSH 46 (2001), Supplement, pp. 57–77 DOI: 10.1017/S0020859001000335
© 2001 Internationaal Instituut voor Sociale Geschiedenis

The Power of Petitions: Women and the New Hampshire Provincial Government, 1695–1770*

MARCIA SCHMIDT BLAINE

There are very few sources available to historians which allow us to hear the voices of Anglo-American women. How can we understand what ordinary women believed were their responsibilities to their families and communities and the responsibilities of their government to them? Petitions provide historians with one of the few opportunities to "hear" non-elite women voice their concerns. In provincial New Hampshire, women regularly approached the royal government with individual requests. By viewing the rights associated with petitioning, the procedure involved, and the variety of applications for petition use, female agency in colonial society becomes more apparent. Through petitions, it is possible to understand under what circumstances women turned to the government for assistance, and under what circumstances the government granted their petitions.

The 1699 petition of Deliverance Derry Pittman is a good beginning for analysis. Pittman was the widow of John Derry and the wife of Nathaniel Pitman, and her petition provides a clear picture of a family destroyed by international disputes. The colony of New Hampshire was on the northern edge of English settlement, bounded by Massachusetts to the east and south, the Connecticut River to the west, and New France directly to the north. Because of its location, the colony was intimately involved in the numerous territorial disputes between the empires of England and France. Native Americans took sides in the disputes, with many New England tribes siding with France. Deliverance Pittman and her family were caught in the imperial and intercultural disputes that resulted in King William's War (1689–1697).

> [I]n the year 1694 the petitioner's house was burnt by the Indians; and our cattle killed; as also most of our Children; my husband, one child, and the petitioner taken captives; in which captivity my husband dyed; none but your petitioner returned; hoping to enjoy what estate was left by your petitioner's husband.

* The author would like to thank Holly Bentley Mitchell, Gregory A. Mark, Frank Mevers, Elaine Forman Crane and, especially, Eliga H. Gould for their comments, advice, and critiques of earlier drafts.

Having managed to bribe her way home, Deliverance learned that her husband's estate was tied up by the men entrusted to protect the estate: Joseph Smith and Jeremiah Burnam, men she felt needed the attention of the government. How could she present the case to the government? Through petition. Smith and Burnam, she protested, have

> [...] violently and contrary to law seized; upon your petitioner's cows and estate; the whole amounting to Ninety Pounds, forty five of which are in Lands; all individuals involved [protested that they were doing so] for the good of my children. But in truth the Petitioner knows of noe such children, being now liveing.

As the apparent sole survivor and thus the representative of her first husband's family, Pittman requested that the government force Burnam and Smith to restore the estate (and cows) to her. While the cattle were apparently neglected in the final settlement or delivered without government intervention, the government returned her land to her possession in 1701. Nowhere else is it possible to learn of Pittman's distress. Pittman's new husband presented the petition to the governing body of the colony of New Hampshire on his wife's behalf – but it was her petition.[1] Pittman turned to the government when she was unable to gain control of the estate.

Many historians view petitions like Pittman's as excellent examples of provincial women's weak legal power. Given the general expectations regarding women and societal acceptance of patriarchy and coverture, it is easy to assume that women had little autonomy or power in any eighteenth-century Anglo-American setting. Elaine Forman Crane emphasized "the long-range negative effects" of patriarchy in her detailed work on women in New England seaports. While noting cases of female agency, she concluded that women, especially widows, "were persistently and effectively marginalized in subtle and not-so-subtle ways" due to their sexual and economic vulnerability over the course of the eighteenth century. Using similar language, Cornelia Hughes Dayton concluded that women in the colonial Connecticut legal system were marginalized by the return of traditional patriarchy during the eighteenth century. These and other studies emphasize women's subservient role in eighteenth-century hierarchy.[2]

1. Petitions, 1699, New Hampshire Division of Records Management and Archives [hereafter NhAr], Concord, NH; Sybil Noyes, Charles Thornton Libby and Walter Goodwin Davis, *Genealogical Dictionary of Maine and New Hampshire* (Portland, ME, 1928–1939; repr. Baltimore, MD, 1972), p. 558. Under the English common law doctrine of coverture, a woman's legal existence ceased with her marriage. Her husband represented the family in the eyes of the law.
2. Elaine Forman Crane, *Ebb Tide in New England: Women, Seaports, and Social Change, 1630–1800* (Boston, MA, 1998), pp. 8, 141; and Cornelia Hughes Dayton, *Women Before the Bar: Gender, Law, and Society in Connecticut, 1639–1789* (Chapel Hill, NC, 1995). See also Joan Hoff, *Law, Gender & Injustice: A Legal History of US Women* (New York, 1991).

After all, women were subject to their husbands' will as part of the colonial hierarchy; (it was Pittman's husband, not Deliverance Pittman, who presented the petition "on behalf of his wife"). Women had no or very little control over property. Certainly Pittman's wording fits such an analysis when she "Humbly Showeth" her complaint and asks the court to "commiserate the Condition of your Petitioner [...] And your Petitioner Shall pray etc".

But New Hampshire women, like Anglo-American women in other British colonies, had more options available to them than such an interpretation may indicate. While cultural expectations of female passivity, irrationality, and dependency existed, the cultural reality of female loyalty, flexibility, and persistence created a corollary set of expectations for women. Lisa Wilson's work on the life cycles of colonial men has shown the pre-eminence of family to all members of colonial society. Families were interdependent, each part tied by mutual responsibilities and obligations to the rest, where "[e]veryone was not equal, but neither was anyone autonomous". Laurel Thatcher Ulrich also emphasizes the reciprocal nature of familial rights and responsibilities where the husband's decisions, while supreme, were expected to include his wife's opinions and interests.[3] Women were expected to care for their households and the individuals within them, as well as to take part in their communities as good neighbors. Domestic duties gave women the power and the ability to petition the government to correct perceived errors and to find justice. In the Pittman example, Pittman's new family needed the property Pittman believed belonged to her. The most efficient way to get the land back was to petition the government. In general, women's petitions tended to be personal, rather than political in nature; yet this is a clear instance of the personal being political. Petitioning was an expression of familial leadership available to ordinary women during the colonial era. It gave women who availed themselves of the right a voice with which to inform the government of their needs, opinions, and quarrels.

Petitioning was an "ancient right" in English society, affirmed by the combined governments of the colonies of Massachusetts and New Hampshire in 1641, ostensibly giving subjects license to request from the government the grant of a private act. As part of the Massachusetts' Body of Liberties which codified the colonists' understanding of their basic liberties, the 1641 law stated that

> [...] [e]very man whether inhabitant or fforreiner, free or not free[,] shall have liberty to come to any publique Court, Councell, [...] and either by speech or writeing to move any lawfull, seasonable, and materiall question, or to present

---

3. Lisa Wilson, *Ye Heart of a Man: The Domestic Life of Men in Colonial New England* (New Haven, CT, 1999), p. 3; Laurel Thatcher Ulrich, *Goodwives: Image and Reality in the Lives of Women in Northern New England* (New York, 1980), pp. 8 and 36.

any necessary motion, complaint, petition, Bill or information, whereof that
meeting hath proper cognizance, so it be done in convenient time, due order, and
respective manner.

The 1641 Body of Liberties was developed while England was caught up in
its Civil War, a time when laws and rights were in flux. Women in England
used the disruption of war to demand the right to petition. "Have we not
an equal interest with the men of this Nation in those liberties and
securities contained in the Petition of Right, and other good Laws of the
Land?" From 1641 onward, through all the changes of government and
governors, petitioning seems to have been an understood or customary
right. While the law did not guarantee the right of petition to female
inhabitants of the province, women in New Hampshire clearly believed
the right applied to them in a more generic sense, either as subjects of the
Crown or as inhabitants of the province of New Hampshire. New
Hampshire women availed themselves of the customary right from the
beginning of settlement.[4] Despite their weakened status under the law,
women understood they had the right to seek aid from the men in
authority. They were assertive enough to exercise the opportunity
petitioning provided for civic involvement. They used the customary
right and political means of petition to explain a personal need. The
women who submitted petitions knew the power of petitioning and the
means necessary to complete the process.

Most New Hampshire petitions were presented by a single person or a
small group of persons directly to, first, the Governor of the province and
his Council and, second, the Assembly. Apparently, the petitioner, or
someone representing her (like Pittman's husband), was often, but not
always, present. It was understood by everyone involved that all petitions
required a governmental hearing and response.[5] It was a way, the most
direct way, for subjects to have their wishes heard, discussed, and debated
by those in power who then generally rendered a decision within a few

4. For the Body of Liberties, see Albert Stillman Batchellor, *Laws of New Hampshire*, vol. 1
(Manchester, NH, 1905), p. 753 [hereafter *Laws of NH*]. For discussion of female petitioning in
England see Crane, *Ebb Tide in New England*, pp. 236–238, quotation p. 238; and David
Underdown, *Revel, Riot, and Rebellion: Popular Politics and Culture in England, 1603–1660*
(Oxford, 1985).
5. Stephen A. Higginson, "A Short History of the Right to Petition Government for the Redress
of Grievances", *The Yale Law Journal*, 96:142 (1986), pp. 142–166, 15;. Gregory A. Mark, "The
Vestigial Constitution: The History and Significance of the Right to Petition", *Fordham Law
Review*, 66 (1998), pp. 2153–2231, 2162–2170; "The government [...] felt a socio-political
obligation to hear those grievances, to provide a response, and often to act upon the complaints",
p. 2160. See also Brian Weiser, "Reconstructing the Monarchy: Access to the King in the Reign of
Charles II", (Ph.D., Washington University in St. Louis, 1999), for a discussion of the role of
petitions in seventeenth-century English society: "To the popular imagination, petitions [...]
formed the essential point of contact [...] between rulers and ruled", p. 8.

days of receiving the petition. With no clear separation of powers, petitions were used for executive, legislative, and judicial matters. A male petitioner in 1697 stated this understanding plainly, for the petitioner knew of no "other way for the fatherless to come by there [sic] undoubted Right but to come to your Honours for releife".[6] Petitioners trusted the provincial government to listen and give each petition due consideration.

The petitioning process began with writing the petition (or having it written) and submitting the petition and the necessary fees to the secretary of the Governor's Council. Elaine Forman Crane found that submitting a petition to the government of another New England colony, Rhode Island, was an "expensive proposition" where charges reached £4 per petition by the mid-eighteenth century, a prohibitive amount for anyone of lesser means.[7] However, in sharp contrast, the New Hampshire provincial government charged far less. In 1718 the government's secretary charged from 2s 6d to 10s, "according to import" of the petition, and the clerk of the legislature charged an additional 4s to read the petition, record the order, and file the records of each action. By 1768 the province had standardized the secretary's fees for petitions to 3s per entry, regardless of the "import". Such fees would not have hampered women's ability to present their grievances to the colonial government of New Hampshire.[8]

The written petition began with a deferential address to the Governor, Council, and Assembly of the province in recognition of the hierarchical order of governance. For example, Pittman's 1699 petition began "To the Right Honble Samuel Allen, Esqr Governor and commander in Chiefe of his Majesty's Province of New Hampshire and Councill Assembled". Similarly, a petition presented by Eleanor Stickney of Hampstead in December of 1755 began "To His Excellency Benning Wentworth Esqr: Governor & Commander in Chief In & Over his majesty's Province of New Hampshire[,] the Honble his Majesty's Council[,] and House of Representatives for Said Province in General Assembly Convend".[9] Given the formality of the address, it is possible to assume many petitioners consulted a source, either human or literary, on the proper format before submitting their appeal.

The petitioner followed the salutation with an explanation of the complaint or problem and the resulting difficulty of her position. Women's petitions covered a wide variety of topics. Some petitions

---

6. Petitions, 1697, NhAr.
7. Crane, *Ebb Tide in New England*, p. 150. Interestingly, Rhode Island seems to have often charged more in government fees. James Kettner found that "[o]nly in Rhode Island were the costs of naturalization consistently high", up to £7, while Massachusetts charged just under 8s in 1731. James H. Kettner, *The Development of American Citizenship, 1608–1870* (Chapel Hill, NC, 1978), p. 113.
8. *Laws of NH*, vol. 1, p. 147 and vol. 3, p. 493.
9. Petitions, 1699, and 1755, NhAr.

covered local land problems, while some women took part in requests for new towns or a tavern license. Individuals may have requested assistance in dividing an entailed estate, limiting the legal trade in alcohol, or regaining losses from wartime efforts.

Whether the petitioner was male or female, each petition was worded in such a way as to gain as much sympathy as possible. Thus it is easy to interpret the wording in petitions as a plea from the powerless because they are full of phrases meant to arouse sympathy: "being in a low condicion [sic] & sickly & weake & not ablt to manage business as formerly", or "My Necesity Oblidges Mee Once More to Recommend My Miserable Circumstances to the Honorbl Generall Court", or "under the Poor Circumstances in which she is left by the Death of her late Husband".[10] However, the purpose of the petitions, to persuade the government to grant the request, made such phrases so common in petitions as to be formulaic. (Even Thomas Jefferson, in writing the Declaration of Independence, wrote "We have Petitioned for Redress in the most humble terms".) Both men and women used a language of subservience in their petitions to the government.[11]

While women used terms such as "powerless" and "helpless" far more often than men, the wording men chose, which usually concentrated on their economic weaknesses, conveyed a similar message of need. There-fore, in individual petitions, when women petitioned for their "fatherless children" or to asked the government to aid them due to "Poor Circumstances", the meaning of the wording in their petitions did not vary tremendously from the wording men used, except, of course, that men spoke of their "motherless [rather than fatherless] children". All petitioners mentioned any other possible difficulty in their lives which might create sympathy among the members of the Council and legislature and cause them to grant the request. Language was used to express the understanding of governmental power and authority. But, consciously or unconsciously, language could also be manipulated to achieve a desired end.

Humble phrases also reminded those who wrote them and those who received them of the paternalistic order of society. Free, white, wealthy males dominated the Anglo-American hierarchy. But status included more than gender; it included class, economic status, access to power, family, and certain other intangibles as well. A certain degree of subservience was expected from petitioners, no matter their age, sex, or economic status; and

10. Petitions, 1693, 1759, and 1745, NhAr.
11. Individual men occasionally appealed to the government by expressing their utter helplessness. Two seamen, Andrew Peterson and Henry Acreman, asked the Governor and Council to "[c]onsider the poor distressed state of your petitioners being altogether helples for want of mony or means or skills"; Petitions, n.d., NhAr.

whether they felt subservient or not. It was simply part of the process. The ritualistic, humble language incorporated into petitions did not negate the impact the petition and the petitioner could have on governmental actions.

Petitions to the provincial government in New Hampshire were common throughout the eighteenth century. But, despite the fact that petitioning was used by all in society, many historians of women have taken the words in women's petitions literally, as illustrations of inherent female weakness in colonial society. In her 1980 study of women of the American Revolution, Linda Kerber conceives of petitioning as an almost purely political act and one that was not used by women before the 1770s. Petitions submitted by individuals Kerber dismisses as mere "individual expressions of opinion". To Kerber, the petitioning process is "the most primitive of political mechanisms" which gave women access only to the least controllable and most cumbersome of grievance procedures. She emphasizes the deferential nature of petitions and women's lack of power in the political process. Deborah Rosen, too, finds petitions to have been a much weaker route to justice. Despite what she takes to be the inherent weakness in petitioning, Rosen finds that it was the route more often chosen by women, instead of the courts, a route men followed.[12]

But both Kerber and Rosen are snared by the submissive language of petitions and miss the importance of the process and the opportunities petitioning gave to women. Petitioning gave women a voice where they would otherwise be voiceless. Petitions provided the opportunity for far greater female assertiveness and civic involvement than either Kerber or Rosen allow. Petitions may be viewed as powerful tools for the disenfranchised, a group that included more than just women. Petitions were often the most direct means of communication between the provincial government and its subjects. They were the means whereby "individuals could seek the employment of public power to redress private wrongs". Since petitions were most often "individual expressions of opinion", they allowed the voices of any private subject to be heard in a way no other political device could. As Stephen Higginson explains, "petitioning meant that no group in colonial society was entirely without political power", even the married woman under coverture. Gregory Mark notes that "even individual grievances embodied in petitions carried powerful political weight simply because of the individual's capacity to invoke public power".[13] Women knew it was the duty of their government to hear and respond to petitions presented to them and they turned to their

12. Linda K. Kerber, *Women of the Republic: Intellect and Ideology in Revolutionary America* (Chapel Hill, NC, 1980; repr. New York, 1986), pp. 41, 98, 287; Deborah A. Rosen, *Courts and Commerce: Gender, Law, and the Market Economy in Colonial New York* (Columbus, OH, 1997), pp. 114–115.
13. Higginson, "A Short History," pp. 144, 153. Mark, "The Vestigial Constitution," p. 2182.

government when needed. It was not legislative or executive power they sought, understanding their place in the overall hierarchy of colonial society. They used the legal custom of petitioning as a means to find an efficient remedy to a situation in which the government could provide a solution.

Since petitions were a means by which the disenfranchised could inform, warn, or otherwise instruct the government, they allowed for broad participatory action at a time when the Assembly as well as the Governor and Council accepted all petitions placed before them.[14] Colonists used the mechanism of petition for a tremendous variety of purposes and the process was open to women as well as men, whether married, single, or widowed, rich, middling, or poor. The fact that most petitions were submitted by individuals, or very small groups of people, did not diminish their importance. Petitioning was a legal custom accepted throughout the colonies.

In New Hampshire, the procedure for dealing with petitions was straightforward. Petitions apparently received two main hearings: one before the Governor sitting with his Council and a second before the Assembly, often on the same day. The notice of action taken on each petition was supposed to be written in the margins or on the reverse of the petition, but unfortunately the casual nature of New Hampshire provincial governance meant that often the clerk neglected his duty. For many petitions no indication exists of approval or disapproval on the petition. But it is possible to discern the unwritten decisions for many petitions through the minutes of the Council or Assembly or through the disbursement lists from the records of the Treasury.

The petitions presented by women to the New Hampshire government tended to be from women who were either widowed or without a male presence in their households, for one reason or another. Of the 153 women whose signatures are clear and who filed petitions between 1695 and 1770 which are still extant, 20 women joined mass petitions to request new townships. But most women (87 per cent) submitted petitions aimed at rectifying individual concerns. Along with five women whose petitions do not fit into any particular category, a handful of women, four, informed the government of abuse they suffered at the hands of their husbands and three others requested a divorce. Seven women disagreed with judicial decisions and wanted the government to order the courts to rehear a case;

---

14. Although he concentrates on petitions submitted with large numbers of signatures, Edmund S. Morgan has written that petitions "nourished the fiction of the people's capacity to speak for themselves. In doing so they renewed the invitation that popular sovereignty unavoidably extended to flesh-and-blood people outside parliament who thought themselves qualified to do the speaking", an interesting thought, particularly when applied to women; Edmund S. Morgan, *Inventing the People: The Rise of Popular Sovereignty in England and America* (New York, 1988), p. 230.

six wanted financial help because they had been captured by Native Americans. Ten women submitted petitions relating to their work as tavern keepers or their desire to keep a tavern. But the largest number of cases may be placed in two categories: 43 women (28 per cent) entered petitions dealing with real or personal property issues, and 55 women (36 per cent) submitted war-related petitions.[15]

Statistics give important information, but the stories behind the stark facts make petitions an unusually good source of information for social historians. Looking at the divorce petitions, for example, is revealing. Divorce, it is generally agreed, was easier to receive in New England than in England. But not in New Hampshire. As one petition put it, "there is no Executive court in this Province [that] has jurisdiction of such a Cause". In New Hampshire, divorce was allowed only by special act of the legislature and special acts began with a petition. Between 1695 and 1770, just three women filed a petition for divorce. The most common problem cited as a reason for divorce was adultery. Eliza Smart's petition for divorce in 1697 indicated a clear need and desire on the part of both parties to end their marriage. Smart "presented her petition desiring a divorce from her husband, he being married to another woman at New York as by testimony from his own hand to Jno. Hinks, Esq. President, as also the testimony of Rob. Almary". Similarly, Eleanor Stickney faced her husband's adultery after a twenty-year marriage. In 1755, Stickney explained to the Governor, Council, and Assembly that her husband had "kept Company with One Mehetable Guile a Single Woman [...] & had Criminal Conversation with her". Then the two lovers had fled to Springfield, Massachusetts "where they lived together as Man & Wife". A shamed Mehetable returned to her home town and confessed to their sins while James fled.[16]

Interestingly, none of the divorce claims use abuse or economic neglect as a reason for divorce. Many women who were, or believed themselves to be, abused or neglected, and who had friends or family willing to house them, simply absented themselves from their hearths and husbands. But, very occasionally, they also alerted the government to their treatment. Ann Foss, wife of the innkeeper Zachariah, informed the government that her

15. New Hampshire petitions may be found at the Division of New Hampshire Records Management and Archives in Concord, NH and in New Hampshire, *Provincial and State Papers*, 40 vols (Concord, NH, 1887–1943) [hereafter *NHPP*]. The archivist for the state is in the process of matching both published and unpublished and unindexed committee reports to petitions.

16. *NHPP*, vol. 2, p. 249 (Smart); Petitions, 1755, NhAr (Stickney). The other divorce may be found in Petitions, 1765 and 1766, NhAr (Barrell). A similarly small numbers of male petitioners requested a divorce. In one very interesting case, Greenwood Carpenter was granted a divorce from his wife, Sarah Leathers Carpenter, in 1771 by the New Hampshire government. Two full years later, the divorce was rescinded by the royal government in England; *NHPP*, vol. 7, pp. 22, 272.

husband "has by a long Course of illusage and Unkind treatment to her [...] Obliged her for the preservation of her health & Safety to leave him & throw herself on the mercy of any Acquaintance & friend for present Support". She feared his "unsteadiness of Temper, and Ungovern'd Passions" and asked the government, not for a divorce, but for protection for herself and her friends. Zachariah replied with an acerbic petition of his own and battle was joined, one that dragged on to no discernable conclusion.

In a case of perceived economic neglect, the widow Mary Macris and her children had lived comfortably on the profits from land inherited from her father and a deceased husband. But then she married Joseph Macris "justly Expecting that he would help me in my difficulties" of widowhood. When she discovered, apparently to her surprise, that her second husband would not allow her to control the income-producing investments she brought into the marriage nor give her the disposable income she controlled before her remarriage, she left him. After living on her own for three years, she petitioned for the right to

> [...] take the said Estate into her own hands, to apply the profits thereof to her own & Infant Children's support, to maintain an Action in the King's Court in her own Name, for the Recovery of the Debts due her while she was Sole, and for any other matter or thing properly belonging to her, & to Dispose thereof as she might do by Law, if not under Coverture.

Macris must have realized that she was treading on thin ice: the government could not condone the actions of a woman who had left her husband. Macris hoped for the opportunity to act as a *feme sole*, an unmarried adult woman. She was disappointed: her petition was dismissed.

In her bid to act as an independent agent, shopkeeper Elizabeth Pascall was more successful. Around 1753, Pascall's husband, Michael Henry, was in some way detained in royal service. In 1763, after supporting herself for the previous ten years, Pascall petitioned the government to sell land she had inherited and, further, for the right to act as a *feme sole*. "Michael Henry Pascall Esq hath been absent from your Petitioner Beyond seas for more than ten years Past & still is Detaind in his majesties Service and it is uncertain when he will return." Pascall reasoned, since she had supported herself without her husband's aid in his long absence, she wanted

> [...] to make sale of her said Land, the whole or any Part, or to dispose of the Same by will & also that she may be enabled to Contract in her own name & to Sue or Defend any action in law as if she were Sole notwithstanding her aforesaid Coverture.

In this instance, the right was granted; however, Pascall's life did not change dramatically. She was able to sell the land, as she requested in her petition. With *feme sole* trader status, she could, with more surety, make contracts with shippers, purchase goods from English suppliers, and provide what her customers wanted, all in her own name. Pascall was the only woman, or the only one for whom records survive, to receive *feme sole* trader status in New Hampshire during the entire period under study and her circumstances were unusual. The ten-year absence of her husband had turned her into a virtual widow without the benefit of dower.[17]

Although women did have the opportunity to use petitions to explain to the government problems within their marriage that they felt warranted attention, most women did not petition for actions which interfered with the duties and legal rights of a husband. Not only were such petitions seldom successful, but women seldom submitted them. Such petitions passed the outer limits of women's acceptable roles. Women's petitions were far more frequent, and more successful, where they requested action that would aid the entire family. Women's accepted role as mistresses of their households, mothers of their children, and consorts of their husbands gave them the power to fight for their families.[18] When women, either as widows or within the understood boundaries of wives, presented cases in which their chief aim was clearly to improve or protect the condition of their families, especially their children, their petitions were well received, well considered, and generally granted.

One of the two largest categories of petitions submitted by women involved property issues. Widows often needed some assistance with the estates of their recently deceased husbands. In 1769 Hannah Jose petitioned as administratrix of her husband's estate for the right to sell some land to pay his debts. Ann Clark asked for the right to cut the entail on her husband's estate and to sell the land in parts. Her adult children were with her when the petition was presented and agreed to the request. When Leah Nutter's husband's estate was divided without regard to his will, Nutter petitioned the government for assistance she was not getting from the probate judge. In 1768 Mary Marston requested the right to have the judge of probate "to Cause Partition & Division of their said Estate to be made in the Same manner [...] as he may by Law do of the Real Estates of Persons dying Intestate".[19] Most requests by widows to ease the sale of land, redistribute an estate, or settle a problem of inheritance were granted.

17. Petitions, 1741, 1743, and 1767, NhAr; *NHPP*, vol. 5, p. 695; vol. 7, p. 148 (Foss and Macris); Petitions, 1763 (Pascall), NhAr; Raymond A. Brighton, *They Came to Fish: A Brief Look at Portsmouth's 350 Years of History; It's Local and World-wide Involvement and the People Concerned Through the Eyes of a Reporter* (Portsmouth, NH, 1973), p. 45; *The New-Hampshire Gazette*, 2 March 1764, p. 3, and 6 March 1761, p. 3; *NHPP*, vol. 6, pp. 866, 885; *NHPP*, vol. 7, p. 44 (Pascall).
18. Ulrich, *Goodwives*. Ulrich concentrates on the many different roles colonial women played in Anglo-American society.
19. *NHPP*, vol. 3, p. 380 (Jose); *ibid.*, vol. 4, pp. 42–43 (Clark); Petitions, 1748 (Nutter), 1768 (Marston), NhAr.

The requests would benefit the family and generally ease the families' transition from one generation to the next while posing no threat to the existing social order.

New widows were not the only ones trying to deal with land issues on the turbulent northern frontier. As times of war repeatedly emptied the land of white settlers while periods of peace pushed the line of white settlement farther west and north, women were forced to fight for their land. The initial illustration in this article is just such a case. Deliverance Derry Pittman requested the return of land taken by the men appointed to settle her first husband's estate. Their legally-appointed control left Pittman without remedy – except through petition. In another land issue, a woman with grown sons petitioned the government with her daughter-in-law to reclaim land lost in the French and Indian War. Judy and Margaret Moore were captured from what is now the Brattleboro, Vermont, area in 1758. In her petition to the New Hampshire Governor and Council, Mother Moore explained, "Your Excleneys Humble Petisoners [...] have under gon a great deall of hardships By the war[...] [F]or in the year 1758 my husband and on[e] of my Sons was Kiled upon the spot". Along with the dead son's wife and children, she was captured but redeemed. Moore petitioned the government for her daughter-in-law and her "three men grown" sons in order to regain title to land the family had worked for the past twelve years. The petition was signed first by the two women and then by the three adult sons, followed by witnesses.[20] Clearly the children, even the adult men, bowed to Mistress Moore's desire to save the land for the family. No other word but respect for the family matriarch seems to fit their actions. As a matriarch, the family turned to her to act as the family agent to provide the leadership, stability, and continuity that the children, despite adulthood, needed.

As in the Moore example, women's role as head of the family was most apparent during wartime and the largest number of petitions were submitted by women affected by war. To date, histories of the pre-Revolutionary colonial wars have focused on the men who fought. Whenever there was any mention of the women the fighting men left behind, it focused on their plight, not the options available to them. This is natural enough, since many women did confront immense difficulties in the loss of their spouses. Mental, physical and, most urgently, monetary challenges faced women during war as they grappled, some more successfully than others, with the work of two. Women took on the work of their departed husbands with the expectation that their extra burdens would end with the return of their husbands and the conclusion of the war.

---

20. Petitions, 1699 (Pittman) and 1760 (Moore), NhAr. Margaret and Judy Moore were mother-in-law and daughter-in-law and the main part of the petition refers to the mother-in-law. It is unclear, however, which was which.

But, in northern New England, warfare was almost constant during the last 100 years of colonization. The imperial wars between France and England: King William's War (1689–1697), Queen Anne's War (1702–1713), King George's War (1744–1748), and finally, the French and Indian, or Seven Years War (1754–1763), were punctuated with several periods of intensified Anglo-Native conflicts in northern New England. In his history of New Hampshire, Jeremy Belknap noted that by 1725 "every man of forty years of age [had] [...] seen more than twenty years of war".[21] The wartime service of fathers, husbands, and sons was a normal part of life for every generation of colonial women.

As the agents of their families, and in their husbands' absence, wives were able to act with the authority that their husbands generally had, guiding their families. They were responsible for the immediate wellbeing of their families. Colonial governments turned to the wives of men who were absent in order to provide stability for individual families and thus order for the entire society. The best example of this is during King George's War (1744–1748), when New Hampshire and Massachusetts leaders decided on a bold plan to use colonial militia to attack the seemingly impregnable French fortress of Louisbourg. Fortress Louisbourg guarded the entrance to the St Lawrence River, the gateway to Canada, from a peninsula in Nova Scotia. New Hampshire and Massachusetts contributed the bulk of the soldiers for the successful colonial attack.[22] To encourage men to enlist in the Louisbourg expedition of 1745–1746, New Hampshire legislation included provisions for widows. "The Widows or nearest relatives of any officer or soldier that is slain or shall otherwise loose [sic] his life in the service, shall be entitled to four months pay." But the legislation also included a further provision to protect the wives left behind. "[T]he wives of any officer or soldier in the Expedition or any other person that appears with a power of Attorney duly authenticated, shall at the end of every month receive out of the Treasury half or all the wages of such officer or soldier as he appears for." The government used the pronoun "he" when referring to those with power to request wages, but the passage started with "wives". Thus encouraged, wives of men in the New Hampshire regiment of

21. Jeremy Belknap, *The History of New-Hampshire*, vol. 1 (Dover, NH, 1812; repr. New York, 1970), p. 217.
22. George C. Gilmore, compiler, *Role of New Hampshire Soldiers at the Battle of Bennington, August 16, 1777 with [the] Roll of New Hampshire Men at Louisbourge, Cape Breton, 1745* (Manchester, NH , 1891 and Concord, NH, 1896; repr. Baltimore, MD, 1995), pp. 15–16, estimated that New Hampshire sent 500 men. William Douglass's pamphlet claimed New Hampshire "contributed of 350 Men under Col. Moor", and later sent 200 reinforcements for a total of 550 soldiers; Douglass, *A Summary*, p. 48. Peckham's study reports that New Hampshire contributed 450 soldiers; Howard H. Peckham, *The Colonial Wars, 1689 –1762* (Chicago, IL, 1964), p. 100.

approximately 500 knew they had the right to petition the government for at least part of the pay of their men – should the need arise. None of the existing petitions that requested payment of the wages of a living relative include a "power of Attorney duly authenticated", so perhaps the reality of wartime need ultimately superseded legal exactions in the eyes of those who wrote and heard petitions. During the later French and Indian War, the New Hampshire legislature ordered "that the Ballance for wages due to each person as carried off against his name be paid to him, his order, widow or Legal Representative". The legal representative was almost always a soldier's wife or widowed mother.[23] The legislatures of northern New England recognized hierarchy within the family as well as the need for wives/widows to act with an understanding of the "mutual responsibilities" of the marriage partnership. Actions taken by the "war widows" of New Hampshire were well within the bounds of traditional female roles; in this case the role as the family's representative or agent. It is also important to note that members of the colonial paternalistic society expected wives to take on this role. No petition from a woman relating to war issues, or any other matter, was dismissed simply because it was from a woman.

The petitions relating to war may be divided into two main sub-categories: petitions requesting an allowance from the husband's earnings, and petitions requiring reimbursement for goods lost in battle or on an expedition. The petitions for allowance emphasized subservience and need and fit the "helpless widow" or at least "helpless female" stereotype. "Sundry Women whose Husbands are gone in the Expedition against Louisburg" petitioned the government in June 1745 for an allowance from the wages their husbands had thus far earned as soldiers. "Your Petitioners families are in Daily Want of Support & are now destitute of the help they used to have by the Day Wages of their Husbands on which only they Depended for Subsistence." The fifteen women who signed the petition stressed the perilous position of their households and their dependent nature as wives. They depended on their husbands' ability to bring in income and to ease the burdens of family life. Without their husband's presence and work, their already heavy workloads were greatly increased.

However, upon closer inspection, the petition may be seen as more than a plea from the powerless. It was a message from women who, while poor and overburdened, knew that the government owed them money and knew how to inform the government of its obligations. And it was more than that: it was the second petition from the fifteen signers. The money granted in the first "being but Small was Soon Expended". They petitioned once again, arguing that "it Seems unreasonable that the Families of those

23. *Laws of NH*, vol. 1, pp. 374, 473–474; *NHPP*, vol. 6, p. 880.

who Expose their Lives daily for the Good of their Country should be left to Suffer".[24] Their households, which had depended upon the "Day Wages" of their husbands, now depended upon the willingness of the wives and mothers to use their right of petitioning to attain needed cash for their families. The government owed the soldiers' families the money and had provided the means for the women to collect. Although no record remains as to the outcome of their second petition, the fifteen "sundry women" willingly approached the seats of power to maintain themselves and their families, fully understanding that since their husbands had earned the money and it was owed to the soldiers' families, there was no reason to fall upon the pocketbooks of their neighbors for charity.[25] Further, as the wives of day laborers, it is also clear that even women of little means understood and willingly used the petitioning process. Usually, twentieth-century historians view women of lower status as virtually powerless. Powerful they were not, but neither were they voiceless. Petitioning was the most efficient way lower-class women could expect their individual needs and the needs of their families to be heard.

Other women, finding themselves in similar circumstances during their husbands' absences, approached the government with similar aims. As a result of the Louisbourg expedition, in April 1747 Ann Brotton, Sarah Tucker, and Sarah Messuere informed the New Hampshire provincial government that "your Petitioners were very nearly affected by and Concerned in the Loss of those Men lately belonging to the Sloop *Warren* [...] One having a Son & the other two their Husbands among the Captives". Along with the anguish they must have felt in fearing the worst for their loved ones, they also felt the need to protect the wages of their men. The only way to do that was to bring the situation to the attention of the government and state their expectations. Their men "had been a Considerable time in the Service before they were taken [by the French] for which the Wages Ramins due". Further, "it Seems to your Petitioners but just & Equal that their Wages Should be Continued till their Return Or if they are dead till there shall be Certain News thereof". Therefore, the women requested all the wages owed "to this time" be paid to them, and that the men be allowed to continue to earn wages until news of their condition was discovered. After stating their case in the most straightforward manner possible, they then added a seemingly perfunctory "Or that you would Grant them Such Relief under their Afflictive Circumstances as in your Great Wisdom & Goodness you See Meet & your petitioners as in Duty bound shall Ever Pray &c". Having couched their words in an acceptable formula, the supplicants felt free not only to ask for the wages

---

24. *NHPP*, vol. 17, p. 225–226. The first petition is no longer extant.
25. In New England, individuals who needed assistance could also turn to their towns for support. However, they then became a public charge. Most people preferred to collect money owed them rather than use town welfare.

owed to their men, but also to explain to the government how wages should be paid and for what length of time. After all, the "Petitioners Families [...] depended on their Respective Relatives [...] for their Subsistence and *their* Wages in the Service was the only Means of the Support of themselves & families". Their predicament was "Occasion'd by their [men] Entering into the Public Service" when the mother country needed sailors. If the needy families did not receive aid, then the women would have to proceed as best they could until their husbands returned or were declared to be dead.[26] Either way, the continuance of the families of the three supplicants was up to them. They were doing the best they could with the means available to maintain their families.

Similarly, the only time Elizabeth Ham of Portsmouth approached the provincial government was to petition for her husband's wages. However, she was a recent widow, not the wife of a living soldier. On 19 February 1746, a petition was entered "per her order", explaining that "Your Petitioner has a family of small Children to maintain & no Estate whereon to Depend they having been hither to Supported by the Industry of their Parents". Through the use of the plural, Ham left no doubt that she provided half of the support for her children through her "Industry". With the other half of that industrious partnership dead at Louisbourg, Ham petitioned the government, asking for, and receiving, the rest of her husband's wages from the soldiers' pay in the Treasury.[27] She entered her request with the aim of self-support. She did not want to become a public charge. Like women in similar circumstances, need drove her actions, but means, and at least a temporary remedy, were available.

Sarah French, a recent widow from Hampton, New Hampshire, used a slightly more aggressive tone in requesting a nonwage allowance from the government. In a patriotic move before leaving for the Louisbourg expedition, French's husband apparently mortgaged all the property they owned "for Security for the Payment of twenty five Pounds of the Loan money which he took up". He had invested not only his life but all that he owned in the expedition, as the "loan" money of which she wrote was money raised by the province to cover wartime expenses. But in doing so he left his "Large family of Small Children" and widow in dire circumstances. "Your Petitioner Can see no method by which She Can Possibly Pay the Interest or Clear the Mortgage unless your Excellency and Honours in Your Great Clemency Shall be Pleas'd to make me some Considerations herein for my Relief." The request here is clear: French was hoping that she "could be Reliev'd herein [of the interest payments]

---

26. Petitions, 1747, NhAr. Also in *NHPP*, vol. 18, pp. 305–306. The italicized word was underlined in the original petition. No notice of action on this petition exists.

27. Like many petitions, Ham's petition and mention of it are found in many parts of the records. The quote is from Petitions, 1746, NhAr, but notice of the petition may be found in *NHPP*, vol. 18, p. 264 and *ibid.*, vol. 5, pp. 406, 795.

for the present that hereafter by Industry and the Blessings of God I Should be able so to Clear the Said Obligations". Without some temporary release from the mortgage interest payments she must "be Strip'd Bare of every thing and turn'd Out of Doors with a Large family of Small Children to the mercies of the world".[28] The implied questions reverberated loudly: did the government want to create another public charge? Had she not paid enough already? She was not planning to renege on her responsibilities: eventually she would pay what her family owed. She appealed to the government to allow her the chance to continue to support her family and delay payment of the debt. The burdens of death had forever altered French's part in the world. Like all widows, her life now depended on her ability to provide the resources for her family's existence.

Requests for aid or a wage allowance had a tone that differed from petitions for reimbursement. Women who asked for reimbursement were more direct and less guarded in their petitions. When Mary Moore, wife of the New Hampshire regiment's commander Colonel Samuel Moore, felt that her husband had overextended their family's finances in the cause of empire, she presented a petition to the colony's government on 27 September 1745. Colonel Moore, she explained, "hath advanced considerable sums [£1,173 old tenor] for the Benefit and advantage of the soldiers at Louisbourg under his Command", and she asked that the government "give your Petitioner opportunity to produce the vouchers for the Sums advanced", as well as an accounting of what was "due to him the said Samuel for him self and servants", so that the government could repay the sum owed to Colonel Moore "[u]nto your petitioner".[29] While no known personal correspondence exists which can confirm the request from husband to wife, the detail given in the petition leads to the logical assumption that Samuel had written to his wife explaining his expenditures and expectations of repayment. Another logical explanation is that Mary kept the accounts herself. Mary Moore was the person her husband chose to act in his stead, and she acted knowing that as a subject she had the right to petition the government and to be heard.

The petitions from women requesting reimbursement for nursing were as straightforward as Moore's petition. Illness attacked almost every expedition of soldiers away from home for any length of time. Thus many of the soldiers who returned home arrived sick and needed nursing. In several petitions throughout the eighteenth century, women requested payment promised by the government for the nursing of soldiers. For instance, in 1763 Susanna Parker of Charlestown appealed to the government in a well-documented petition regarding her care of a sick soldier who was "helpless as an infant" for much of the time. The distance

28. Petitions, 1746, NhAr.
29. Petitions, 1745, NhAr.

from Charlestown on the Connecticut River to the seat of government in Portsmouth on the Atlantic seacoast meant Parker did not appear personally, and her case had to be as strong as possible if there was any hope of success. In an itemized account, she charged £22 11d for candles, wood, bed, bedding, and board of the soldiers. Finally, she included a petition from William Hanson, the father of one of the sick soldiers, supporting her claims and verifying that Parker cared for his son for seven months. It was Hanson, a lieutenant in the New Hampshire militia, who presented the petition to the Governor, Council, and Assembly. Parker included a note from the Charlestown Justice of the Peace. "[T]here appeared Susannah Parker Subscriber to the above Accompt and made Solemn oath that the same was Just [and] True." Similar petitions regarding the nursing of nonrelated soldiers were not unusual. For instance, Hannah Osgood of Concord who was paid for nursing soldier Samuel Houston for forty-one days in her tavern in 1754 while he began to mend from a broken leg; and the Widow McClanen of Brentwood who was paid over £100 in 1761 for nursing James Moody, who returned from his stint in the militia with smallpox.[30]

Some women considered the nursing of their returned ill or injured family members warwork worthy of compensation by the government. Elizabeth and Mary Drown, wife and daughter respectively, presented a bill to the New Hampshire provincial government for nursing Samuel Drown, who had been wounded while scouting in the Rochester area in May 1748. Their petition was sent to the government along with Samuel's separate petition for aid. Samuel explained to the representatives that he was "now Extrem Ill at portsmo[uth] & being under Low Sircumstances Borth [both] of Body & purse & being wounded in the province Service Beg you would make Some provision for me to prevent my Soffering & for my Comfortable Sorport". His wife and daughter were less circumspect in their approach to the government. "The Province of New Hampshire Debtor to Elizabeth Drown for nursing the said Drown in the year 1747 when he was wounded by the Enemy and Car[ri]ed Down to Portsmouth [...] we expect the Common wages that is allowed for nursing." Elizabeth had nursed her husband for ten weeks and Mary had attended her father for eight. The petitions had the desired effect because the government agreed to support its wounded scout "in the most frugal manner" and to pay his family the customary allowance for their nursing services.[31]

A petition from the French and Indian War attracts more attention (and

30. Petitions, 1763, NhAr; Donna-Belle Garvin and James L. Garvin, *On the Road North of Boston: New Hampshire Taverns and Turnpikes, 1700–1900* (Concord, NH, 1988) p. 138; Petitions, 1761, NhAr.
31. Petitions, 1748, NhAr, and *NHPP*, vol. 18, pp. 307–308. The government "voted that Elizth Drown be allow'd & pd twenty shills & Mary Drown ten shills in full of their accts for Nursing of Saml Drown"; *NHPP*, vol. 5, p. 579.

pity) from the twenty-first-century researcher. In 1762, the widow Bridget Clifford of Brentwood petitioned for "money to get her sick soldier son home from Albany". We can imagine her distress, knowing her son was too ill to return home himself where she could look after him. Then she added a line to her petition that shed light on the difficulties the war had caused her: "I Lost two Sons that went in the Expedition that way already".[32] She was eager to nurse her sole surviving son to health if the province would just bring him home. The only means she had available to let the government know of her willingness, desire, and ability to do so was to petition.

As the weeks stretched into months and their men did not return, women who were related to injured, lost, or killed combatants learned that the temporary burdens they shouldered could become permanent ones. Death was no stranger to soldiers away from home – or their wives. Petitions from women who had suffered the deaths of their spouses had the greatest air of urgency. Usually unknown in public records before the deaths of their spouses, widows, now *femes sole*, became the public speakers and, if without an adult son, the sole representatives of their households. In order to succeed in their petitions they had to rely on memory, the testimony of friends and comrades, and itemized accounts. Deborah Dunn of Portsmouth entered the official government records when she petitioned the government in 1746. Her husband, a carpenter named Nicholas, had volunteered for the 1745 Louisbourg attack and there had died in battle. She used the usual words to explain her helplessness: "Your Petitioner is a poor helpless widow & Nothing but her hands to get [...] her living". But after that she placed formulaic helplessness aside in this, her only appeal to the provincial government. Dunn enclosed a detailed list all the items lost by her late husband, "one of the Bold Adventurers in the Attack of the Island Battery", that included a gun, a knapsack, a cartridge box, a hatchet, five pairs of hose, three pairs of breeches, three jackets, one coat, one shirt, one pair of silver buckles (worth £3 10s alone), and a hat. The total value of all the goods came to £37 4s old tenor. The government apparently agreed with her accounting and allowed her a generous £15 new tenor within a week after hearing her petition.[33]

---

32. Petitions, 1762, NhAr. Although no known action was taken by the governor, council, or legislature, the request to transport sick soldiers once they were well enough to move was well within the norm.

33. Petitions, 1746, NhAr and *NHPP*, vol. 18, pp. 283–284, 287, and *ibid.*, vol. 5, p. 451. In 1742 New Hampshire revalued its currency and created new tenor currency with a four to one exchange rate with old tenor, an exchange rate which continued to rise. Yet for some reason, in most petitions in which specific debts were enumerated, the petitioners continued to use old tenor in their accounts throughout the colonial period. Thus the £15 new tenor that Dunn received was very generous and/or may have included other debts owed to Dunn by the government.

When Olive Russell of Litchfield petitioned the New Hampshire government in 1758, she included an itemized list and a sworn statement signed by Justice of Peace Matthew Patten. Lieutenant Pelatiah Russell left home in 1757 with

> [...] [a] good new Beaver hatt, two new worsted Caps and one woolen shirt, three good Jackets and one Coat and two Pairs of Leather Breeches, three Pair of Stockings and one Pair of Shoes and one Pair of Magezens [moccasins], one Silk handkerCheif and one Cotton hander Chief and a Gun and Snapsack [knapsack?] and Powder horn.

Either Widow Russell had an extraordinary memory or she and her husband had written it all down just in case Olive needed to produce such a list. The sworn list worked. The legislature approved payment of £100 for the missing articles and three months wages.[34] It was Russell's first and last known official contact with the provincial government. Despite her lack of any other communication with the general government, she knew and understood the power of petition and used it when she needed to.

Elizabeth Goudy of Portsmouth tried a similar approach when she became a widow upon the death of her husband, James, who was also killed while serving at Louisbourg. She delivered a petition to the government explaining that her husband had been "charg'd by Capt Mason with two Guns one of which he return'd to Capt Mason & the other into ye Province Store for the Expedition against Canada". She received 50s new tenor for the mistaken reduction of her husband's final wages. Goudy did not stop with her attempt to seek redress for gun money. She also sent an itemized list of goods that her husband had taken with him to Cape Breton but "that I never received", including a shirt, hat, shoes, "the lace about the Hat," a pair of stockings, "waring Cloathes", and a chest – for a grand total of £20 18s old tenor.[35] But, interestingly and sadly, this was not the last time Elizabeth Goudy came before the government. In 1760, during the French and Indian War, her son Hugh was killed. Perhaps because her petition during the previous war had been well received by the provincial government, Goudy sent an itemized list once again this time asking for £83 10s old tenor for "Sundry Articles her Son lost when in the Army in the year 1760". Once again the government honored her request and paid her what was by then the equivalent amount in new tenor: £15. On the eve of the American Revolution, she again petitioned the government, explaining that her husband and son had been killed in the service of the province and asked for her son's remaining unpaid wages of £8 5s. Then she added to her 1774 petition a request "that

34. Treasury Records, 1758, Box 8, NhAr.
35. The petition may be found in *NHPP*, vol. 5, p. 457 and the itemized list in Treasury Records, Miscellaneous Treasury Account, NhAr.

your Excellency and Honors would be pleasd to consider whether your Petitioner is not equitably entitled to some allowance from the Government for the time her husband spent in said Expedition before his Death, for which neither he or She ever received any Consideration".[36] Tenacity in the face of grief paid off for this strong northern New England woman.

Like the petitions of war widows to the colonial New Hampshire government, petitions from women were requests that required special governmental action. Not every woman with a case exercised her option to petition, nor did every man. But the individuals who did knew petitioning could produce the results they desired. They were informants and, as such, petitioners were the government's most direct contact with the needs and expectations of the populace. As members of society, as subjects of the British colonies, women, as well as men, took advantage of their opportunity to inform their government. At the same time, they respected the distance social position placed between ordinary citizens and the governing elite. Lacking the status to have their needs and expectations met without the necessity of a petition, petitioning gave individuals without any other direct contact with the government a legal mechanism to urge the government to fulfill its obligations.

Those who made the effort to petition did so knowing the government would give due consideration to their petitions. Women understood their qualifications as petitioners and their rights before the government. Using societal assumptions of dependence and helplessness in their communications with the government, women were able to use the traditional language of petitioning to put forward their individual needs and demands, all within the acceptable bounds of patriarchy. Many female petitioners had lost their normal family spokesman but remained to face the world for their household, no matter what extra work it entailed. After all, if they did not do it, who would? They knew their families' needs could be addressed, not through the vagaries of the court system, but through the *right* of petition. The petitioning process gave ordinary women direct access to the highest levels of provincial government and the power of a traditional form of governmental address to rectify a wrong. It was a customary political device that the limitations inherent in coverture and patriarchy did not deny to women.

36. The lists are found among the scraps of bills and receipts filed by year in the Treasury Records, 1764, Box 8 and 1760, Box 8, NhAr. Petitions, 1775, NhAr.

IRSH 46 (2001), Supplement, pp. 79–106 DOI: 10.1017/S0020859001000293
© 2001 Internationaal Instituut voor Sociale Geschiedenis

Officially Solicited Petitions: The *Cahiers de Doléances* as a Historical Source

GILBERT SHAPIRO AND JOHN MARKOFF

INTRODUCTION: THE *CAHIERS DE DOLÉANCES*

The *cahiers de doléances* of 1789 have generally been regarded as unique historical documents. In convening the Estates General, the royal government followed centuries-old precedent in asking the nation not only to elect representatives to an assembly, but to provide them with lists of the demands, wishes, and grievances of their constituents as well. One could hardly describe these documents as resources unknown to historians. Apart from a very few who have seen these documents essentially as fraudulent,[1] historians have generally seen them as uniquely *vox populi*. Tocqueville, for example, described them as "an authentic account" of the ideas and feelings of the nation drawn up "in perfect freedom". More recently, Guy Chaussinand-Nogaret saw them as "the truest sampling of opinion ever realized in the France of the Old Regime".[2]

The procedures by which deputies were selected to represent the clergy, nobility, and commoners at the Estates General of 1789 were quite complex, and differed for the three estates. In most of France, rural communities met in face-to-face assemblies to elect their delegates to a higher assembly, the assembly of the commoners – the third estate – of the basic electoral circumscription, the *bailliage*. There they met with town delegates chosen at a town assembly, who, in many towns, were themselves elected by the town's corporate groupings, such as its guilds and professional bodies. The *bailliage* assembly often chose delegates for the Estates General; sometimes, however, it sent its delegates to an assembly composed of the representatives of several *bailliages* and it was this latter "*bailliage* cluster" that deputed to Versailles.[3]

For the nobility the process was far simpler; eligible nobles met in the main town of the *bailliage* or *bailliage* cluster at the same time as the

---

1. Notably Augustin Cochin, "Comment furent élus les députés aux États Généraux?", ch. 5 in *idem, Les Sociétés de Pensée et la Démocratie Moderne* (Paris, 1924), pp. 209–232.
2. Alexis de Tocqueville, *The Old Regime and the French Revolution*, trans. Stuart Gilbert (Garden City, NY, 1955), p. 262; G. Chaussinand-Nogaret, *La noblesse au XVIIIe siècle: de la féodalité aux lumières* (Brussels, 1984), p. 181.
3. We have coined the term "*bailliage* cluster" as an English equivalent of the rather clumsy French phrase, "*bailliage principal avec secondaires*" used by Hyslop and Brette.

highest stage meeting of the third estate, and elected delegates to the Estates General. (Even the nobles' procedures were not devoid of complexity: Paris had an aberrant two-stage process and women nobles with fiefs could choose a male delegate to represent them, making the small permitted female noble participation multistep.) For the clergy, parish priests could be represented either in person or through a delegate at the corresponding meeting of the *bailliage* or *bailliage* cluster, and ecclesiastical corporate bodies (chapters, monasteries, nunneries) could choose delegates. All of the assemblies just mentioned (and some of the individual participants in some stages) had the right to draw up a list of grievances, a *cahier de doléances*, and many did so.

Several characteristics of the *cahiers*, especially when considered together, have made their use by historians of France extremely common.

(1) They are very numerous. Some 40,000 rural communities drew up *cahiers*; so did many towns and, within the towns, urban corporations (such as guilds); so did hundreds of assemblies of France's upper strata – its clergy, its nobility, and its urban commoner elite.

(2) They are accessible. As quasi-sacred texts from the founding crisis of modern France, very many have been published in finely edited official editions. Graduate students learning French revolutionary history are likely to be exposed to them in seminars around the world, even if they never get the funds to travel to France, where many other *cahiers* await them in the archives.

(3) They are in a fairly standard format. The national regulations spelling out the electoral process in considerable detail helped impart a standardized structure to the crafting of these documents, as did a familiar culture of legal document forms. This standardization was powerfully reinforced by an energetic campaign by the many parties who sought to influence the documents by circulating models. This campaign reached out into the depths of the countryside. A startled official in Provence lamented the effort of the urban notables of Sisteron to "address the peasants and workers in their usual language in order to get them to take an interest in present affairs";[4] the nobility of Brittany made their case for peasant support against King and urban elites in Breton.[5] All over France, people had broadly similar notions of what a *cahier* ought to look like. The achievement of a common culture of *cahier*-writing makes one confident that differences among *cahiers* may be attributed to differences in the social composition of the assemblies that wrote them, as well as differences in the economic, social, and political challenges across the map of France, rather than differences in understanding

4. Quoted in Monique Cubells, *Les horizons de la liberté: La naissance de la Révolution en Provence, 1787–1789* (Aix-en-Provence, 1987), p. 68.
5. Roger Dupuy, *De la Révolution à la Chouannerie: paysans en Bretagne, 1788–1794* (Paris, 1988), pp. 24–32.

what a *cahier* was. There were some important differences, however, concerning the degree to which a *cahier* was intended to control the delegate who carried it, an important matter which we discuss below.

(4) They cover almost the entire map of France. With few significant lacunae, peasant communities, clergy, urban notables, and nobles drew up *cahiers* throughout the country. A very small number were produced by such aberrant procedures as to make the comparability of their contents with those of the overwhelming majority difficult; for example, the Provincial Estates of Dauphiné, Béarn and Navarre were permitted to choose delegates and write their own *cahiers*.[6] The nobility of Brittany refused to participate altogether. Some guilds in some towns did not write the *cahiers* they were permitted – but probably almost every rural community did so.[7] Parish priests, allowed to bring their personal *cahiers* to the *bailliage* assembly of the clergy, often seem not to have done so. And the fortunes of document loss mean that significant numbers of *cahiers* have not survived. Nonetheless, there is a very large proportion of the general *cahiers* of the clergy, nobility, and third estate available to historians; there is also a very large number of the parish *cahiers* extant, from which it is possible to draw a representative national sample of parish *cahiers*. Towns in many parts of the country have surviving *cahiers* from their corporations. Other *cahiers* have been less well-catalogued, and therefore their sampling characteristics are far less clear.

(5) They are almost simultaneous. The overwhelming majority of the tens of thousands of documents were drawn up within a few weeks of one another in the spring of 1789, providing an unrivalled snapshot of the views of the nation.

(6) The assemblies drawing up the *cahiers* can be identified with major social groupings. Because the documents emerged as an integral part of the electoral process, that process provides convenient, and very meaningful, social labels for those who adopted each *cahier*. They come to the historian readily identified with a rural community, an urban guild, a parish priest, local nobility. While much debate continues over just which peasants, or nobles, or clergy are those whose views prevailed in particular assemblies, and whose voices we therefore encounter in these documents, broad contrasts of different social categories, or of similar social categories in different parts of the country, are extremely easy to extract from these sources. Researchers who wish to know how the complaints of villagers in one part of France differed from those in another, or on what subjects nobles and commoner elites agreed, and on what they differed, will be almost certain to consult

6. Beatrice Hyslop, *A Guide to the General Cahiers of 1789 with the Texts of Unedited Cahiers* (New York, 1968), ch. 1.
7. Gilbert Shapiro and John Markoff, *Revolutionary Demands. A Content Analysis of the Cahiers de Doléances of 1789* (Stanford, CA, 1998), pp. 233–235; Gilbert Shapiro, John Markoff, and Silvio Duncan Baretta, "The Selective Transmission of Historical Documents: The Case of the Parish *Cahiers* of 1789", *Histoire et Mesure*, 2 (1987), pp. 115–172, 119–120.

relevant *cahiers*. But social categories that had no distinct assemblies in the convocation process (for example, protestants), as well as social categories whose members were largely excluded from participation at any of the assemblies (for example, women) cannot be studied in this way.

(7) The writing of the *cahiers* occurred at the beginning of one of the world's great social upheavals. Had there been no French Revolution, the snapshot of views on a national scale of a large and varied early modern European society would still be an unrivalled source of data. Had there been only a haphazard and unstandardized collection of a large number of miscellaneous petitions at the beginning of such a great social upheaval, nevertheless those petitions would be minutely scoured for what they reveal of the social forces generating such a momentous event. But the combination of a nationally standardized and readily accessible collection of documents from identifiable and significant social categories at the onset of the great upheaval makes the *cahiers* virtually irresistible to students of French revolutionary history.

But if the *cahiers* are a widely used resource for social history they have not always been a wisely used resource. The potential for systematic comparison could be realized only if pursued following rational sampling principles and a content analysis featuring a comprehensive coding scheme. Our recent effort to meet these requirements will be drawn upon and cited repeatedly below. The sample consists of 748 rural parishes (clustered in 46 *bailliages*), the 166 extant *cahiers* of the nobility, and 198 documents, virtually all of the extant "general *cahiers*" of the third estate (those drawn up in the final stage of the convocation and actually carried to Versailles). The database holds over 27,000 grievances expressed in the documents of the nobility, over 47,000 grievances in the documents of the third estate, and over 28,000 grievances in those of the rural parishes.

These 100,000 grievances are recorded in a code which reflects the *semantic structure* of a grievance: a designation of the *subject* of the grievance (ordinarily an institution or problem area, such as the church's finances, or the salt tax); a code for the *predicate*, which consists of the *action* demanded (for example, the abolition or reform of the subject), and an optional *object*, which is sometimes required to complete the meaning of the demand; and a code for any *qualifications*, such as: COND, a conditional demand; ALT, an alternative possible action; LO, a demand addressed to local conditions; or PV, one addressed to provincial conditions. The code has 1,227 institutional subjects (organized in a four-level hierarchy), 91 standard actions 76 standard objects and 45 code categories to deal with qualifications.[8]

---

8. Shapiro and Markoff, *Revolutionary Demands*, chs 10 and 12.

THE *CAHIERS* VIEWED AS PETITIONS

While the combination of characteristics itemized above is unique, we propose to view the *cahiers* here as "petitions", thereby enabling us to gain insights from comparisons with other petitions, including other petitions in the early modern world. While a petition is always a statement of wishes addressed to some authority, the character of that authority and the relationship of the petitioners to that authority are subject to great variation. To properly appreciate the sort of petitions represented by the *cahiers* of 1789, we need to focus on three critical dimensions of petitions in the abstract:

(1) the circumstances of a petition's origin;
(2) the manner of a petition's composition; and
(3) the role of the petition-bearer.

The circumstances of a petition's origin

First, we must consider the circumstances in which a petition comes into existence. Petitions from below may be strictly forbidden, intermittently accepted, generally permitted, plainly encouraged, or even demanded from on high. We see this as a continuum of increasing openness of those on high to public expressions of the wishes of those below. From the point of view of the freedom for autonomous action of those down below, however, matters are far more complex than such a simple linear progression, for it is in the intermediary zone, where petitioning is generally permitted, but not encouraged, let alone demanded from above, that the act of petitioning may be seen to be most autonomous. It is probably the case as a general sociological proposition, however, that whenever some right to petition becomes widely recognized, some in positions of power will discover that it is in their interest to sponsor petitions. Such solicited petitions, addressed to other power-holders, may be a significant means of exerting pressure on rivals; addressed to oneself they may constitute a resource in intra-elite debates, as when Members of Parliament in the English revolution discovered the power of evidence that "the People" were demanding something of them. Parliament "drew up petitions to itself", as one satirist put it.[9]

As petitions, the *cahiers* are toward the high end of this continuum, well beyond the halfway point between state encouragement and state insistence. Their significance must be assessed against the background of severe limitations on the right to petition in Old-Regime France. The absolutist state provided no general right of assembly, no general right to

---

9. Edmund S. Morgan, *Inventing the People: The Rise of Popular Sovereignty in England and America* (New York, 1988), pp. 227–228.

debate official actions, and a vigorous, if porous, censorship apparatus.[10] Not only were the *cahiers* a unique opportunity for the public expression of positions, a privilege not normally enjoyed even by the nobility, but the convocation regulations literally mandated that certain assemblies must provide their delegates with *cahiers*. Article 25 of the basic regulation is unambiguous: "The parishes and communities [...] shall assemble [...] to join in drawing up of *cahiers* and nominating deputies".[11] We think it noteworthy that France's rural communities, required by the convocation regulations to produce *cahiers*, probably were nearly unanimous in writing these documents.[12] We might well wonder what happened if a rural community opted, intentionally or inadvertently, to send off its delegates with no *cahier*. At one Norman *bailliage* assembly, a few rural delegates did show up without these documents, according to the records of the proceedings – but, nevertheless, we actually have *cahiers* from those parishes. It seems very likely that someone told those delegates after they arrived to get, or make, a proper *cahier* – unless they realized on their own that they ought to do so.[13]

The town assemblies that chose deputies for the *bailliage* meeting of the third estate, as well as the *bailliage* assemblies of the clergy, nobility, and third estate that chose deputies to the Estates General were also required to provide those deputies with *cahiers*.[14] High up in the electoral scheme, few assemblies with the right to send *cahiers* and delegates to Versailles failed to so. The major exception was the nobility of Brittany, who, as we stated above, boycotted the proceedings.

Other participants were *permitted* but not *required* by the official rules to write *cahiers* (for example, ecclesiastical corporations sending deputies to the *bailliage* assembly of the clergy, or parish priests attending in person). For still others, most importantly the urban corporations, nothing very specific is said at all. Preliminary *cahiers* of the clergy and guild *cahiers* were often not written,[15] although an absence of any thorough

10. Robert Darnton, *The Literary Underground of the Old Regime* (Cambridge, MA, 1982) and *The Business of Enlightenment: A Publishing History of the Encyclopedia* (Cambridge, MA, 1979); Daniel Roche, "Censorship and the Publishing Industry", in Robert Darnton and Daniel Roche (eds), *Revolution in Print: The Press in France, 1775–1800* (Berkeley, CA [etc.], 1989), pp. 3–26.

11. Jacques Cadart, "Règlement fait par le Roi pour l'exécution des lettres de convocation", in idem, *Le régime électoral des Etats Généraux de 1789 et ses origines (1302–1614)* (Paris, 1952), p. 197.

12. See note 7.

13. Emile Bridrey, *Cahiers de doléances du bailliage de Cotentin (Coutances et secondaires) pour les Etats généraux de 1789* (Paris, 1907), pp. 11–12, 28–30.

14. Cadart, "Règlement", arts 25, 28, 33, 40, 43–45, pp. 197–199.

15. Charles Porée, *Cahiers des curés et des communautées ecclésiastiques du bailliage d'Auxerre pour les Etats généraux de 1789* (Auxerre, 1927), pp. 2ff.; Philip Dawson, *Provincial Magistrates and Revolutionary Politics in France 1789–1795* (Cambridge, MA, 1972), pp. 150–151.

inventory of these types of document makes it impossible to be terribly confident about the precise proportions. There are no known surviving documents from urban corporate groups in seven-eighths of the towns where such groups were required to meet.[16]

The manner of a petition's composition

Second, the manner of a petition's composition, including the recruitment of petitioners and the contents of the petition may be unregulated by the state, arrived at by tacit understandings of the permissible, or formally governed by official regulation. In the more democratic states at the beginning of the twenty-first century, petitioning is rather close to the unregulated end of this particular continuum. Pretty much anyone may decide to circulate a petition or sign one circulated by others; and the petitioners are free to put almost anything they wish into their petition, perhaps occasionally restrained by libel laws. The *cahiers* were towards the opposite extreme in regard to who might petition, although not in regard to content; only definite groups were permitted to submit them, but their contents were extremely free. The government announced in richly complex detail how the tens of thousands of assemblies drawing up *cahiers* were to be constituted, who would have the right to attend which meetings, who would preside over each meeting, with very different rules for who chaired, say, a meeting of clergy and who chaired a village assembly, and how decisions were to be made. The initial announcement was followed by a long series of decisions that accepted, or – far more often – rejected claims by various groups to deviate from the modal pattern, usually by writing their own *cahier*. (The government agreed, for example, to permit the provincial estates of Béarn, Navarre, and Dauphiné to draw up *cahiers*, but refused to allow other provincial estates to do so.)

Unlike the close regulation of participation and procedures, the contents of the *cahiers* were not officially dictated. Indeed, there was some effort to keep government officials from overtly injecting themselves into the debates of the assemblies. The basic regulation barred most officials from any such effort.[17] Those who did have a role in convening local assemblies, and in presiding over meetings, varied somewhat in the degree to which they saw themselves as permitted to advocate any particular content for the *cahiers*.[18]

Against a background in which getting around the police and the censorship was a well-honed art, however, we may be confident that there were tacit understandings about what ought not to be said and how things

---

16. Dawson, *Provincial Magistrates*, p. 151, n. 37.
17. Cadart, "Règlement", arts 8, 30.
18. Hyslop, *Guide*, pp. 53–55.

ought to be phrased. We may be skeptical about whether all those who agreed to *cahiers* praising the King's many virtues believed their own words.[19] But we may be quite certain that to the extent that there was antimonarchical sentiment, the *cahiers* were not the place to express it. The noble deputy Count Beugnot, whose memoirs have a number of interesting observations on the drafting of the *cahiers* of his *bailliage*, quotes a very exceptional parish *cahier* that he turned over to the relevant authorities for criminal prosecution: "We give our deputies power to ask the lord-King's consent to the preceding demands; and should he grant it, to thank him, but should he refuse, to unking him".[20] (If this document really existed, we have not been able to find it.)

But while some things may have been virtually impossible to get into the *cahiers*, we also need to realize that assemblies were often willing to defy authorities. The rules required many parish assemblies to be chaired by a seigneurial judge. Although some historians have contended that the mandated presence of such a judge as chair must have inhibited the peasants from expressing their views of the seigneurial regime, we find evidence that complaints about seigneurial rights were just as numerous and just as strong when a seigneurial judge presided as when he did not.[21]

The royal invitation to participate was virtually a wide-open invitation to address whatever concerns the assembly wished, and contained only the most limited suggestions about appropriate general themes. In his letter of convocation the King called on his "faithful subjects to help us overcome all the difficulties in which we now find ourselves in regard to our finances", which certainly suggested, in a very general way, what he and some of his top advisors hoped for from the Estates General. But anyone who might have wondered about the prudence of raising other issues could note that the King also expressed the hope "that abuses of any kind be reformed", and that he promised his subjects "to listen favorably to their advice on everything that might concern the well-being of our peoples".[22] Many high-level *cahiers*, moreover, reflect defiance of the King's expressed disapproval of "binding mandates", as we explain below.

The assemblies certainly found in one aspect of state finances a favorite topic: many of the most common demands in the *cahiers* of the nobility, third estate, and parishes alike, concern taxation.[23] But the assemblies also made use of the considerable latitude provided in what subjects they might address. In designing our code, we found we needed to distinguish over 1,000 institutions under discussion in the *cahiers* collectively.

---

19. Shapiro and Markoff, *Revolutionary Demands*, pp. 369–376.
20. Jean-Claude de Beugnot, *Mémoires du Comte Beugnot, 1779–1815* (Paris, 1959), p. 94.
21. Shapiro and Markoff, *Revolutionary Demands*, pp. 150–155.
22. Jacques Cadart, "Lettre du Roi pour la convocation des Etats Généraux à Versailles le 26 avril 1789", in *idem, Le régime électoral*, pp. 202–203.
23. Shapiro and Markoff, *Revolutionary Demands*, pp. 380–381.

The role of the petition-bearer

Third, the role of the petition-bearer has, in the history of petitions, been subject to great variation. Petition-bearers might be limited to delivering the document into the hands of the authority. If so, they are clearly replaceable by modern, effective postal systems. Petition-bearing might itself become a form of political action, and this action might vary in the degree to which it is improvised or ritualized. If the bearers become numerous, march from one location to another, assemble to hear speeches, carry signs, and chant slogans, we have, no doubt, an origin of the demonstration as a form of social action, which, eventually, can even do without the petition.

In the case of the *cahiers*, the role of their bearers was the occasion of considerable disagreement at the time. As we have seen, that role was embedded within the convocation of the Estates General. Deputies chosen by lower-level assemblies carried *cahiers* to higher ones; at the highest levels, deputies of the three orders carried *cahiers* to the Estates General where, had the standard model been followed, three ultimate *cahiers*, one from each order, would have been produced. (This last step was short-circuited in the revolutionary crisis of 1789.)

In the monarchy's crisis, a significant debate took place over the relationship between the deputy and the *cahier*. That debate pitted against one another two rival conceptions of the Estates General's purposes and activities, rival conceptions of who or what was to be represented at the Estates General, and in consequence rival conceptions of the purposes of the *cahiers*. We will present some evidence below that the assemblies who wrote the *cahiers* took different positions on this cluster of issues.

In the first view, what was to be represented were the *corporate bodies* out of which a society was constructed: its towns and villages, its provinces, its urban guilds, its nobility, its clergy. The *cahier* was where the views of such a group were recorded. The job of a deputy was:

(a) to carry that *cahier* to some higher body;
(b) to join with fellow deputies in collating the various *cahiers* that body received into a summary super-*cahier*; and
(c) to join with fellow deputies in choosing those who would carry that super-*cahier* further up the hierarchy.

At the end of this process lay the Estates General itself, which would aggregate the *cahiers* its members bore with them and present the ultimate compendium to the King. The King would study this material to know the state of his subjects, and their advice, but the decision rested with him. In this conception, a deputy, even at the pinnacle, the Estates General, is not a legislator, engaging in horse-trading with his fellow deputies and joining them in collectively hammering out bargains with the King. He is a conduit by which the views of those below arrive at the ear of the sole legislator, the King of France. This entire conception was an extremely idealized reading of the history of Estates General past; such Estates General in fact were sometimes able to bargain with kings, and, indeed, a main reason for calling them, as in the crisis of the late 1780s, was that the royal government found that it needed someone with whom to strike a bargain.[24]

Embedded in this first conception of the deputy, the Estates General, and their relationship to the King was the conception of the *cahier* as a *binding mandate*.[25] The *cahier* bound the deputy to advocate the demands it contained. The monarchy might like such a conception, to the extent that it inhibited the possibility of an Estates General striking out in some unexpected direction. And constituents might favor such a notion in a world without any way to monitor the behavior of their delegates afar, with no newspapers reporting deputies' positions, no future elections to lead a deputy to fear antagonizing constituents, and no organized parties imposing discipline. To the extent, moreover, that constituents saw the King as an opponent, they might favor mandates, not so much in order to bind the deputies as to give them leverage in dealing with the King. Those *cahiers* that enjoin the deputies to accept no new taxes without a constitution utilize just such a strategy.

Aspects of this first conception of a *cahier* were embodied in the royal convocation order:

(1) Describing deputies primarily as carriers of *cahiers* to a higher assembly, as, for example referring to the "deputies who shall be chosen by the rural parishes and communities in order to carry their *cahiers*".[26]
(2) Describing a higher assembly as engaged in "the amalgamation of the *cahiers* of the towns and communities into a single one",[27] rather than as engaged in making a collective decision to forge a new document.

But a further view of the role of the deputy was also under consideration as the Estates General of 1789 was being planned. In this view, society is made up of a collection of *individuals* who were to be represented. No person had a right to be a deputy by virtue of rank or office; a deputy had to be chosen by some constituency. Wisdom was to be found in debate among individuals and in assemblies, and an Estates General was a place

24. The delegates to the Estates General of 1484 were clearly engaged in independent bargaining with the monarch, and show few signs of restraint by their constituencies. See James Russell Major, *Representative Institutions in Renaissance France, 1421–1559* (Madison, WI, 1960), pp. 64–71.
25. We use the term "binding mandate" for what Hyslop calls an "imperative mandate."
26. Cadart, "Règlement", art. 31, p. 198.
27. *Ibid.*, art. 34, p. 199.

for reasoned debate, a place in which distinguished delegates could reflect on the debate thus far and advance the national discussion. Since wisdom emerged from a process of dialogue, deputies were not to be bound by those who chose them. In such a conception, the hierarchy of assemblies might refine and improve upon the views submitted to them, not merely summarize them and collate them for transmission upwards. An Estates General was a protolegislature, engaged, in the last analysis, in a re-definition of the constitution of France. And such an Estates General would most certainly bargain with the King, especially about the scope of its own authority. In this conception, a *cahier* could not be a simple mandate, because deputies had to be able to horse-trade, to innovate, and to do more in dealing with royal authority than to pass on the views of those down below. But the monarchy, too, might favor such a conception, to the extent that binding mandates might seem a way to stiffen resistance to royal initiatives.

This view, too, found its way into how the convocation was framed by the King. In stressing that he will not "interfere, in any way, with the freedom of their deliberations", something beyond merely summarizing the views of those down below is acknowledged; and in committing himself to carrying out "what shall have been worked out in concert between us and the said Estates", he implies negotiations.[28]

While some were advocating what they believed to be the traditional conception, others, like Dauphiné's Mounier, opposed any constraint on the freedom of action of the representatives of the people, and rejected mandates. And, if the *cahiers* were not mandates, why, he reasoned, have them at all? Sieyès urged what amounted to a compromise position: *cahiers* without mandates.[29] This was the view adopted by the King, and strongly insisted upon in the basic convocation regulation: "His Majesty is persuaded that the confidence appropriate to an assembly that represents the entire nation forbids giving the deputies any instruction that could halt or trouble the course of deliberations."[30] Thus, in one of the many ways competing conceptions of the Estates General were embodied in the rules of 1789, the King expressed disapproval of mandates, which, for some, were virtually synonymous with the *cahiers*, while retaining the *cahier* itself. And, as one of the many signs that assemblies thought things through for themselves, quite a number of them ignored the royal dis-approval and restrained their deputies with a binding mandate. As we elaborate below, this was especially pronounced among the nobility: drawing on information provided by Beatrice Hyslop, by our count we

28. *Ibid.*, p. 193; Cadart, "Lettre du Roi", p. 203.
29. Philippe Sagnac, "Les cahiers de 1789 et leur valeur", *Revue d'histoire moderne et contemporaine*, 8 (1907), pp. 329–349.
30. Cadart, "Règlement", p. 193.

can say that about three-quarters of the nobles' documents carried binding mandates, about two-fifths of the third estate's did, and about one-third of the clergy's.[31]

Mounier, Sieyès, and the King no doubt, rejected mandates because they expected that, in the lineup of forces in the crisis, binding the deputies would have been a barrier to the innovations in finance and taxation required to meet the monarchy's fiscal crisis. At the height of the crisis of June, when the King ordered the privileged estates to join with the third in a common assembly, a large number of nobles held that this would violate their mandates and, in response to the King's orders, returned to their constituencies for new instructions. While most of those who sought new powers did so in the first half of July, a good number of noble or clerical deputies attempted to meet separately for some weeks, but most eventually joined in the common meeting. A few of the more recalcitrant were seeking new powers from their constituents as late as the fall, keeping alive the notion that a deputy was an agent of those who elected him.[32]

Since the question of mandates would not only have a significant impact on how the new National Assembly went about its business but also on whether there would be any business at all on which it would be able to make binding decisions, the mandates were among the very first topics of its debates, virtually from the moment, in late June, 1789, that deputies claimed they were a National Assembly. Harriet Applewhite's study of the positions of those deputies who spoke to that question in the early summer of 1789 shows that: "Mandates, one of the earliest substantive questions before the National Assembly, divided the embryonic left from the embryonic right".[33] Those opposing binding mandates were later found on the left, those in support on the right, and those favoring the eventually winning compromise of having deputies with mandates seek new powers took a variety of political paths down the line. Future revolutionary electoral procedures generally retained assemblies, rather than isolating individual electors to cast votes in secret,[34] but such discussions as might take place were not, as a matter of law, to bind the deputies, a point clearly stressed in the constitution of 1791: "The representatives named in the departments shall not be representatives of an individual department but of the entire Nation, and they may be given no mandate". As if for someone

---

31. See note 46.
32. Timothy Tackett, *Becoming a Revolutionary: The Deputies of the French National Assembly and the Emergence of a Revolutionary Culture (1789–1790)* (Princeton, NJ, 1996), pp. 151–165; Hyslop, *Guide*, pp. 101–102.
33. Harriet B. Applewhite, "Citizenship and Political Alignment in the National Assembly", in Renée Waldinger, Philip Dawson, and Isser Woloch (eds), *The French Revolution and the Meaning of Citizenship* (Westport, CT, 1993), pp. 43–58, 45.
34. Patrice Gueniffey, "Revolutionary Democracy and the Elections", in *ibid.*, pp. 89–103.

who might have missed the point, the next article begins: "The functions of primary and electoral assemblies are limited to electing".[35]

HOW TO READ THE *CAHIERS*

Following the historians' classic injunction to engage in "criticism of sources", a good deal of ink has been expended on what sorts of information can be reliably mined from the *cahiers*. At various points historians have debated whether the *cahiers* are a source of "objective", factual information or are limited to the realm of the "subjective", the wishes and hopes of those who wrote them. An even longer discussion has been carried on about the "sincerity" or "authenticity" of the views expressed in either particular documents, particular kinds of *cahiers*, or even in the *cahiers* as a whole. If a village assembly was presided over by the local seigneurial judge (a likely possibility under the official rules), could their document be held an authentic expression of the community's views? If the community enlisted the advice or even the pen of a local priest or local attorney? If the document showed evidence that one or several locally circulating "model *cahiers*" had been read and some of its (or their) suggestions followed? While we agree that all such aspects of the context of *cahier*-writing are important to study, we believe that a great deal of this criticism suffers from an inadequate understanding of what sort of documents these texts are, an understanding that is essential to their proper interpretation as historical sources. Many criticisms derive, we think, from a notion that individual opinions are both the essential building blocks of historical processes, and the entities that are knowable through proper document study. The *cahiers* are not however some sort of X-ray into the hidden soul of French peasants, French clergy or French nobles. They are doubly *public* documents.

They are statements of collectivities. They were arrived at as the decision of some group of people, whether villagers, urban professionals, clergy, or nobles. They are statements that required an assembly's assent (but not necessarily, as the record makes abundantly clear, its unanimous assent to each and every statement). They, therefore, are inevitably the product of horse-trading, of deliberate omission of the concerns of some participants in the interests of securing the agreement of others, of debate in which we may be confident that the voice of some was weightier than the voice of others. The *cahiers* are not an aggregate of individual voices. They are a collective political act. This may be readily verified by observing that higher-level *cahiers* are not mere compendia of the lower-level *cahiers*, as

---

35. "Constitution du 3 Septembre, 1791", in Maurice Duverger, *Constitutions et documents politiques*, 2nd edn, (Paris, 1960), p. 10.

one idealized conception of the transmission of views from his subjects to the King would have had it.

They are addressed to higher bodies at a specific moment. The *cahiers* were not produced in an institutional vacuum. They were written in order to produce desired outcomes in the midst of a great crisis in which, for many, change seemed possible, and from which, therefore, there was much to hope and much to fear. Assemblies had to consider what sorts of articles in a *cahier* would help bring about desired change and ward off undesired change. This is by no means the same thing as a compendium of an assembly's deepest wishes. Moreover, they were written in a time and place in which freedom to speak out was hardly a national tradition, and in a moment of crisis in which the group in command of force tomorrow was a matter of considerable uncertainty. If we impute even a minimal level of rationality to participants in those assemblies, we may be confident that considerations of prudence and of effectiveness played a significant part in what was put into the documents. One third-estate deputy later recalled the moderation he and his associates felt they had to display in their *cahiers*: "It was necessary to be cautious so as not to frighten despotism too much".[36]

The *cahiers*, then, are strategic statements of collectivities. They are not to be confused with what peasants or nobles said to their fellows at those meetings, but shrewdly omitted from the documents. To insist on some point might hopelessly divide the assembly, or to make another point might be impolitic, or ineffective. In many cases, it is possible that whatever peasants or nobles said to themselves, they would not even say to their fellows.[37] Let us consider two concrete examples.

Peasant reticence on food prices

The parish *cahiers* usually make no mention of the soaring price of food.[38] It is inconceivable that this shows a lack of interest in France's villages. Skyrocketing grain prices, caused by a catastrophically poor harvest, have been amply documented by historians, and sometimes even been held to be the critical trigger of revolution.[39] Not only did France have a long

36. Quoted in Timothy Tackett, "Nobles and Third Estate in the Revolutionary Dynamic of the National Assembly, 1789–1790", *American Historical Review*, 94 (1989), pp. 271–301. Quotation on p. 276.
37. Very helpful in thinking about such matters: James C. Scott, *Weapons of the Weak: Everyday Forms of Peasant Resistance* (New Haven, CT [etc.], 1985).
38. Shapiro and Markoff, *Revolutionary Demands*, p. 424. In fact, only 11.4 per cent of the parish documents complain about the supply or price of any articles of consumption, and less than 1 per cent about food.
39. Camille-Ernest Labrousse, *La crise de l'économie française à la fin de l'Ancien Régime et au début de la Révolution* (Paris, 1944).

tradition of popular mobilization in times of scarcity, with extensive rural involvement, but during the very weeks when the *cahiers* were being written, these kinds of popular actions constituted the major form of rural mobilization.[40] So why do the villagers who wrote the *cahiers* not address more often than they do the fear of hunger that was such a frequent catalyst to collective action? We conjecture that this was a rather divisive matter within village communities, where some families had enough land to produce a marketable surplus and others did not. Avoiding the subject, and indeed avoiding many other subjects that divided a village's haves and have-nots,[41] may have been a political decision to produce a more consensual *cahier*. As it happens *cahiers* that take up subjects that were likely to be contentious within rural communities[42] tend to be from regions whose peasants engage in none of the many forms of mobilization found in the spring and summer of 1789. The connecting thread that links a *cahier* addressing such topics and the absence of collective action may well be the lower level of village unity.

Noble reticence on seigneurial rights

More than one-fifth of the noble *cahiers* have not a word to say about seigneurial rights.[43] Among those noble *cahiers* that do take up the seigneurial regime, there are considerably fewer grievances on that subject than found in the *cahiers* of the third estate (on the average 5.5 vs. 17.4). Seigneurial rights were a source of income and of pride for many lords. In light of the multifaceted critique of those rights from champions of monarchical power, economic development, peasant wellbeing, and judicial reform, under discussion for some time and now being incorporated into many third-estate *cahiers*, it is inconceivable that the one-fifth of noble assemblies who remain silent simply had other things on their minds. But unity may have been difficult to achieve: examining those noble *cahiers* that do treat the seigneurial regime, we have found that this is actually one of the subjects on which those nobles who express themselves disagree most with each other.[44] We would expect such intranobility division to inhibit saying very much in their *cahiers*. Not only that, but the

---

40. Cynthia Bouton, "Les mouvements de subsistance et le problème de l'économie morale sous l'Ancien Régime et la Révolution française", *Annales historiques de la Révolution française*, 319 (2000), pp. 71–100; John Markoff, *The Abolition of Feudalism: Peasants, Lords, and Legislators in the French Revolution* (University Park, PA, 1996), p. 287.

41. Shapiro and Markoff, *Revolutionary Demands*, pp. 424–426.

42. Besides agricultural prices, these include communal rights, which divided those who benefited from those whose livelihoods were injured by them, and the auction agents whose sales of the meager possessions of the bankrupt were opportunities for the better off.

43. Markoff, *Abolition of Feudalism*, p. 41.

44. Shapiro and Markoff, *Revolutionary Demands*, pp. 288–289.

nobles, meeting in the same town at the same time as the third estate, were likely to be keenly aware of their inability to frame a defense in terms that would generate much assent from anyone. The prudent course may well have been to say as little as possible, or even nothing at all. The nobility is, in fact, far more likely to dare urge that a particular seigneurial right be maintained if the third estate has relatively little to say about it. In more precise statistical terms: if we consider the dozen specific seigneurial rights most discussed in the noble *cahiers*, there is a negative correlation between the proportion of noble *cahiers* demanding that the right be maintained and the proportion of third-estate *cahiers* that discuss that particular right, a substantial 0.69.[45] So noble assemblies, we suggest, acted with a calculated prudence: if the third estate was particularly focused on some specific right, this was not the right to try to defend; and some assemblies opted to say nothing at all.

Cahiers as collective and strategic

All this implies that an understanding of these documents, and their contents, demands something very different than any assumption that we are looking for the aggregated wishes of independent, isolated individuals. The crafting of *cahiers* was embedded in social relationships. The *cahiers*, therefore, are to be understood as collective and as strategic. Searches for the authentic individual or the sincere voice of the heart are as inappropriate as they would be if we were looking at the platforms of contemporary political parties. Even that countermodel, the modern public-opinion poll, in fact produces statements that are embedded in social relationships and in which strategic speech plays a role. Public-opinion professionals are keenly aware, as a major methodological problem, of the degree to which respondents give systematically different answers to men and women interviewers, young and old, those well dressed and those in casual attire, and so forth, because human beings cannot help attempting to create impressions and wish for different impressions on members of different categories. What makes this a problem, rather than a fascinating object of research in its own right is that we are trying to find that pristine, uncontaminated, sincere, individual opinion – which does not exist.

BINDING MANDATES

In judging the character of the *cahiers de doléances* of 1789 as petitions, and their proper uses in research on the Revolution, the prevalence and the

---

45. Markoff, *Abolition of Feudalism*, p. 131.

Table 1. *Noble mandates by third estate mandates from the same* bailliage

Noble mandate	Third estate mandate		Total
	Absent	Present	
Absent	29.35%	17.19%	24.36%
Present	70.65%	82.81%	75.64%
No. of cases	92	64	156
	100.00%	100.00%	100.00%

Chi-Square = 3.0291
P = 0.082

meaning of the binding mandates are of major significance. Their study can tell us to what extent these documents were regarded as constraints upon the actions of elected deputies, and to what extent they were provided as guidance to a modern representative, elected to make decisions and bargains in the interests of his constituents. We turn first to the simple question of how many assemblies passed mandates. Of the noble assemblies whose *cahiers* are available, 74 per cent did so, as did 41 per cent of the third-estate assemblies, and only 31 per cent of the assemblies of the clergy.[46] While the predominance of nobles would seem to support the common notion of the mandate as a means of resistance to change on the part of the privileged orders, the fact that a greater number of third-estate assemblies passed mandates than did assemblies of the clergy seems to require a different interpretation. One hypothesis might be that the clergy were reluctant to put controls on their superiors in the church hierarchy, but we find that the proportion of assemblies issuing mandates is no different where their deputies are members of the upper clergy than when they are not.

The geography of mandates

While there is some slight tendency for any estate to be more likely to pass a binding mandate if another estate of the same *bailliage* does so, in no case does this relationship reach the 5-per-cent level of significance by the Chi-Square test. The strongest of these weak relationships is between the third estate and the nobles, which is presented in Table 1.

Despite the weakness of this relationship, it does appear that the binding

46. Hyslop, *Guide*, pp. 471–473. Our proportions differ from Hyslop's because we include only cases with extant *cahiers*, lacking which one cannot be sure whether there was a binding mandate or not, since the mandate might sometimes be given in the *cahier* itself rather than in a separate document.

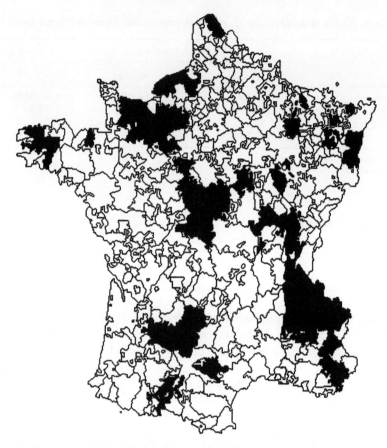

Figure 1. Clerical mandates (Dark areas have mandates.)

mandates come from definite restricted geographic regions. The similarity
of the geographic distributions shown in Figures 1 to 3 is striking, indicating that while there is only slight, if any, tendency of mandates of
different estates to come from the same *bailliages*, they do seem to
frequently come from the same *regions*.

Mandates and committees of correspondence

Beatrice Hyslop summarizes the variety of purposes that led assemblies to
form committees of correspondence: "a desire to keep tab on the deputies,
to furnish the deputy with supplementary information about the *bailliage*,
to perpetuate the electoral assembly, and to secure a method of receiving
information from the deputies which could be relayed to the constitu-

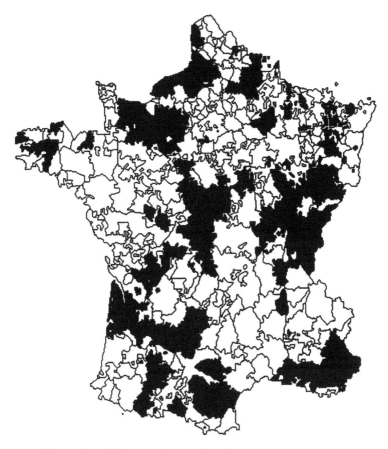

Figure 2. Noble mandates (Dark areas have mandates.)

ents".[47] Insofar as these committees were designed to restrain, and not merely to inform the deputies, it is not surprising that, where they were established, the assemblies also frequently wrote mandates for the same purpose. There is a very strong relationship between the presence of a binding mandate and the establishment of a committee of correspondence in a *bailliage*. This relationship is well beyond the 1-per-cent level of confidence in all three estates.

In fact, the establishment of such a committee went a step beyond a mandate as a means by which the assembly could control the deputy; it was a mechanism by which, faced later with a new, unanticipated situation, he could be given new instructions.

47. Hyslop, *Guide*, p. 99.

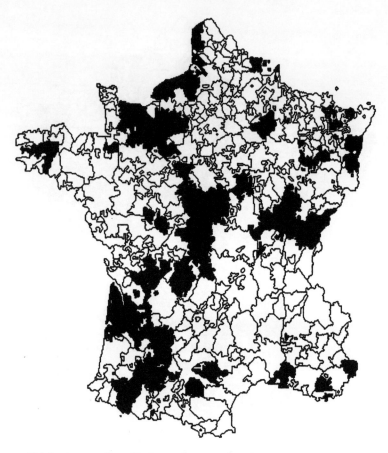

Figure 3. Third-estate mandates (Dark areas have mandates.)

Mandates and voting in the Estates General

The literature on the French Revolution concentrates on the role of the mandates in the crisis of June 1789. After the failure of the government to coerce the third estate into acknowledging three independent estates, with separate deliberations and vote by estate, the King gave in to the demand of the commoners to recognize them as a National Constituent Assembly, and ordered the clergy and nobility to join with the third. At this time, a large number of noble deputies claimed their inability to obey such an order because of their mandates, and the King ordered them to return to their constituencies for new instructions. Because of these dramatic events, many narratives of the Revolutionary period either describe the mandates

Table 2. *Committee of correspondence established by the clergy, by binding mandate*

Binding mandate	Clergy: committee of correspondence		Total
	Not formed	Formed	
Absent	77.03%	5.56%	69.28%
Present	22.97%	94.44%	30.72%
No. of cases	148	18	166
	100.00%	100.00%	100.00%

Chi-Square = 38.5159
P = 0.000

Table 3. *Committee of correspondence established by the nobility, by binding mandate*

Binding mandate	Nobility: committee of correspondence		Total
	Not formed	Formed	
Absent	30.88%	3.33%	25.90%
Present	69.12%	96.67%	74.10%
No. of cases	136	30	166
	100.00%	100.00%	100.00%

Chi-Square = 9.7187
P = 0.002

Table 4. *Committee of correspondence established by the third estate, by binding mandate*

Binding mandate	Third estate: committee of correspondence		Total
	Not formed	Formed	
Absent	68.71%	11.76%	58.88%
Present	31.29%	88.24%	41.12%
No. of cases	163	34	197
	100.00%	100.00%	100.00%

Chi-Square = 37.6817
P = 0.000

as restricted to the issue of vote by head or estate, or mention the mandates only in connection with this conflict, leaving the impression that they were concerned only with this issue.

Our examination of mandates does not confim this impression. We find some mandates applying to an entire *cahier*, containing dozens or even hundreds of grievances on different subjects. In other cases, the mandate applies to a group of grievances particularly selected, which may or may not contain the issue of vote by head or by order. By way of illustrating a bit of this variety we note a few examples.

The third estate of Charolles, having taken a firm stand in favor "of a constitution that does not permit the establishment of any law without the authorization of the prince and the consent of the representatives of the people" goes on to "forbid [...] their deputies to vote on any matter before such a constitution is granted", and declares "that they will withdraw all their powers should they contravene the above mandate".[48]

The nobility of Agen present some sixteen items on which their deputies are not to deviate under any circumstances, while allowing them to concede some ground on others if after a good fight they see they will lose. With regard to the mandated sixteen items: "Our intention is to limit the powers that our deputies receive from us in regard to the matters just set forth [...]. We disavow them in advance, should they be guilty of not fulfilling their undertakings to strict obedience to our will, without in anyway adding, deleting or modifying." With regard to the remainder of the *cahier*, however,

> We have too much confidence in them and believe them too enlightened not to leave them in complete freedom with regard to the following articles. We do urge them, upon their honor, to formally insist upon each of the demands that are going to be expressed – and not to abandon any unless the general sentiment makes it impossible to resist longer.

(Apparently not quite willing to simply trust the good judgment of their deputies, the assembly added a nuanced discussion spelling out circumstances in which the deputies will be permitted to back down from an insistence on vote by order.)[49] This is in considerable contrast to the nobility of Aix, who give their deputies instructions but "leave to their conscience to decide on all matters according to their patriotism and their honor, giving them full and sufficient power to propose, remonstrate, advise and consent".[50]

Thus, the scope of mandates is highly varied, as are the subjects covered under them. In fact, it is not even true that noble mandates are significantly more common when there is a demand for vote by order, or that third-estate mandates are significantly more common when assemblies demanded vote by head. (See Tables 5 and 6.)

While both tables show tendencies in the conventionally expected

48. J. Mavidal and E. Laurent, *Archives parlementaires de 1787 à 1860 (première série)* (Paris, 1879), vol. 2, p. 619.

49. *Ibid.*, vol. 1, pp. 680–681.

50. *Ibid.*, p. 693.

Table 5. *Binding mandates by vote by order, noble* cahiers

Binding mandate	Noble *cahiers* demands for vote by order		Total
	Absent	Present	
Absent	32.35%	21.43%	25.90%
Present	67.65%	78.57%	74.10%
No. of cases	68	98	166
	100.00%	100.00%	100.00%

Chi-Square = 2.4961
P = 0.114

Table 6. *Binding mandates by vote by head, third-estate* cahiers

Binding mandate	Third-estate *cahiers* demands for vote by head		Total
	Absent	Present	
Absent	71.43%	56.17%	58.88%
Present	28.57%	43.83%	41.12%
No. of cases	35	162	197
	100.00%	100.00%	100.00%

Chi-Square = 2.7668
P = 0.096

direction, in neither case does the relationship attain the 5-per-cent level of significance which would leave us with some confidence that it is more than a chance occurrence.

Mandates and the ideology of the cahiers

One might suppose that those noble assemblies that were especially conservative would have utilized mandates to reinforce this position and that third-estate assemblies that were especially radical would have done the same. But it is also not the case that noble mandates are associated with *cahiers* which are notably conservative, or that third-estate mandates are to be found in *bailliages* with especially radical views. We may take the proportion of all actions that call for an institution to be maintained as a general indicator of conservatism and the proportion calling for outright abolition as a general indicator of radicalism. Tables 7–10 show the mean frequency with which noble and third-estate *cahiers* call for actions (on any subject) entailing the abolition of social institutions, or their maintenance.

While Table 7 shows a slightly greater conservative tendency among the

Table 7. *Mean number of grievances to "abolish" institutions in the noble* cahiers, *by presence of binding mandates*

Binding mandates	Noble *cahiers:* no. of grievances to "abolish"		Frequency
	Mean	Std. Dev.	
Absent	0.11076047	0.06008692	43
Present	0.0956626	0.04479788	123
Total	0.09957349	0.04946605	166

t = 1.73 with 164 d.f.
P > |t| = 0.0849

Table 8. *Mean number of grievances to "maintain" institutions in the noble* cahiers *by presence of binding mandates*

Binding mandates	Noble *cahiers:* no. of grievances to "maintain"		Frequency
	Mean	Std. Dev.	
Absent	0.01808372	0.02620214	43
Present	0.01318049	0.01513846	123
Total	0.0144506	0.01867753	166

t = 1.49 with 164 d.f.
P > |t| = 0.1389

Table 9. *Mean number of grievances to "abolish" institutions in the third-estate* cahiers *by presence of binding mandates*

Binding mandate	Third estate *cahiers:* no. of grievances to "abolish"		Frequency
	Mean	Std. Dev.	
Absent	0.14539483	0.05802291	116
Present	0.14552963	0.04713166	81
Total	0.14545025	0.05368455	197

t = −0.02 with 195 d.f.
P > |t| = 0.9862

noble *cahiers* with mandates, it is not significant by the standard t-test criterion of 5-per-cent probability and, furthermore, this finding is not supported by Table 8, where it actually appears that the noble *cahiers* without mandates are slightly more conservative than those with mandates, though the difference is not significant. Tables 9 and 10 show no differences at all in conservatism or radicalism between third-estate *cahiers* with and without mandates.

Table 10. *Mean number of grievances to "maintain" institutions in the third-estate* cahiers *by presence of binding mandates*

Binding mandate	Third estate cahiers: mean no. of grievances to "maintain"		Frequency
	Mean	Std. Dev.	
Absent	0.01108448	0.00933398	116
Present	0.01291728	0.01003254	81
Total	0.01183807	0.00964459	197

t = −1.31 with 195 d.f.
P > |t| = 0.1901

Table 11. *Demand for doubling the deputies of the third by binding mandate: third-estate assemblies*

Binding mandate	Double the third		Total
	Absent	Present	
Absent	51.58%	65.69%	58.88%
Present	48.42%	34.31%	41.12%
No. of cases	95	102	197
	100.00%	100.00%	100.00%

Chi-Square = 4.0433
P = 0.044

Mandates and the organization of the Estates General

Although the demand for vote by head is not significantly related to the presence of a mandate in the third estate, two closely related demands, also addressed to the organization of the Estates General, do have significant relationships. While the convocation regulations of 1789 provided for twice the number of deputies from the third estate as were authorized for either of the other two estates, there were frequent demands in the third-estate *cahiers* for such an arrangement, presumably addressed to the longer term constitutional question of how the estates would be organized in the future. Table 11 shows that, in the third estate, this demand is significantly more common where there are binding mandates. And many third-estate documents called for the permanence of the Estates General as an institution, or for regular meetings of the assembly, instead of the traditional arrangement whereby they met at the will of the monarch. Table 12 shows a significant relationship between these demands in the third estate and the presence of a binding mandate. The nobles show no such relationships.

Table 12. *Mean number of demands for permanence or regular meetings of the Estates General in the third estate* cahiers, *by presence of binding mandates*

Binding mandates	Third estate *cahiers:* demands for permanence for estates		Frequency
	Mean	Std. Dev.	
Absent	0.71551724	0.6158209	116
Present	0.91358025	0.77777778	81
Total	0.79695431	0.69207678	197

t = −1.99 with 195 d.f.
P > |t| = 0.0478

Table 13. *Mean number of demands that powers and functions be assigned to the Estates General in noble* cahiers, *by binding mandates*

Binding mandates	Number of demands		Frequency
	Mean	Std. Dev.	
Absent	2.9767442	2.6230514	43
Present	4.0406504	2.6716434	123
Total	3.7650602	2.692118	166

t = −2.26 with 164 d.f.
P > |t| = 0.0252

However, they do frequently insist upon specific powers and functions to be exercised by the Estates General, and these demands are significantly more frequent in *bailliages* with mandates, as shown in Table 13. The third estate shows no relationship.

   If mandates are a clue, a part of the third estate is taking a firmer stand on the autonomy of the Estates General, while a part of the nobility digs in its heels about its precise powers. This amounts to a two-pronged assault on absolutism. For those who like to speculate on history's might-have-beens, this interesting datum points up how difficult it would have been for the monarchy to abort the crisis by successfully allying with either nobility or third estate against the other. But it also suggests that, in the spring of 1789, the challenge posed by the third estate was more fundamental. Although some of France's aristocrats had long been at the center of struggles to maintain arenas of autonomy from monarchical control, it appears that, in the spring of 1789, it was the commoners who were more intransigent over the establishment of a newly independent Estates General, the fundamental departure from absolutism.

CONCLUSION

While the *cahiers de doléances* of 1789 are, as commonly believed, unique documents, we find it methodologically useful to regard them in a comparative framework as petitions, in some respects like other petitions in the early modern period. In particular, like all petitions, they must be understood in the light of the circumstances of their origin, the way in which they were produced, and the role of the petition bearer. In evaluating the last of these considerations, a detailed look at the mandates often passed by the assemblies helps to clarify France's struggles as it slid into revolution.

As French assemblies made their different decisions about whether to treat their deputies as free to negotiate on their behalf or as agents bound in detail to their expressed will, they anticipated some of the difficult tensions between mobilized citizens and elected representatives that was to characterize the entire revolutionary period. Was an election the device for choosing an assembly whose decisions would constitute the only occasion on which the voice of the sovereign people would be manifest? Or would an election be but one channel through which the people would speak, with other channels open through which the people could make clear that deputies were merely their agents? Was popular sovereignty to be identified with parliamentary sovereignty? Champions of popular sovereignty might make different stands at different moments – the Left might be sympathetic to pressures upon the national legislature from the mobilized sections of Paris and even claim a right to insurrection, for example, yet reject the notion that the ultimate decision on the fate of the King be taken out of the hands of the Convention and lodged in a national referendum.

If we may look beyond the French Revolutionary context and glance downstream over the next two centuries in which the institutions of contemporary democracy were forged, we may note a deep significance in this neglected and long-forgotten debate over the details of just what kind of petitions the *cahiers de doléances* were to be. In claiming that the right to rule could and should rest on popular will, late eighteenth-century revolutionaries opened up the question of precisely what were to be the institutions of the new democratic order, a question in no way settled by their general rejection of Athenian models (the assembled citizenry, the agent chosen by lot) and substitution of a scheme of representation.[51] The question of whether a *cahier* was to be a binding mandate was one occasion on which the nature of that representation was fought out, and, along with

---

51. John Markoff, *Waves of Democracy: Social Movements and Political Change* (Thousand Oaks, CA, 1996), and "Where and When Was Democracy Invented?", *Comparative Studies in Society and History*, 41 (1999), pp. 660–690.

it, the nature of the relationship between the democratically governed and those who claimed to govern democratically. The annulment of the mandates, and the subsequent abandonment of *cahiers* in French elections, were a piece of the multisided and multicontinental process by which democracy has come to be defined. But – for ill or good – not defined beyond question: the growth of state referenda in the United States today,[52] and the development of popular consultative assemblies in Brazilian cities,[53] are just two of the signs that the relationship of citizens and governors is again in question at the beginning of the twenty-first century.

52. Lars-Erik Nelson, "Watch Out, Democrats!", *New York Review of Books*, 20 July 2000.
53. Gianpaolo Baiocchi, "Activism, Civil Society, and Politics: The Porto Alegre Case and Deliberative Democratic Theory", *Politics and Society* (forthcoming).

IRSH 46 (2001), Supplement, pp. 107–129 DOI: 10.1017/S0020859001000347
© 2001 Internationaal Instituut voor Sociale Geschiedenis

Revolt, Testimony, Petition: Artisanal Protests in Colonial Andhra*

POTUKUCHI SWARNALATHA

This paper examines the form, content, and role of petitions in the context of protests occasioned by the handloom weavers of colonial Andhra, particularly the northern districts of the northern Coromandel region, between 1770 and 1820.[1] Minor and major protests and revolts by weavers erupted with increasing frequency from around the middle of the eighteenth century, whenever their socioeconomic structures and conditions of work and trade were under threat from the old and new elites, as well as from the commercial interests of the colonial state. On these occasions, weavers expressed their grievances through petitions and representations, either in combination with other strategies or independently. These petitions therefore offer opportunities to study and identify the economic and social conditions that prompted weavers to resort to collective action. Careful analyses of the petitions yield considerable insights with respect to the causes of the protests; their spatial and social diffusion; the social profile of contending parties, and their mentalities; the changing organizational structure of the textile industry; the petitions' consequences; and, finally, the attitude of the colonial state towards these petitions.

The existing literature on law and society in colonial India discusses extensively the impact of colonialism on agrarian relations and social reform issues.[2] However, with a few exceptions, the implications of law and the impact of new legal provisions on the nonagrarian economy

---

* This article is based on material collected while working on a Ph.D. dissertation at the University of Hyderabad. I wish to thank the staff of the Andhra Pradesh State Archives and Tamil Nadu State Archives for assistance. Some of the arguments are presented in the author's forthcoming work, *World of the Weaver in the Northern Coromandel: 1750–1850* (Hyderabad, forthcoming). The assistance and advice of D. Parthasarathy in the preparation of this manuscript is gratefully acknowledged.
1. The northern, predominantly Telugu-speaking districts of the Madras Presidency in colonial India constituted the Andhra region.
2. David Washbrook, "Law, State and Agrarian Society in Colonial India", *Modern Asian Studies*, 15 (1981), pp. 649–721; Janaki Nair, *Women and Law in Colonial India: A Social History* (New Delhi, 1996) and Sudhir Chandra, *The Enslaved Daughters: Colonialism, Law and Women's Rights* (Delhi, 1998).

remains unexplored.[3] Here, therefore, the emphasis is on those factors that compelled the weavers to accept the "petition" as the ventilator of grievances by the beginning of the nineteenth century. In this process, it is intended to outline the way in which the art of writing and presenting petitions evolved, and how it turned out to be a crucial determinant for the success of weavers' revolts and movements.

Four major "disturbances" or "revolts" are examined that took place in the textile world of the Godavari and Visakhapatnam districts between 1775 and 1820 – the weavers' revolts of 1775 and 1798 in Godavari district, and revolts of 1796 and 1816 in Visakhapatnam district. Prior to the acquisition of political authority by the British, there was intense competition among the major European trading companies – English, Dutch and French – for control of the textile trade from these districts.[4] Principal merchants, head weavers, *copdars*, and *senapaties* were the main intermediary groups with whose assistance European trading companies conducted their trading operations.[5] Except for merchants, the remaining three mainly belonged to the major weaving communities of the region. In these two districts the principal weaving communities included the Devangas, Padmasales, Pattusales and Kaikalavallu castes.[6] However, more than caste, it was product specialization that constituted the major divisions among the weavers during the period, namely between fine cloth and *punjum* cloth weavers. Textiles that were manufactured and traded in the region included white piece goods, long cloth of various denominations, popularly called *punjum* cloth, and *salempores*, ranging from superfine quality to ordinary coarse varieties.[7] Around the 1760s, the demand for coarse varieties gradually increased in European markets, compelling the English East India Company to import these varieties. By the end of the eighteenth century, with the virtual decline in demand for

3. See for instance, Hameeda Hossain, *The Company Weavers of Bengal: The East India Company and Organization of Textile Production in Bengal: 1750–1813* (New Delhi, 1987).

4. Tapan Ray Chaudhuri, *Jan Company in Coromandel, 1605–1690: A Study in Interrelations of European Commerce and Traditional Economies* (The Hague, 1962); S. Arasaratnam, *Merchants, Weavers and Commerce on the Coromandel Coast, 1650–1740* (Delhi, 1987); Sanjay Subrahmanyam, "Rural Industry and Commercial Agriculture in Late Seventeenth Century South Eastern India", *Past and Present*, 126 (1990), pp. 76–114; and Sanjay Subrahmanyam, *The Political Economy of Commerce in South India: 1500–1600*, (Cambridge, 1990).

5. The head weavers were the principal and prosperous weavers, and in some areas they were called *senapaties* (literally heads of armies); the *copdars* were essentially brokers between the merchant and the weaver and were also contractors for supplying long cloth.

6. D.F. Carmichael, *A Manual of the district of Vizagapatnam in the Presidency of Madras* (Madras, 1869), p. 65; and F.R. Hemingway, *Madras District Gazetteer: Godavari* (Madras, 1907), pp. 102–104.

7. *Punjum* cloth was the local name for long cloth. It refers to plain white long cloth, popular in Europe on account of its length of about 37 yards or 72 cubits and width of 2 1/4 cubits; *punjum* literally denotes 120 threads.

superfine and fine cloth, all the weavers working for the Company were categorized as weavers producing long cloth and *salempores.*[8]

The English acquired political control over the region in 1766, and, using its political leverages, the incipient colonial state attempted to extend its control over the production process of the textile economy.[9] These changes occurred during a significant period when the textile trade reached both its peak and ebb.[10] Its effects were felt in the form of the elimination of merchant groups in the organization of the production process, reinforcing community and caste linkages. They also resulted in the elimination of precolonial patron–client relations between landed elites and weavers at one level and between merchants and weavers at another level, the creation of administrative units of weaving villages, and the creation of legal institutions to enforce major bonds between the weaver and the state.[11] In due course, the objective conditions created by the emergent colonial state reinforced and reproduced social categories which opposed as well as accepted the changes, depending on the benefits they derived from these transformations. Each of the changes initiated by the colonial state alarmed the weaving community, and thereby impelled them to organize protests on a continuous basis. An analysis of petitions that were submitted by weavers on these occasions reflects their awareness both of new possibilities in the realm of political and legal action and the possible outcome of their collective action.

During the mid-eighteenth century, weavers used petitions along with other weapons: foot dragging, desertion, and relocation. In these instances, "testimony" – giving oral reports of their problems to committees constituted by the Company – was popular. By the last decade of the eighteenth century, when revolts turned violent and organized protests for the redressal of grievances became the norm, the colonial state began to accept and consider petitions as the sole legitimate action to be taken by the weavers. With the introduction of new juridical systems and legal provisions by 1799, weavers were constrained to utilize the petition as the

---

8. The term *salempores* is derived from *salembarigudda*, the local name whose usual dimensions were a length of 16 yards and width of one yard, and the quality of which varied between an ordinary variety of 12 ½ *punjum* to superfine quality of 36 *punjum* cloth. *Salempores* were mainly used for block printing in England.
9. The region of Northern Circars, which the Company acquired through the Mughal grant in 1765, was confirmed by a treaty with the Nizam of Hyderabad in 1766. Sarojini Regani, *Nizam–British relations, 1724–1857* (New Delhi, 1988), provides a detailed account of this.
10. The demand for textiles from Andhra region, *chay* goods (coloured varieties) from Masulipatnam, and white piece goods (*salempores* and long cloth) from the Injeram, Maddepollem, and Visakhapatnam factory areas reached a peak during the last decades of the eighteenth century, but started declining continuously between 1810 and 1830, when the factories were finally abolished.
11. For more details on these changes see the author's forthcoming work, *World of the Weaver*.

only method that had a cognizant position under the law. Petitions draw attention to the colonial juridical structure and the mechanisms that were put in place to discipline the so-called "fugitive", or "rebel" weavers and to bring them into accord with colonial structures.

WEAVERS' REVOLTS IN 1775, 1796 AND 1798

Soon after acquiring political authority in the region, the colonial state was much perturbed by a major revolt in 1775 by the *punjum* cloth weavers under the jurisdiction of the Visakhapatnam, Injeram, and Maddepollem factories.[12] Changes initiated in the production organization of the textile economy were essentially responsible for this revolt. In order to ensure greater concern among weavers for the Company's investment, Anthony Sadleir, the Commercial Resident of the Injeram factory, initiated changes in production organization in 1774.[13] Until then, three main European trading companies – English, Dutch and French – were operating in the trading arena of the textile economy of the region through the mediation of principal merchants, under whose charge the primary producer, the weaver, was working.[14] Among the changes, the first was to place all the weaving villages falling under the jurisdiction of the Visakhapatnam, Maddepollem, and Injeram factories under the management of newly-created administrative units called *mootahs* which were managed by native agencies – namely *gumastahs*, *kanakupillais*, and head weavers.[15] In this process, the informal networks, in which merchants were mediating between the weavers and the market, were replaced by a formal mechanism involving administrative intervention. Thus the role of merchants was suddenly diminished.

Secondly, with the ever-increasing demand for coarser textile varieties in Europe, weavers weaving superfine, fine and middling varieties were forced to weave coarser cloth – namely 18-, 16- and 14-*punjum* varieties – thus reducing their skill and specialization.[16] Further, the sorting out

---

12. Until 1774, major sections of weavers were producing fine cloth. The revolt of 1775 was organized by those weavers who were made to weave coarse cloth – the *punjum* cloth weavers. A section of fine-cloth weavers, who still continued to weave fine cloth, were called upon by the state to be a witness to the proceedings.

13. Proceedings of the Enquiry into the conduct of Sadleir, while Resident at Injeram, 28 November 1775 to 30 March 1776, Public Department Sundries [hereafter PDS] 25, Tamil Nadu State Archives, Madras, vols 24 A and 24 B.

14. *Ibid.*, PDS 24A, pp. 111–115.

15. *Ibid.*, PDS 24A, pp. 70. Proceedings related to Enquiry into Conduct of Sadleir, PDS 24 A, p. 70. *Concoply* or *kanakupillai* were native accountants in charge of various functions at the factories. The types of *concoplys* included beating *concoply*, washing *concoply*, and sorting *concoply*.

16. Testimonies given by the head weavers of Peddapuram, Amalapuram, Hasanallybadah, Arrivatum, Dungalooroo, Rustumbadah, PDS 24 A, pp. 12–15.

method was introduced, mainly to ensure a regular supply of quality fabric.[17] Under this method, each specific variety was sorted into four types based on quality. The cloth that was categorized as the third and fourth quality was rejected. The cloth that was rejected was not returned to the weaver but was taken by the officials, both foreign and native, for their private trading. It is evident from the data presented in Table 1 overleaf, that while weavers found it profitable to work and produce *punjum* cloth if the pieces were accepted in the first sort, prices offered for rejected cloth did not even cover the cost of production. Thus restrictions on the quality of a specific variety led to severe constraints on the work and economic opportunities of the weavers. Moreover, weavers were forced to accept advances, and were later on ordered not to weave fine cloth for any merchant, foreign or native.[18] Under the new system of advances introduced by the Company, the earlier reliance on local merchants for investment operations ceased, and after 1765 the involvement of merchants was deliberately reduced by Company officials. This was done through the *mootah* system, by which the weaving villages came under the management of a hierarchy of Company officials who actually managed all advances of cash and the account of cloth received from common weavers. Gradually, however, the Company brought back the *copdar* as an intermediary to fulfil the weavers' contracts with the merchants, either through direct purchase or by advancing cash on their looms. In the Visakhapatnam district, the Company functioned mainly through the *copdars* and head weavers, eliminating the mediation of merchants, a system that came to be known as the *aumani* system. By 1800, the *copdar* was made completely responsible for the Company's investments and advances. A percentage of the advances went to the *copdar*. The new system thus placed a lot of power in the hands of the *copdar*, who often used it to delay payments, or force grain, cotton and other articles of merchandise on to the weavers. This was particularly so when traders from the Bania caste (the traditional trading community), took over as *copdars* in place of members of weaving castes. These changes led to what is frequently referred to in petitions and records as "economic severity" among the weavers, as they became indebted for huge amounts to the English Company.

Disturbed by the constraints imposed on their organization of production, weavers of the region, with support of their caste members, resorted to the various options available to them. They quit their work, did not accept new advances, and fled to nearby French and Dutch factory

---

17. *Ibid.* The term "sorting out method" refers to the inspection and sorting out of cloth submitted by weavers, according to quality. If the piece did not conform to the required standard, it was rejected and it was supposed to be returned to the weaver.
18. *Ibid.*

Table 1. Cost of production and price data for various punjum varieties and sorts (in pagodas)

Variety (punjums)	Price of thread per piece	Cooly hire per weaver for each piece	Total cost of cloth, per corge	Price for Company's cloth per corge			
				1 sort	2 sort	3 sort rejected	4 sort rejected
14	1.25	0.375	32.5	32.5	30.0	28.75	–
16	1.375	0.5	37.5	37.5	35.0	33.75	32.5
18	1.5	0.625	42.5	42.5	40.0	37.5	36.5
22	2.0	0.812	56.25	56.25	53.75	50.0	–
24	2.125	0.812	58.75	58.75	56.25	53.75	50.0
36	5.5	3.0	170.0	170.0	160.0	140.0	–

Note: One pagoda equals four rupees. A corge equals 20 pieces.
Source: Public Department Sundries, Tamil Nadu State Archives, Madras, vol. 24 A, pp. 113–116. Testimonies preferred by the weavers of Hasanally badah before the committee meeting on 2 December 1775, PDS 24 A, pp. 29–31.

areas. They also organized a *samium*, an association consisting of the four main weaving castes of the region, for collective action and represented their plight in the form of a petition.[19]

The economic impact of the new policies and structural changes on the weavers provoked in 1775 a reaction from the weavers of the area, who organized collective action through their caste networks. Such a congregation was made possible due to the efforts of head weavers, who wanted to express their grievances to the Company's officials.[20] On this occasion, the Company's peons attacked 4,000 weavers of Kottapalli who assembled and prepared to go to Injeram to express their grievances. The fine-cloth weavers were further forced to accept advances to weave coarse cloth. When they stated that they did not know how to make it, "Mr Sadleir in answer told them that they must now learn it".[21] Some weavers, who did not know the art of weaving coarse cloth, bought the same from other places and submitted those to *gumastahs*. In due course, they faced losses. To expose this sort of economic oppression, they fled to Yanam and Palakollu, the nearby Dutch and French territories.[22] Given the new circumstances and the administrative structures initiated by the state, the weavers considered petitions as a major mechanism for grievance redressal, as will become clear. Weavers resorted to other methods only in the event of the failure of petitioning to yield results.

Detailed information relating to their oppression under the new system was brought out by the weavers through oral testimony, which they preferred to the enquiry committee appointed on this occasion. Though they also sent a delegation with a petition asking for redressal, it was not accepted by Anthony Sadleir on the ground that the weavers had not placed their signatures on the petition. To this the weavers forwarded a precise and effective reply, bringing out the exact nature of colonial intervention in their means of subsistence:

> You are pleased to write us that we have not set down our names to the letter we wrote you. The names of all the weavers as far as Rajahmundry and Ellore, you have note down in your book. You may be induced to think that this *Samium* is made by one man – by one it cannot be done. We have done this for want of victuals and not to hurt your business. You will be please to introduce a method to procure us victuals as you are pleased to give us the same price as the merchant

19. *Ibid.*; "No. 2. The answer to the above translation", PDS 24.
20. *Ibid.*; also PDC 116 B, 17 December 1776, pp. 814–815.
21. Committee meeting on 4 December 1775; 150 weavers of Amalapuram preferred their grievances to the committee; PDS 24A, p. 46.
22. Committee 9 December 1775, Rustumbadah weavers' testimony, PDS 24 A, pp. 106–110; also testimony given by Appagunta Veeresha, head weaver of Peddapatnam in front of the committee headed by Mathew Yeats. This report contains 40 testimonies given by nearly 120 weavers from 39 villages under the control of 27 *mootahs*; PDS 24A, pp. 43–104.

did. Likewise you should sort our goods as they did, but if you sort them as you do and sum all our goods to lower number, how can we subsist? You write, as you will not take the notice of our petition. We are like your children, you are like our parents. If you will not have our petition, who then will? Remove our hunger and support us.[23]

Besides disclosing clearly the hardships of the weaving community, this petition also indicates that the weavers, though not having a mastery over written English, had yet mastered the art of petitioning, realizing that posing as humble supplicants is a necessary aspect of petitioning. The primary concern of the weavers was to obtain and sustain ways to maintain their livelihood, and so they were at pains to state that their movement was not intended to hurt the Company's investment. The petition also indicates the loss of the patron–client relationship that had existed between artisans and the state in the precolonial period.

When the weavers declined to accept any advance towards the Company's investment, a committee was appointed to inquire into the conduct of Anthony Sadleir as Commercial Resident of the Injeram Factory. The list of witnesses in the committee proceedings included commercial officers of Maddepollem, Cuddalore, and Masulipatnam, military officials, native officials, *dubashes*, linguists, all the *gumastahs*, head weavers, fine-cloth weavers, and *concoplys* belonging to the two factories as well as all the Company's old servants.[24]

In the course of the inquiry, the efforts of Sadleir to bribe the witnesses into silencewere revealed. When the investigation committee was record-ing the witnesses' statements, weavers from different *mootahs* used petitions to place before the committee the daily conduct of the corrupt officials – both foreign and native.[25] *Dubashes* and merchants testified that they did not buy superfine cloth without Sadleir's permission. In the course of the committee's investigation, the voices of the weavers, and their collective account of their grievances, turned out to be effective. The committee, and later on the Council of the Board of Trade, passed a resolution to the effect that Mr Anthony Sadleir's management of the investment at Injeram was injurious to the Company: "(Sadleir was) cruel and oppressive towards the weavers and unwarrantable towards the agents of the French and Dutch. Resolved for these reasons that Mr Sadleir do

23. "No. 2. The answer to the above translation", PDS 24.
24. Proceedings of the committee to inquire into the complaints against Anthony Sadleir, Resident, Injeram, PDS 24A; William Hamilton to Committee, 27 November 1775; a list of witnesses is enclosed with this letter, pp. 11–12.
25. William Hamilton's letter to the committee, 17 January 1776, briefing the summary of a letter; petition given by eighteen weavers of Penumallem; a list of the weavers is provided in PDS 24 A.

stand suspended from the Company's service until judgement of Court of Directors can be known".[26]

Thus, the organization of collective action by the weaving community spread over twenty-seven *mootahs* clearly demonstrated the possibilities inherent in political action. From inception, whether it was by sending verbal messages, petitions, organization of the *samium* or taking to flight, the mechanisms for their movement were clearly thought out. When the committee asked the weavers to present their grievances at Nalapalli, near Injeram, a huge gathering collected in the place. From each *mootah* a contingent of weavers, in certain cases as large as 150 members, went to Nelapalli to place their grievances before the investigation committee. Seventeen to eighteen hundred weavers represented their problems in person. From each of the twenty-seven *mootahs*, six common weavers represented their grievances along with head weavers, *gumastahs*, *concoplys* and peons. Weavers belonging to thirty-seven villages gave nearly fifty-five testimonies.[27] Unlike later revolts, which were mostly led by specific castes, this particular revolt represents the collective action of the entire weaving community, with participation from all the weaving castes and others involved in the textile industry and trade.

A more serious "revolt/insurrection" took place among the weavers of the Visakhapatnam district in 1796. This was against the influence of Chinnum Jaggapah (a Bania caste *copdar*) over the production process, the low prices offered by the merchants for the *punjum* cloth, and the imposition of the *salempore* variety, which was opposed strongly.[28] In 1795, Company officials introduced some changes to ensure the quality of cloth. Earlier, the weavers were accustomed to follow a system through which they got a certain price for their cloth (18- and 14- *punjum*), and the contractor met losses incurred on account of inferior quality. Under the new system, the Resident of the factory issued notes specifying the number (representing the quality of the cloth) at which the cloth is to be received with the prices the contractor had to deliver for it.[29] Strict enforcement of

26. PDS 116 B, 17 December 1776, p. 81–86.

27. The price of thread and weavers coolie (hire) as for second and third sort of cloth is the same as first sort. Committee meeting on 4 December 1775; 150 weavers of Amalapuram presented and testified to the same effect; PDS 24A, p. 46. The list of witnesses, total number of weavers, head weavers, *gumastahs*, *concoplys*, peons, and common weavers present from twenty-seven *mootahs* to prefer their testimonies to the committee; PDS 24 A, p. 180–189.

28. W. Brown, Collector, Cassimcotah, to Robert Malcolm, Commercial Resident [hereafter CR], Visakhapatnam, 24 July 1796; Board of Revenue (Proper), [hereafter BORP], Tamil Nadu State Archives, 162, pp. 8058–8068.

29. Robert Malcolm, CR, to Mr Webb Coll of Northern Division of the Visakhapatnam, 27 July 1796, Visakhapatnam District Records, [hereafter VDR], Andhra Pradesh State Archives, Hyderabad, vol. 3706, pp. 325–327.

rules and regulations by the native agency placed greater burdens on the weavers as they had to pay extra charges. Thus, the economic hardships bound together the weavers of the district, who stopped their work for the Company and incited other villagers to join them. Such an act was made possible by the leadership provided by caste leaders belonging to the Devanga caste and other *senapaties* to induce the weavers to join the movement.[30]

Since the weavers expressed their grievance through sudden action, without bringing it to the notice of the officials, the entire incident was dubbed an "insurrection" by "fugitive" weavers. Company officials felt that the proper way to express their grievances was "to state them in person, which if possible would be redressed". The Collector stated that the weavers were still continuing their action, without yielding to any sort of appeal, "no overtures have been made on the part of the fugitive weavers, who continuing still more or less intent on their purpose of extorting, rather than petitioning for redressal of grievances". He further expressed the hope "they would yield to reason, and insisted on the senapaties of the several parties to represent their story in a quiet submissive manner".[31]

In 1798, weavers of the Godavari district "revolted" against major changes initiated by the state in its investment policies. Grievances came to the fore, such as inadequate prices for their work, particularly when there was an acute scarcity of thread, and a new policy of the Company to collect balances due from the weavers at the time as advances made during the early part of the year. However, the immediate cause of this revolt seems to have been the harsh treatment meted out to Company weavers by Company merchants, who began collecting balances due from the weavers with much rigour.[32] Nearly 15,000 pagodas was owed to the merchants, who were advised by Richard Dillon, the Commercial Resident of the Maddepollem factory, to collect from the weavers according to their economic circumstances. The merchants decided to collect one rupee monthly from better-off weavers, half a rupee from poorer weavers and one-quarter rupee from the poorest. Secondly, weavers did not want to confine their contracts to one merchant to whom the Company provided advances. They wanted the right to be granted to any merchant to make advances both on Company looms and on private looms. The Commercial Resident expressed his inability to take any measures, and requested that a

30. BORP 162, pp. 8063–8074.
31. John Snow, Collector, Cassimcotah, to Robert Malcolm, CR, Vizianagaram, 26 July 1776; VDR 3706, pp. 330–332.
32. Richard Dillon, CR, Maddepollem to William Fallofield, Board of Trade [hereafter BOT], Godavari District Records, [hereafter GDR] 830, Andhra Pradesh State Archives, pp. 19–46.

few from their caste represent their grievances in the form of a petition to the Madras government.[33]

Changes in the structures, whereby Bania-caste *copdars* assumed a significant position in the textile trade, provided a common platform for the head weavers, caste leaders (*senapaties*) and common weavers to air their grievances. Head weavers, and *senapaties* in particular, played a crucial role in this particular disturbance, led by head weavers belonging to all four major weaving castes of the region. Soon after the revolt's inception, the Collector recommended that these "tumultuous assemblies should disperse, leaving behind them ten head weavers comprising all four major weaving castes, with one weaver from each important weaving village. After hearing their grievances, he would recommend to redress them".[34] Weavers opposed this suggestion and continued their movement, bringing weavers from various villages into the fold. Weavers moved from one village to another and, with the support of their principal and head weavers, strictly refused to undertake Company's work. From Daglooroo village in Godavari district, they marched towards Masulipatnam, bringing under their banner the weavers of all the villages situated on the route.[35]

The Board of Trade took serious note of this crisis, as the merchants working for the Maddepollem factory refused to enter into contract for the year owing to the disturbances. In such a situation, the official perceptions regarding the weavers' movement, and its ability to express problems in a written complaint, instead of causing a better result appears to have resulted in further apprehension in the colonial mind. The concern of the authorities about the troubles, and their surprise at the tumult caused by weavers and their organizational capacity was made obvious when the officials stated,

> [...] by what means people so miserably poor as weavers are generally known to be, could now contrive to keep so long together [...]. The original copy of a representation sent to [...] appears to be written in so masterly a style [...] that knowing the weavers as well as me, I confess that I did not imagine them capable of such a superior production.[36]

Weavers who had decided on "insurrection" appear to have sent a

33. Richard Dillon, CR, Maddepollem to Benjamin Branfill, Collector, 8 January 1798, GDR 847, pp. 141–142.
34. Richard Dillon, CR, Maddepollem to William Fallofield, BOT, GDR 830, p. 32.
35. The "insurrection" disturbed the state of affairs in the 1st, 2nd, and 3rd Divisions of Masulipatnam and thereby affected investments at the Maddepollem factory; 300 weavers gathered in the village of Daglooroo in the mootah of Chintapurroo in the 2nd division under the leadership of two head weavers – went to Relingy and their number rose to 500; they then proceeded to Yellindeperma in the Nidadavole Parganah of the 3rd division.
36. Richard Dillon, Maddepollem Factory to William Fallowfield, BOT, Madras, 19 January 1798; GDR, 830, pp. 19–23.

representation to the authorities specifying the economic grievances that forced them to act on this occasion. This particular revolt is also significant from the viewpoint of state action. The state, instead of insisting upon them resubmitting their cases peacefully, as had happened in the case of the 1796 revolt in Visakhapatnam, tried all methods to put down the revolt. In this case, this problem was further complicated when the weavers cut across the existing revenue districts and tried to bring other weavers under their control. Consequently, the officials were left with no policy measure to deal with such a situation, which caused confusion and rifts between the revenue and commercial interests of the districts.

As a result of these disturbances to the production process, the Company considered many changes in the weaving world of the region during the late 1790s, to protect its investment. Eliminating the merchants and according official recognition to *copdars* of the weaving caste – the main agents in the commercial activity – were some of the changes that were adopted, along with the more powerful judicial regulations.

In the early nineteenth century, under the impact of these changes, the only mechanism left to weavers to express their grievances was through legal procedures, without which their grievances were not attended to by the state. The idea of putting in place legal mechanisms was first adopted in 1794, when the Company noticed the unprotected nature of manufacture in its jurisdiction as the District Collectors were not able to act, due to the nonavailability of any kind of guidelines. The Board of Trade considered the importance of applying a set of judicial regulations similar to the ones that were already in existence in Bengal. The issue came up before the Board of Trade again in 1799, when it decided to adopt regulations for the conduct of Commercial Residents and agents, and all persons employed or concerned in the Company investment, along with changes at the level of production organization.[37]

The regulations adopted concerning weavers were, in general, "sufficiently severe".[38] They were prohibited from working for individual Europeans or native agencies or for bazaar sales until they would complete their engagements in relation to the investment they had agreed upon. "Peons may be placed over such as fail in their engagements mainly to ensure a quick delivery"; in case of any deficiency and incurring of losses the weavers were made to clear the debts they owed to the Company in preference to the claims of any others. All contracts with weavers were to be made in writing, in the presence of at least two credible witnesses; weavers were asked to give fifteen days advance notice if they decided not to take any more advances. Further, if the weaver acted in a way

37. Boards Proceedings on the Introduction of the Judicial and Revenue System of Bengal, Board of Revenue Miscellaneous, 190, G.No.18288, Tamil Nadu State Archives, pp. 316–319.
38. *Ibid.*

contradictory to these stipulated rules and regulation, he was liable to be prosecuted in the Court of Adawlat.

These new legal procedures initiated by the colonial state were intended to put an end to sudden protests. "Disturbances" and weavers' "unwarranted" actions were no longer to be tolerated by the state. Weavers were provided with a new mechanism to put forward their grievances to the state, namely the petition. Only in certain circumstances were the weavers given a chance to sue the officials or persons concerned in court. One of the clauses of the new regulation that enabled them to sue the Commercial Residents, and their native officers of any category, in the Court of Adawlat specified the following grounds. First, when a proper and agreed price was not paid for the cloths they submitted; second, when their accounts were not settled on fair terms; and third, when they were forced to pay unjust fines on account of peons placed over them. However, the aggrieved party, the weaver, had to prefer the complaint to the Commercial Resident, and only if that complaint was not redressed within a reasonable time could the weaver sue the Resident.[39]

A petition to the authorities was thus the only means left to the weavers of the region to get any relief against oppression that was directly related to the activities of the Company's investment operations. However, under the new judicial regulations, the state restricted the weavers' actions to economic grievances, and further, grievances that could be petitioned were clearly specified along with a procedural hierarchy for preferring complaints.

Hence, the weavers started using petitions very judiciously and cautiously, more so in cases against the Company's officials. When they filed a petition, they included every minute detail about the activities of all those connected with the Company's investment in the region. One such occasion during which weavers of the Visakhapatnam district depended entirely on the use of petitions was the 1816 Revolt.

THE VISAKHAPATNAM REVOLT OF 1816

The Company's investment received a great setback in 1816 when nearly 20,000 weavers in the Visakhapatnam district stopped their work and assembled at the Simhachellam Hill Temple near Visakhapatnam. Since congregations were forbidden under the new law, their main purpose for such a gathering was "to attract the attention of higher authorities" to the severe oppression put on them by the native agency, with the support of

39. *Ibid.*

the Commercial Resident of the Factory.⁴⁰ Petitions submitted by weavers to the Board of Trade throw light on the economic history of the weaving community. At the organizational level, issues such as individual- as well as community-level consciousness, individual leadership, and temporal and spatial aspects of writing a petition, can be analysed from these "humble" petitions.⁴¹ The form and tone of petitions submitted during the revolt of 1816 show that the weavers had come to terms with the new rules and regulations of the colonial state, and were trying to retain their place within the new economic system by reference to their "humble" stature in relation to the Company and the state. The need for a trained person to be employed in the writing of such petitions – one who had mastered the new legal terminology and procedures – was understood, and indeed weavers managed to find such persons.

This particular revolt appears to have been caused by the overall unhappiness of the weaving community with a few powerful persons who were not giving due consideration to the changes in work organization brought about the Company. Perhaps because of this, the weavers recognized the necessity of using petitions as the only way to resolve long-standing grievances. Through their petition dated 19 March 1817, twenty-eight weavers, acting as agents to the Company's weavers in Visakhapatnam district, went to Madras and requested the Board of Trade to place their petition before the Governor-in-Council.⁴²

It constituted an account of the economic severity which the weavers of the district suffered at the hands of Chinnum Jaggapah, the Head Servant of the Company since 1811. In that year Chinnum Jaggapah, a Bania, was appointed as head servant or *copdar* of the factories by the Commercial Resident, Henry Taylor, and his relatives were placed in charge of a number of looms under their control. From each and every *copdar* of the district, Jaggapah extracted half a rupee per loom whenever advances were made. Every year, he was collecting the pay of those peons who were employed to guard his house at the time of "disturbances". Moreover, whenever the weavers attempted to obtain justice from the Commercial Resident, they were severely ill-treated. Unable to get justice from the immediate authority, they assembled at Simhachalam temple in Visakhapatnam district.⁴³

---

40. The Humble Petition of the Head Weavers and Weavers employed in Company's *punjum* Cloth investment in the Vizagpatnam Zillah, presented by the undersigned Agents to the Whole Body, to Hugh Elliot, Governor in Council & Others, Fort St. George, Commercial Department Consultation, [hereafter CDC] 10, Tamil Nadu State Archives, Madras, dated 19 March 1817, pp. 1249–1257.
41. This represents one of the first instances when the term "humble" was used by the weavers in a petition.
42. *Ibid.*
43. *Ibid.*

The nature of complaints made by the weavers against the *copdars* shows very clearly the actual history of the weaving trade in Vizagapatnam during the late eighteenth century and early nineteenth century. In their first petition of 29 November 1816, they explained the rates established by the government, which were paid to the *copdars* by the Company for its investment. Earlier, they were getting Company-established prices but since 1811 lower prices were being paid to them.[44]

Once cloth was rejected and returned to the *copdars*, they collected Rs. 3 to Rs. 20 for each piece of 18- and 14-*punjum* cloth that was rejected. The weavers thus incurred a heavy loss when the rejected cloth was not returned to them, but was sold by the *copdars* to private merchants at an higher price. Soon after the Company disbursed advances to the *copdars*, the latter usually lent the money to the *soucar* (merchants) and *zamindars* (tax farmers) for interest. They got back the money from the *soucars* both in grain and money, the former being supplied at a cheap rate. This grain was forced upon the weavers at high prices.[45] Weavers were thus paid in cash and grain, even though in the account books the full price was mentioned.

On this occasion, to their surprise, the weavers noticed that the Commercial Resident was supporting the cause of his *dubash* Chinnum Jaggapah and his relative *copdars* – Grundy Vencataramoodoo and Motamurry Paupiah. They therefore sent their agents to Madras to represent their case before the Presidency.[46] They demanded a new Resident for Visakhapatnam to investigate and redress their grievances, and wanted the amount that had been held back since 1811 by the *copdars*, on account of the *punjum* cloth, to be paid to them. On this occasion the petition was seen not only as an instrument by which the weavers brought their miseries to the notice of government, but as a weapon to make known what they wished to achieve.[47]

The weavers then sent a second petition to the Board of Trade, dated 13 December 1816, which sought to place before the Board the daily ill-treatment that they had to face. When Henry Taylor, Chinnum Jaggapah, and other *copdars* came to know of this petition, they went to their *macaums*, and with the help of 130 pariah peons, placed in confinement all

44. Petition of the weavers' agents to the body of Company's *punjum* gents to the body of Company's *punjum* cloth weavers, to Board of Trade [hereafter BOT] 29 November 1816; CDC 10, pp. 1257–1263. Also translation of a petition from Emenda Jagapa, Davoleree Romoodoo, Emunda Mulliah, weavers of Coderee Macaum in the district of Visakhapatnam, to the Magistrate, 30 July 1816; CDC 10, pp. 1264–1268.

45. In this petition, the weavers brought out the deterioration in the economic conditions of their community due to the low price offered for their cloth by Henry Taylor, since the time Chinnum Jaggapah was reinstated in 181; petition dated 19 March 1817 to BOT, CDC 10, pp. 1249–1257.

46. *Ibid.*, p. 1251.

47. *Ibid.*, pp. 1251–1252.

those weavers pointed out by Chinnum Jaggapah and other *copdars*. They forced these weavers to give *sunneds* (deeds or agreements) to testify to information opposing the weavers' problems addressed to the agents in Madras.[48] The *copdars* sought this kind of information and documents from those weavers who were poor. Those who refused to give such information were forced to discharge their balances demanded by the *copdars*. The weavers then suggested that they would pay for all the charges incurred for investigation, and would accept any punishment, if the charges against those *copdars* "were not proved through investigation".[49] This petition shows the limitations of petitions as a historical source, and the need to be careful in using these sources, for petitions can also be falsified accounts, as some weavers were brought forcibly by the *copdars* to sign the papers.[50]

When their ill-treatment intensified by the day, the weavers sent yet another petition, dated 2 February 1817, this time by *Tappal* to the Board of Trade, which placed before the highest authority the intensity of ill-treatment meted out to them by the *copdars*.[51] This particular petition is useful in that the weavers, while describing the situation under the jurisdiction of a factory, also reveal the history of an individual – Chinnum Jaggapah – who rose to an important position in his locality owing to the unlimited favours bestowed on him by Company officials. It also brought to the fore the issue of corruption and bribery that rapaciously engulfed the commercial affairs of the Company. Jaggapah was removed once from the Company's service, but returned to the same position with more powers due to his "crafty nature". He concocted false evidence before the court of Adawlat and refuted all the allegations against him.[52] Jaggapah was also responsible for the removal of previous *copdars* from the Company's service, and he placed all these *macaums* under the leadership of his relatives – his own brother-in-law and the father-in-law of his brother, along with other Banias and Devangas of his liking. Most of the servants in the Company's service were appointed according to his choice. During Henry Taylor's tenure, Jaggapah rose from a servant employed on a salary of 14 rupees per month to the man with full control over factory affairs, who carried on extensive trade, and "purchased landed property and vessels".

48. *Ibid.*, p. 1251.
49. *Ibid.*, pp. 1249–1256. Petition of the weavers' agent to the Body of the Company's *punjum* cloth weavers in the district of Vizagapatnam, to BOT, 16 December 1816; CDC 10, pp. 1264–1273; petition dated 29 November 1816 to BO; CDC 10, pp. 1257–1264.
50. *Ibid.*
51. Reference to this petition is provided in CDC 10. *Tappal* is a system of post wherein articles and letters are transported through a relay system.
52. Weavers' petition to BOT dated 29 November 1816; CDC 10, pp. 1257–1264.

Based on the information provided in these petitions, the Board summarized the entire issue as follows and gave appropriate instructions for redressal. (a) Ill-treatment of certain weavers by persons connected with the factory at Visakhapatnam, and complaints related to this – weavers (petitioners) were ordered to prefer their complaints to the Magistrate in the Zillah. (b) Payment of just dues withheld by the *copdars* – petitioners were asked to complain to the Resident in the first instance for the recovery of the dues, and if not satisfactorily decided by the Resident, to appeal then to the Zillah court. (c) The influence of the native agency on the public establishment who were the leading cause of promoting the irregularities – petitioners' agents were ordered to appear before the Resident to enable him to investigate the charges against the servants of the factory, viz. Chinnum Jaggapah, and other *copdars*.[53]

The weavers, however, expressed their inability to accept the three Board of Trade orders on two grounds. The first was:

> It is notoriously known in this part of the country that the weaver class is the most ignorant and meekest part of the community. Consequently, your petitioners can never dare to complain to the magistrate against the Resident for the ill treatment the weavers at various times unjustly and undeservedly received from that office.

In relation to the second article of the order, the weavers stated that it was not possible to prefer their complaints to the Resident. To offer individual complaints was impracticable as they were "very poor, illiterate and ignorant, and to recover such a huge amount from the *copdars* they had to starve themselves, and put their families to death, as the daily work was the only source of sustenance for them".[54] Moreover, they felt that this process would affect the Company's investment. Therefore, the petitioners accepted only the third order of the Board of Trade.

The response of the petitioners to the orders of the Board of Trade shows an awareness of legal mechanisms and the appropriate methods of dealing with Company officials, and shows the overall clarity with which they carried out their "movement". It also demonstrated the contradictory images they projected about themselves. They considered themselves as the "meekest and ignorant elements of the community", who had no strength to prefer their complaints in the district court. Further, they stated that they were too "poor, illiterate and ignorant" even to pursue their complaints related to the recovery of dues. Before the colonial state, they considered themselves as weak elements, a strange situation when compared to the late eighteenth century. For instance, in 1796 they were

53. *Ibid.*
54. Weavers' petition to BOT dated 16 December 1816; CDC 10, pp. 1269–1273; weavers' petition to BOT dated 2 February 1817; CDC 10, pp. 1273–1277.

objecting to even a slight change in the organization of the production process and were considered by the colonial state as fugitive, rebellious and barbarous. From a situation where they perceived the Company as being intrusive in their economic activity, the weavers had reached a stage where they saw the Company as, in fact, being of assistance in expanding economic opportunities. However, in order to protect their interests while at the same time reaping the benefits of colonial trade, they resorted to various methods of redressal of their grievances while at the same time taking care not to offend Company officials too much.

Thus the organization of the 1816 movement indicates the strength of caste and community networks, and the weavers' strategic abilities, although they do not admit this openly, and instead portray themselves as poor, meek, and humble clients of a new patron. The weavers appear to have been meticulous in understanding the procedures relating to investigations, and therefore asked the Board of Trade to see that Chinnum Jaggapah not only be distanced from the commercial affairs of the factory, but be removed from the area of Visakhapatnam itself. Further, they stated that they would provide the necessary proofs for the grievances and charges levelled against the *copdars*. They said that they had not passed these to the Board of Trade out of fear that the Board would forward them to the Commercial Resident for examination, which would then result in a tampering with the proofs and other evidence by Chinnum Jaggapah. The weavers therefore reserved those complaints to be brought forward before the Enquiry Committee.[55]

Thus, apart from complaining to the Board of Trade, the weavers also took pains to state the authenticity of their cause, and promised that they would pay off all the expenses incurred in connection with the conduct of the investigation and enquiry. They were only too acutely aware of the corrupt practices and mechanisms used by *copdars* and Company officials to shield themselves from accusations.

When the weavers were asked to send twenty representatives from their gathering at Simhachellam, these were taken to Visakhapatnam where they were confined. Upon this, the weavers thought it proper to bring to the notice of the Magistrate their situation and requested that measures be adopted to relieve the weavers from their oppression; they also asked that they might receive the Company's price for their cloth at established prices, and that the earlier balance be paid back, and finally that the entire advance was to be paid only in cash.[56] The Magistrate's office totally rejected these demands stating:

[...] as the petition was not written conformably on a stamp paper, [...] even if

55. Petition to BOT dated 19 March 1817; CDC 10, p. 1255.
56. *Ibid.*, pp. 1255–1256.

they written it was a civil complaint but not a criminal one. Moreover they had not specified the amount which for they were due. In fact as agreeable to the petition, it had to be delivered to the Adjunct Court but as it lacked regulation it is rejected totally.[57]

The weavers, who had hoped for quick justice from their first petition, dated 21 November 1816, and not receiving any redress, on becoming aware that the weavers had sent their agents to Madras, dispatched their second petition on 16 December 1816 specifying the increased harassment caused to them by Henry Taylor and Jaggapah. With the help of 130 pariah peons whom they hired on an hourly basis, these men had forced the weavers to give false *sunneds*, negating whatever they had said earlier. On this action, "the petitioners further stated that if the *copdars* and Jaggapah had not done any evil then there was no necessity for them to employ 130 pariah peons to make the weavers to give a certificate".

The agents presented another petition that they received to the Board of Trade, in which the weavers specified that the certificate had been obtained by compulsion and that "to save their property, houses and weaving tools from being put up for public auction, they gave such certificates". Weavers who refused to furnish certificates were forced to pay off other balances by auctioning their property. In this third petition, dated 2 February 1817, the weavers gave an account of the illtreatment they were made to suffer and told how the *copdars* exacted *sunneds* from the weavers by compulsion and outright torture.

The weavers clearly demonstrated the oppressive character of Jaggapah and the influence he had been exerting over Henry Taylor. They expressed their regard for other commercial and revenue officials whom they compared favourably with their oppressors, by requesting of the Board of Trade,

> [...] the appointment of a gentleman like Mr Thackeray, Mr Brown, or Mr Robinson, because the weavers thought that these people would not "mind" any rich natives or give weightage to the recommendation of any European in the administration of justice. If the board would send any one of the persons, they would come to know that it was not thousands but lakhs [hundred thousands] of rupees that had been taken unjustly from the weaving community.

By not casting any aspersions on officials as a category and by differentiating between good and bad officials, they perhaps hoped to project the impression that they were not opposed to the Company and its activities *per se*, but were only opposing the behaviour of specific officials.

In this particular revolt therefore, the weavers dispatched a series of petitions to put pressure on the authorities to redress their grievances. The

---

57. Petition of the weavers agents to the Body of the Company's *punjum* cloth weavers in the district of Vizagapatnam, 29 November 1816; CDC 10, pp. 1257–1264.

officials in Madras, however, prior to initiating any plan to consider the issues, imposed a precondition that all the agents camping at Madras should return to their respective places. Written orders were issued to this effect.[58] On their return, however, the weavers were abused and assaulted by the Bania *copdars*, and were moreover, pressurized by Henry Taylor to pay back their outstanding balances to the Company. They were also not given any fresh advances, thus severely impacting on their economic condition. In this situation, the weavers submitted a common petition with 201 signatures affixed.[59] The text and content of this petition enable us to observe the indignation, as well as the anxiety, on the part of the weavers, when the state was delaying consideration of their grievances.

> We presented many petitions praying to direct a discontinuance of the interference of the *copdars* [...]. We are poor people and live by earning by our labour. We therefore request you will protect us [...]. In consequence of our having made complaints we are deprived of the advances of money for weaving clothes [...]. We have suffered a great loss and how come we conduct our business if we be put under those who dislike us. We complain of our case to your Board and beg you will be pleased to appoint any gentlemen you think proper to inquire into our grievances. When Mr. Mango Dick was here and in the Board he treated us as the children of the Honourable Company and ever since his departure to Europe, Chinnum Jaggapah now of great influence and the present gentleman (Mr. Taylor) has been doing great injustice towards us and we live now as children without parents. We pray that you will be pleased to depute some gentleman to render us justice and you will we hope protect us.[60]

This, then, was the first time that the weavers openly displayed their feelings regarding the inordinate delay by the authorities in taking cognizance of, and acting upon, their petitions. It was also the first instance in which they attacked the Commercial Resident for his "unjust" actions.

The weavers' remarkable consciousness regarding the use of various judicial and legal mechanisms and their organizational abilities are also reflected in these petitions. Sending representatives from each *macaum*, ensuring proper authorization, collecting signatures from thousands of affected weavers, they ensured that their petitions were not rejected on legal or procedural grounds. It was due to this thorough and methodical process that the enquiry committee finally agreed upon, and corroborated, most of the complaints of the weavers.[61] This particular revolt turned out

58. Translation of a petition from Emenda Jagapa, Davoleree Romoodoo, Emunda Mulliah, weavers of Coderee Macaum in the district of Vizagapatnam, to the Magistrate, 30 July 1816; CDC 10, pp. 1264–1268.
59. Petition of weavers' agents to BOT dated 16 December 1816; CDC 10, pp. 1269–1273.
60. *Ibid.*; also weavers' petition to BOT dated 29 November 1816; CDC 10, pp. 1258–1264.
61. *Ibid.*; also petition dated 17 May 1817; CDC 10, pp. 565–570.

to be a success, as the enquiry committee recommended the dismissal of Chinnum Jaggapah and other Bania *copdars*, and ordered that the old-established division of *macaums* under the command of a head weaver *copdar* should be revived. The entire management of the factory was to be placed under a committee of two members, the senior member to be in full charge of the factory, who would also (1) investigate the dismissal of weaver-caste *copdars*; (2) examine the minute details of the accounts of actual deliveries and advances by the weavers; (3) investigate exaction collected by the head servant of the factory; (4) examine the possibility of instituting legal proceedings against the head servant and others for recovery of money exacted; and (5) assess and investigate the accusations of personal violence committed by the *copdars* with the sanction of the Commercial Resident.

The committee arrived at the conclusion that "a course of fraud and plunder had been pursued for years" by native agents, in association with their European superiors, which led to undue suffering of the weavers and denial of their just dues. More important perhaps was its statement that it is necessary to find out why, despite the establishment of a judicial system, weavers chose to follow the older mechanisms of flight and assembly to get their grievances brought to the notice of the authorities, and in particular the "causes which militate against weavers having recourse to the Courts of Justice".

CONCLUSION

The social history of the weaving community, their concerted efforts and solidarity in times of crisis, comes out clearly from the weavers' revolts recounted above. Weavers used their traditional community organizations such as caste associations and *samiums* in the 1775 Godavari district revolt and in the 1816 Visakhapatnam revolt. In both these, weavers cut across caste groups in launching their movement. In contrast, in the 1796 revolt, the participants almost entirely belonged to one caste – Devangas. However, despite all the obstacles of illiteracy, lack of power, and resources, the ability of weavers to successfully obtain and maintain community support across space and time stand out.

Other than caste and community-based groups, skill-based groups also came to the fore in these revolts. On occasion, socially and economically marginalized sections tended to have lower ranks in the social hierarchy. But when it came to opposing the deskilling processes, affected weavers from different castes came together to oppose the new structural and trading arrangements. Thus, these revolts presented contradictory images. Throughout the period, weaving castes opposed interventions that affected their skills, as these would lower economic and opportunity structures. On the other hand, this very process provided greater scope for all the weaving castes to unite and oppose the "undue" interference in their productive and trading activities, be it from local elites, intermediaries, or government officials. Thus, while divisions based on caste, skills, and specialization were a dominant feature of the textile world prior to the establishment of the East India Company, the structural changes brought about by the Company made it possible for different groups to unite.

Another feature that is established is that both the weaving community and the state accorded importance to the petition as a mechanism for redressing grievances, and, in fact, it progressively became the dominant mode of expressing grievances. Moreover, these petitions gave voice not just to economic complaints but were also directed against social and political exploitation, as well as voicing certain incipient "human rights" issues, including the right to subsistence, freedom from physical abuse, and the right to be heard. For the state, petitioning was not only a more convenient and efficient form of considering grievances, but petitions were also the means by which state officials learned about popular feelings and discontents regarding the new policies and structural changes that were being effected. This was important since, apart from economic changes, the new systems were creating and destroying certain social categories, and transforming the organization of the production system in the region, resulting in shifts in the native power structures.

The petitions also demonstrated the perceptions of colonial officials regarding the colonized. The language and tone that is used in response to the petitions provide indications of this. Weavers are "poor and illiterate", and therefore their ability to write a petition is questioned. Their linguistic and communication skills were suspect, but also a cause for apprehension, as they posed a threat to colonial domination. Western superiority over "barbarous and uncivilized" weavers could be preserved only if they conformed to the images adopted by their colonial masters.

But perhaps the most important conclusion to emerge from an analysis of weavers' petitions is that weavers learned, over the course of time, the methods of dealing with colonial officials and the "best" methods for achieving their objectives. Initially, they took to desertion, flight, assembly, and mutiny, and publicly questioned the authority of colonial officials. Especially when their community members were displaced from leadership positions in the organization of production, and replaced by Bania caste *copdars*, they protested violently. However, gradually perhaps realizing the importance and benefits to be derived from colonial trade, and their structural weaknesses in the face of an increasingly powerful state, they began to resort to more peaceful and "legal" mechanisms. Therefore, the use of petitions is a mirror of structural changes taking place in early colonial Andhra – increasing subordination to colonial commercial interests and resentment against this, expanding economic opportunities, disintegration of traditional patron–client relations, and the possibility of collective action for grievance redressal rooted in legal and judicial principles, rather than being subjected to the whims of feudal patrons.

IRSH 46 (2001), Supplement, pp. 131–150 DOI: 10.1017/S0020859001000359
© 2001 Internationaal Instituut voor Sociale Geschiedenis

Deference and Defiance: The Changing Nature of Petitioning in British Naval Dockyards

KEN LUNN AND ANN DAY

INTRODUCTION

Petitioning as a method of expressing grievances in British history was not peculiar to any particular set of individuals, but was widely used by all sections of society for a range of issues. Given its origins, however, it became ritualized as the means of labour negotiation for workers who were employed by the state, and, by the nineteenth century, by municipal authorities. This was before the institutionalization of trade unions and their recognition as representative agencies for industrial bargaining. One of these groups of workers in the state sector were naval dockyard employees, engaged in the construction, repair, and maintenance of British naval ships. For these workers, the nature of labour relations, and the importance of petitioning as an instrument of negotiation between employees and employer, was both complex and dynamic.

It was the state as employer which characterized the context of work in the Royal Dockyards. Although it is the case that the yards never had a monopoly on the building of the nation's ships – commissioning in private yards was always an element, particularly in times of impending conflict – it was the unique nature of the employment relationship in these yards which set them aside from private shipbuilding concerns and gave the petitioning system a particular set of meanings. This system, tying workers into "the service of the state", contributed, therefore, to forms of bargaining which were peculiar to national and local government employment.[1] The hierarchy of "management" and the concept of being a worker for the state gave a particular relevance to the use of petitions. Rates of pay, conditions of service and levels of employment were seen, from the very early days of the dockyards, as in the domain of the monarch and/or his or her representatives within the structures of dockyard government. This meant that, whilst the yards were directly controlled by the Navy Board, which was answerable to the Board of the Admiralty, the ultimate authority was the monarch. The particular nature of the British parliamentary system, one which has effectively retained the medieval

1. For examples, see M. Daunton, *Royal Mail: The Post Office since 1840* (London, 1985), and P. Beaumont, *Public Sector Industrial Relations* (London [etc.], 1992).

concept of "the Crown" at the apex of the system of government, contributed, in the seventeenth and eighteenth centuries, to stamping dockyard workers as ultimately responsible to the monarch, and impacted significantly on forms of defiance, particularly when resorting to strikes as a method of resistance. Although, as will be shown, strikes were used at various times alongside the petition system, many dockyardmen and their governing officers viewed this type of action as a treasonable offence, even in the twentieth century.

The discussion that follows will focus on the key symbolic role played by petitioning in the changing dynamics of labour relations within the dockyards. In this way, patterns of both deference and defiance to authority and, in particular, to the state, can be identified. Notions of "moral economy", legitimation, and resistance are all revealed by the analysis of the petitioning process. The historical legacy of petitioning, long after it had ceased to be a formal part of the bargaining process in the twentieth century, will also be demonstrated.

"A PRIVILEGED COMMUNICATIVE SPACE"

The origins of petitioning in the British context date back to medieval times, when public discussions of overtly political issues were disallowed. Parliament met as high courts to receive grievances, in the form of petitions, and to make decisions on appeals.[2] Given these origins, the language and means of presentation of the petition were couched in deferential terms which symbolized the hierarchical relations of subject and monarch (or monarch's representatives). The granting of petitions indicated the bestowal of favour, as petitioning was deemed to be entering "a privileged communicative space".[3] Zaret has argued that such an approach was a conscious choice, presenting the petition as a spontaneous reaction to a specific situation, not a "factious", premeditated, or organizational grievance. The latter was deemed to undermine the validity of the appeal and to lessen the chances of acceptance. It was the rhetoric of deference in petitions which defined them as ostensibly apolitical and therefore less challenging to the authority of the monarch.[4]

Although petitioning was seen as an inviolate right for all subjects, its use was necessarily defined and redefined through the centuries. At the time of the English Civil War, "petitioning became a device that constituted and invoked the authority of public opinion as a means to

---

2. D. Zaret, "Petitions and the 'Invention' of Public Opinion in the English Revolution", *American Journal of Sociology*, 101 (1996), pp. 1497–1555.
3. *Ibid.*, p. 1512.
4. *Ibid.*, pp. 1513–1515.

lobby Parliament".[5] The state responded to this more openly political style of petitioning by introducing the Act against Tumultuous Petitioning in 1661. This sought to curb forms of mass petitioning from politicized groupings formed in taverns and coffee houses.[6] Thus, whilst the ritual of deference in the language of petitions was maintained, its use as a quasi-political tool developed considerably. The late eighteenth century saw the beginnings of a huge upsurge in petitions to parliament, such that, by 1832, changes in procedure were required to limit once more the rights to present and debate petitions which effectively restricted their usefulness in broader political decision-making.[7]

The nature of petitioning had thus shifted in the nineteenth century, with a focus more on ways of "creating and measuring a necessary condition of success, namely, bodies of organized opinion".[8] Towards the end of the century, petitioning as an effective means of expressing grievances began to decline as other methods of formulating demands and seeking redress emerged. The slow evolution of parliamentary democracy, representative political parties and access to legal procedures all came to have an increasing role in the mediations between "the people" and "the state". These changing patterns of petitioning in the wider British context can be clearly demonstrated in the development of labour relations and administrative structures in the Royal Dockyards from the eighteenth through to the twentieth century.

PETITIONING AS INDUSTRIAL BARGAINING: THE CASE OF BRITISH NAVAL DOCKYARDS

Before the fifteenth century, British monarchs had relied on private merchant ships for their sea-based strategies in times of war, and it was not until the time of the first Tudor king, Henry VII, that a permanent navy was established,[9] with the subsequent need for bases where the state's ships could be constructed and maintained. In 1495, Portsmouth, on the south coast, was chosen as the site for a purpose-built dry dock, making it effectively the first Royal Dockyard in Britain. By the end of the eighteenth century, there were seven British dockyards, three of which had already been in existence for over 200 years: Portsmouth, Chatham (on the Medway) and Sheerness (on the Thames).[10] What makes the British

---

5. *Ibid.*, p. 1499.
6. M. Knights, "London's 'Monster' Petition of 1680", *The Historical Journal*, 36 (1993), pp. 39–67.
7. C. Leys, "Petitioning in the Nineteenth and Twentieth Centuries", *Political Studies*, 111 (1955), pp. 45–64.
8. *Ibid.*, p. 62.
9. P. MacDougall, *Royal Dockyards* (Newton Abbott, 1984).
10. For details see *ibid.*

Royal Dockyards remarkable is not so much their existence as large-scale industrial complexes (as by the late eighteenth century there were also a number of large manufacturing sites elsewhere in Britain), but that they were among the first locations specifically established by the state for its own needs, and this factor influenced the shaping of employment strategies and forms of deference and defiance undertaken by dockyard workers.

DEFIANCE AND DEFERENCE

The first significant development of the petitioning process, which was established as a form of individual negotiation for dockyard workers, came at the start of the eighteenth century. The Board of Admiralty introduced a system of formal visitations to the yards, providing an identifiable physical presence to the representational monarchical authority which dominated employment relations.[11] This heightened the sense of importance that petitions held in the presentation and redress of grievances. Not only were these now constructed by individuals but also saw the coming together of groups of workers to voice their common grievances. Towards the end of the eighteenth century, this form of protest and claim against the state as direct employer became more dramatic. Knight notes that, in the 1770s, petitioning by dockyardmen increased 300 per cent. The main grievance was the decreasing purchasing power of the established wage rates, as the cost of living rises of the 1750s and 1760s began to have an effect. It was essentially the inequality of the state sector, which seemed to be failing to keep up with what might be termed "market forces", which was the main grievance. Whilst other trades outside the dockyards had seen wage increases, and most relevantly in this case, the private shipyards, wages for the dockyards had remained the same and thus, it was argued, were contributing to hardship.[12] What is noteworthy from these petitions is this sense of relationship with the state, the monarchy and the difficulties of its distancing from the market economy. Although the Board of Admiralty might argue that security of employment was virtually guaranteed in the Royal Dockyards through the system of establishment,[13] and that this was

11. Visitations were initiated by Lord Sandwich (First Lord of the Admiralty) in 1749 as part of a move to make the dockyards, and their workforces, more efficient. See R. Middleton, "The Visitation of the Royal Dockyards, 1749", *Mariner's Mirror*, 77 (1991) p. 21.
12. R. Knight, "From Impressment to Task Work: Strikes and Disruption in the Royal Dockyards, 1688–1788", in K. Lunn and A. Day (eds), *History of Work and Labour Relations in the Royal Dockyards* (London, 1999), p. 17.
13. In the Royal Dockyards, workers were employed either as "established" or "hired". Established workers were virtually guaranteed "a job for life" and a pension on retirement, whereas hired men could be taken on or dismissed at any time and only received a gratuity for some years of their service, with no pension rights.

adequate compensation for wage rates which might not always match those for skilled craftsmen elsewhere, the tone of petitions suggested a responsibility which the Admiralty held to ensure adequate payment and provision for workers' families, particularly since their employment was in defence of the nation-state. This particular form of moral justification for wage demands was to be a central feature of the later petitions and of more direct action.

Knight notes that, in 1739, a large number of shipwrights at Chatham Dockyard went out on strike over the withdrawal of what they saw as a traditional right; the right to take small pieces of wood, or "chips" out of the dockyard for their own use. In the same year, smiths at Deptford and Woolwich combined to petition and went on strike briefly, after which the Navy Board approved their demands. Their show of solidarity was a clear factor in the success of the petition, but may also have alerted the Lords of the Admiralty to the power of workers' collaboration. Further strikes followed at Deptford and Woolwich Dockyards in 1742 and 1744 and in 1745 at the ropeyards over the same issue. However, the most significant strike occurred in 1775, with the introduction of task work instead of day rates, a system which was opposed so vigorously that the Admiralty had to abandon it and reintroduce it years later. As Knight points out, "it illustrated very definite limits upon government control and discipline administered by the Navy Board", limits that were defined by a sense of moral economy and personal rights.[14]

Morriss's studies of dockyard labour moves on to the turn of the eighteenth century and into the period of the Napoleonic wars and their aftermath. Closer scrutiny of the petitions in these years shows demands for higher rates of basic pay, as food prices rose. The 1790s had seen considerable rises in earnings, as a system of piecework was introduced to encourage the necessary output. However, a dramatic rise in prices, culminating with the bad harvests of 1799–1800, saw the cushion which had protected dockyard workers and their families disappear.[15] It was then that the agitation for improved basic rates of pay, the subject of the petitions in the 1770s, was renewed. Since many of these rates dated from the 1690s, increases were clearly an overdue issue for many of the skilled tradesmen in the yards. However, it was here that some of the specific significance of dockyard petitions emerged. The British state was becoming particularly concerned about the threat posed by groups of workers organizing the protests. The introduction of the Combination Acts (1799–1800) were specifically designed to prevent these forms of organized strikes or other types of industrial and political action, and to

14. Knight, "From Impressment to Task Work", pp. 9–10. See also B.M. Ranft, "Labour Relations in the Royal Dockyards in 1739", *Mariner's Mirror*, 47 (1961), pp. 281–291.
15. R.A. Morriss, "Labour Relations in the Royal Dockyards, 1801–1805", *Mariner's Mirror*, 62 (1976), pp. 337–346.

strengthen existing legislation against union activity.[16] This had a particular resonance within the dockyards, where overt resistance could so obviously be defined as treasonable activity.

Interdockyard forms of petitioning seen in the late eighteenth century, and culminating in the petitions for higher basic rates of pay at the time of national food riots in 1801, were viewed by the Admiralty as an alarming precedent, and representatives from the Navy Board visited six of the main dockyards to dismiss those men who had led the strikes and riots. These discharges in 1801, followed by reductions at the end of war in 1802, resulted in an overall 10 per cent reduction in the total dockyard workforce.[17] From 1815 onwards, the economic impact of the postwar depression and the decline in the need for ship construction and repair brought a range of particular hardships. Both Morriss and MacDougall have noted the upsurge in petitioning,[18] although there is some disagreement as to the longer-term implications of this action. For Morriss, it would seem to represent, by 1830, the reduction of the dockyard workforce to "an emasculated factor of production",[19] at least in comparison to the militancy of the eighteenth century. MacDougall opts for an interpretation which favours a pragmatic switch of tactics from the strike to the petition and the associational culture which could be seen by the middle of the nineteenth century, a culture which could cross the various trades and link the different yard workforces.[20] A detailed analysis of the different forms of petition and the language used suggests a rather more complex picture, one which reveals both the wide range of attitudes displayed by dockyard workers and the broad sweep of grievances which were deemed worthy of petitioning.

As has been suggested, one of the most significant features of the postwar petitions was the severity of the economic difficulties following the end of the wars. Rising prices, shortages of food, reduced wages and discharges from work all contributed to distress of varying degrees in dockyard towns. As a group of shipwrights from Pembroke Dockyard begged in May 1817:

> That your Petitioners are in very Great distress occasioned by the Dearth of provisions and house rent, That your Petitioners are Destitute of Necessaries of Life. We therefore have Ventured with Humility to lay our Distress Cases before

16. E.P. Thompson, *The Making of the English Working Class* (London 1963, repr. 1970), p. 174.
17. R. Morriss, "Government and Community: The Changing Context of Labour Relations, 1770–1830", in Lunn and Day, *History of Work*, pp. 21–40.
18. Morriss, "Government and Community", and P. MacDougall, "The Changing Nature of the Dockyard Dispute, 1790–1840", in Lunn and Day, *History of Work*, pp. 41–65.
19. Morriss, "Government and Community", p. 35.
20. MacDougall, "The Changing Nature", pp. 56–57.

you Humbly Praying your Lordships will Consider our Distressed Circumstances and allow us to Get a Little more wages what your Lordships may please to think proper.[21]

Such an appeal demonstrated very graphically the deferential language of the petition and it represented the most basic aspect of dockyard petitioning, the appeal for "a little more wages", couched in terms which indicated the crucial economic necessity for an increase and not one which was in any way assertive of the skill and bargaining power of militant workers. Pembroke Dockyard had only been established in 1814, at a strategically-placed location on the western side of Britain (Pembrokeshire in west Wales).[22] This petition clearly indicated the hardships experienced by what was a very new dockyard, with many workers living some distance from the newly-established site. It was likely that these dockyardmen had had little chance to establish themselves before the downturn in the economy and, thus, their petition reflected a degree of tentativeness in its approach.

Other petitions around this time, however, demonstrate rather different attitudes and concerns. As might be expected in the difficult times of the 1820s, they do not display the solidarity of earlier periods. Indeed, often their concerns lie with the distinctiveness of one group of workers from another, with an emphasis on status and craft differentials, and with the fear of social and economic decline. For example, in 1822, Chatham Dockyard shipwrights petitioned against the proposal to redeploy them as sawyers and scavelmen. The main complaint was the lower wages, which they claimed "entirely renders them incapable of paying taxes and puts many of them to the greatest straits to maintain their numerous families".[23] However, it was clear that, at least in the language of the petition, that part of the appeal was to do with the loss of respectability and status which would accrue. The shipwrights were keen to identify themselves a "respectable Class of Mechanics" and emphasized that "all without exception paid their quota of the Assess'd Taxes".[24] Similar sentiments, even more exaggerated, came from the Woolwich Dockyard shipwrights the same year. They too had found their hours cut and wages reduced. Some had to take on the duties of other mechanics, which entailed difficult

21. Petition of shipwrights, Pembroke Dockyard, 23 May 1817, Public Record Office [hereafter PRO], ADM1/5132.
22. A. Day, " 'Driven from Home': The Closure of Pembroke Dockyard and the Impact on its Community", *Llafur*, 7 (1996), p. 79; P. Carradice, *The Book of Pembroke Dock* (Buckingham, 1991). A later petition of 1820 suggested that rates of pay at Pembroke were 20 per cent less than other dockyards, and rising prices, travel costs, and housing shortages in the new dockyard town were illuminating this discrepancy; 27 April 1820, PRO ADM1/5132.
23. Petition of shipwrights, Chatham Dockyard, 26 September 1822, PRO ADM1/5132.
24. *Ibid.*

work and the purchase of new tools. The worst experience, and "one most degrading in its character and tendency" was being forced to work as scavelmen and labourers, some of whom were deemed to be felons "hardened in guilt, and [...] of the worst description". The skilled shipwrights begged to be spared "The disgrace, which must attach to mixing with Felons" and to be retained in their appropriate work and status.[25]

Petitions in this period could also reflect the concerns of higher-ranking officials in the yards and those officers who found that their anticipated "pensions" and allowances were not materializing. Again, apart from financial concerns, it was loss of status which featured strongly. Quartermen (supervisors) from Portsmouth Dockyard, on being retired from service, sent a particularly heartfelt statement to the Admiralty, indicating that their situation was:

> [...] at one blast reduced from respectability and comparative affluence to a state bordering on starvation and to be the scorn of our neighbours – Whole families, who heretofore through the munificence of the Government enjoyed every comfort, are now doomed to linger out a miserable existence upon the very inadequate stipend of £32 per annum [...].[26]

A similar group of workers, from Sheerness Dockyard, were even more eloquent in their pleas:

> Your Memorialists hoping their late responsible situations would have been permanent, during their *capability* of performing the several duties annexed thereto, had buoyed up themselves, with the pleasing hope, of reaping a competent remuneration, when *Age and Infirmity* should *disable* them from filling their respective Stations.[27]

The Admiralty papers show petitions from these groups of workers from every British dockyard, indicating a common grievance and some degree of cooperation across the dockyards to make their difficulties known. What seems most apparent, overall, is the disgruntlement not simply with their financial situation, but also with what is seen as the state's refusal to recognize the nature of their service and their loyalty to the British nation. For some, this was expressed in pride in their artisanal skills – Woolwich Dockyard shipwrights proclaimed the acquisition of "knowledge of an art and mystery universally allowed to be of the highest importance to this great maratime (sic) nation which throughout a protracted contest for naval ascendancy has fully proved the superior

25. *Ibid.*
26. Petition of quartermen, Portsmouth Dockyard, 18 December 1822, PRO ADM1/5132.
27. Petition of quartermen and foremen, Sheerness Dockyard, 28 October 1822, PRO ADM1/5132.

character of their workmanship, which has materially contributed to the safety of the Country".[28] The quartermen of Portsmouth Dockyard had been expecting more in the way of superannuation, and felt they were owed more because of the "long and efficient services, upon our former respectability in the Community, and upon our faithful discharge of the Trust and Confidence reposed in us".[29] The Woolwich Dockyard shipwrights had "cherished the expectation that services so often acknowledged in cases of emergency, would secure for them protection".[30]

What this study of the period immediately following the Napoleonic Wars indicates is the ways in which petition appeals had become formulaic, but also that within such expressions a complexity of situations and attitudes can be discerned.

By the 1830s, many of the petitions had become much more sharply focused on limited issues and the apparent minutiae of industrial relations negotiations through the only available agency. Different groups of workers from different locations raised questions about rates of pay and tried to negotiate equality of conditions between established and hired men, debating, in particular, the problems raised by the "classification" system, where men in the same trade were paid at different rates according to their ability.[31] One major dimension, revealed through a petition in this period, draws attention to conflict between dockyardmen and their self-help organizations and the dockyard communities, particularly traders, "outside the walls". In May 1837, a group of bakers, flour dealers, and millers from the "three towns", which at that time constituted the hinterland of Plymouth Dockyard, petitioned the Admiralty for intervention against a cooperative venture established by dockyardmen. Their target was the Dock Union Mill Society, set up in 1817, to supply workers and their families with flour and bread. The substance of the complaint was the success of this enterprise, and its expansion into trade with superior officers, clerks, and even those who had no connection with the yard. An earlier complaint, in 1830, had produced an Admiralty directive that the Society confine its sales to its existing members (c.600 people). This, it was claimed, had now been ignored: membership had doubled and sales to the general public had become commonplace.

It is the language of this petition which is so revealing about the sentiments behind the attack on the cooperative venture and about the perception of the Royal Dockyards as an enterprise. As a study of early nineteenth-century petty bourgeois notions of laissez-faire and state intervention, it offers much to reflect upon. The Society was seen as,

28. Petition of shipwrights, Woolwich Dockyard, 22 August 1822, PRO ADM1/5132.
29. Petition of quartermen, Portsmouth Dockyard, 18 December 1822, PRO ADM1/5132.
30. Petition of shipwrights, Woolwich Dockyard, 22 August 1822, PRO ADM1/5132.
31. MacDougall, "The Changing Nature", pp. 58–62.

> [...] pregnant with the greatest evils to the Trading Community – for it cannot be denied that the Founders and active Managers are composed of Persons who receive their support from the Public, through your Lordships, and are able to supply part of their *surplus income so derived* to this profitable speculation – whilst on the other hand it must be admitted that your Memorialists (who are not maintained from the Public Purse but obliged to apply both their Labour and Capital to earn a frugal livelihood) cannot fairly compete in their *lawful* callings with their Opponents [...].[32]

The petitioners went on to argue that they paid taxes to the state without any support in return and argued that the Society be declared a monopoly and abolished, or at least that its trade be limited only to the artificers and labourers who were currently members. What is interesting from this particular instance is the growing sense of hostility towards the state enterprise, the perception of it as a drain upon financial resources and its eccentricity located within the "free market forces" notion of mid-century British capitalism, at least from the small-scale producers of southwest England. Although, as state enterprises, and unlike the commercial sector, the Royal Dockyards were not tied to a profit-making ethos, the Board of the Admiralty was nevertheless answerable to the state for its level of expenditure and to ensure efficient production, particularly as public opinion became a greater force.

These concerns with costs saw the Admiralty tighten both its administrative processes and its responses to petitioning demands in the first half of the nineteenth century. The absence of strikes in the dockyards in the first six decades has been taken by some commentators as a sign of the emergence of a deferential and passive workforce. A more subtle interpretation would recognize a perceptive tactical shift by dockyardmen. As MacDougall notes, by mid-century, the petition as a negotiating tool had been "carefully honed"[33] by the workers and, when appropriate, employed to voice quite militant demands. These surfaced quite dramatically in the second half of the century.

TOWARDS TRADE UNIONISM

By the 1860s, it was becoming clear that both the nature of work, as characterized by the shift from wood to iron in shipbuilding technology, and the system of labour relations were changing. There were a number of differing influences, ones which were to change fundamentally the petitioning culture that had developed over the previous centuries.

The petition continued to be the chief agency for the negotiation of

---

32. Petition of Bakers, Flour Dealers and Millers of Devonport, Stonehouse and Plymouth, 18 May 1837, PRO ADM1/5137.
33. MacDougall, "The Changing Nature", p. 62.

grievances but its symbolic nature became increasingly divorced from economic and political "realities". Predominant among the new influences was the growth of trade unionism. Although, as already indicated, dockyard workers had demonstrated many of the characteristics of eighteenth- and nineteenth-century trade associations seen elsewhere in British manufacturing, unions were not formally recognized by the Admiralty for the purposes of negotiation. As will be shown, there was also an unwillingness to ease their presence within the yards. What can be seen, therefore, in the period leading up to the First World War, is an increasing use of petitions in the contestation of wages and conditions, but also a growing pressure to challenge the system of bargaining symbolized by the petitions themselves and their replacement with a more "modern" system of labour negotiation and recognition.

The 1862 strike at Chatham dockyard, ostensibly about rates of pay for platers brought in to construct the hull of HMS Achilles (the first ironclad battleship to be built in a Royal Dockyard),[34] demonstrated the ways in which trade-union attitudes were coming to influence labour relations. In part, this was due to labour mobility between public and private sectors. This had always been an aspect of dockyard history: workers with experiences outside the state sector were drawn in to more secure employment in the Royal Dockyards and brought with them a work culture which was perhaps more confrontational. In addition, the changes in technology – essentially the shift from wood to iron – also drew in new workers and different expectations and patterns of labour representation and consciousness. The conventional historical wisdom, too, of trade-union growth percolating down from the skilled artisanal limitations of mid-century to the "semiskilled" and "unskilled" sectors of the workforce, applied to the dockyard as much as anywhere else. These broader trade union developments, and their impact on the yards, was "a subject much on the Admiralty's mind in this period".[35]

Overall, the second half of the nineteenth century is a period of considerable industrial unease within the Royal Dockyards. The late 1850s and early 1860s saw discontent swelling, with the number of petitions increasing, peaking in 1865, by which time the shipbuilding boom had diminished. The following year, the Conservative government cut construction, closed the establishment list for dockyard workers and there were layoffs of hired men. By 1870, the dockyard workforce had slipped to just over 11,000 from its 1865 total of over 18,000.[36] Nonetheless, petitioning was still the predominant form of labour negotiation, not only

---

34. M. Waters, "Changes in the Chatham Dockyard Workforce, 1860–90", *Mariners's Mirror*, 69 (1983), p. 55.
35. J.M. Haas, *A Management Odyssey: The Royal Dockyards, 1714–1914* (Lanham, MD, 1993), p. 102.
36. *Ibid.*, pp. 103–104.

from male workers, but from a growing number of women who were also employed in the Royal Dockyards, mostly as flagmakers in colour lofts or as ropemakers in spinning rooms. Petitions were received by the Lords of the Admiralty in 1875 from a number of women workers in Chatham and Portsmouth Dockyards about decreases in their hours of work and the hardship this would place on their families.

The first record of female employees in the nineteenth century can be found in the papers of Commissioner Cunningham in 1816:

> Having determined that in future the Signal Flags required by His Majesty's ships and vessels shall be made in the Dock Yards by women entered for the purpose, We desire that you will inform us, after a sufficiet *(sic)* store shall have been provided, what number of women it will be proper to continue to meet the demands for these Flags.[37]

Four women were taken on for the work and, according to the files, they were paid "two pence per hour" and started work at six o'clock in the morning. These first women employees worked in the colour loft and in the 1860s women were also taken into the roperies, when steam-powered machines were brought in for ropemaking and the work was less heavily manual.[38] Both these types of employment, in the colour loft and spinning room, were initially given to the widows of sailors or dockyardmen, as a way of enabling the Admiralty to carry out its responsibilities in providing for the wives and children of seaman and dockyardmen beyond the grave.

Thus, the employment of women was extended as a privilege rather than as a right, and the language of deference seen in a petition brought before the Board of Admiralty in 1875 by women workers aptly illustrates their supplicant status. Under the 1874 Factory Act, the Admiralty was required to make changes in the hours of work of women employees. The amended hours would allow a break of four and a half hours between meals; four whole days leave in addition to Christmas and Good Friday; and working hours not to extend beyond 6am or 6pm or after 2pm on Saturdays. The Admiralty's system of amending the working day according to the season resulted in a contravention of these requirements, and, in order to comply with the Act without incurring any loss of working time, it was proposed to extend the summertime working hours for female employees in the spinning rooms and the colour loft. In response, women workers at the ropery in Chatham and in the colour loft at Portsmouth sent a memorial in 1875 to the Lords of the Admiralty, via their Captain Superindent, protesting at these changes in their hours of work.

---

37. Chatham Letter Book, January–December 1816, National Maritime Museum, CHA/F/29.
38. B.H. Patterson, *"Giv'er a Cheer Boys": The Great Docks at Portsmouth Dockyard, 1830–1914* (Portsmouth, 1989), p. 21.

We the undersigned beg most respectfully to state that we have heard with regret and alarm the alteration of working time that is about to take place in the Spinning Room, and we beg you most seriously and earnestly to use your powerful influence in preventing the same from being carried out, for the following reasons. A great portion of us are widows, with families and would be injured in a pecuniary point by a longer absence from our families than at present, for we shall be compeled to pay more for the care of our children. Many of us take them to nurseries for the day but then we should be prevented, for they would not be open early enough in the morning and they are closed before six at night, besides the money received for our day's work is not sufficient for the maintenance of our families, and we are compeled to work at night. And if retained in the Yard until a quarter to six instead of a quarter past five o'clock it will deprive us of the money we should earn in the time, hence starvation would exist and the Workhouse would follow [...].[39]

At the same time, the colour women complained about the longer hours and the reduction of the dinner break from one hour to half an hour, stating that "our absence all day must in a measure be detrimental to their wellbeing [of their children]".[40] The memorial from the ropery workers was signed by eighty-eight women and there were twenty-five women in the colour loft at this time. The Admiralty decided that, under the Factories Act of 1874, the new summer hours would stay in force but that the women could come in half an hour later in winter and have an hour dinner break. The Admiralty's response was clearly aimed at recognizing the need to adhere to the regulations laid out under the Factory Act, but also to save themselves any loss of working time. It is ironic that the 1874 Act was introduced to improve the working conditions of women and juvenile workers, but that, because of the nature of dockyard working practices, the changes required worked against the best interests of women employees, necessitating a petition to rescind the required changes.

Although appeals can be found in the 1820s and 1830s from male workers, which also refer to the Admiralty's moral responsibility in ensuring that levels of pay did not result in starvation and the workhouse, there is an interesting, and significant, difference with these memorials from women workers. The concern is focused on their roles predominantly as mothers and their domestic responsibilities rather than their role as workers. Disputes about wages and working conditions continued throughout the 1870s, as the transition to iron shipbuilding developed, and issues of demarcation and pay amongst male workers were again high on the petitioning agenda. Arguments about a growing gap between rates in private yards and those paid in the state sector became more powerfully

---

39. Petition from women in the spinning room, Chatham Dockyard, May 1875, PRO ADM116/159.
40. *Ibid.*

articulated by the workforce. In return, various Admiralty committees began to articulate the notions that the dockyards were inefficient in comparison with the public sector and that idleness was a key feature of the dockyard workforce. Graham's Committee of the 1880s also wanted to see harsher powers of dismissal allowed to individual Admiral Superintendents, delegating authority away from the Board of the Admiralty itself.[41]

By 1892, the figure for annual petitions had risen to 252, and in that year a committee was set up under Rear Admiral Fane (Admiral Superintendent at Portsmouth Dockyard) to look into the whole issue of wage levels, working conditions, and objections to the system of classification which had been reintroduced in 1891.[42] The rise in petitions was undoubtedly related to the establishment of a Royal Commission on Labour in 1891, and the Admiralty's reaction was to set up the Fane Committee, which included a representative from the Labour Department of the Board of Trade. On giving evidence before the Commission, the Director of Dockyards expressed his views on classification, stating that,

> [...] where gradations of pay have not existed in certain trades [...], I have frequently felt that I was perpetrating an enforced injustice to the best and most conscientious workmen, because I could only pay them the same wages as I paid to the least skilled and lazy men of their class.[43]

He also stated that, although classification had been introduced for some trades in private shipbuilding yards, "the shipwrights in private yards have always set their faces against what is known as classification", and that in the dockyards, "the trades unions stepped in and said that all men were to be paid alike", with most trades objecting strongly to graded levels of pay. There is clear evidence here that some trade unions were able to influence decisions on certain aspects of dockyard work and, despite the Director of Dockyards's viewpoint, the Lords of the Admiralty decided to abolish the system of classification in 1893 because it was felt that the "men's discontent is justified and that the system must be abandoned".[44]

Confrontation continued into the 1890s, when there were rumours of a strike threat, although it came to nothing. The articulated issue was wages, although the underlying tensions about the whole system of employment were apparent. To defuse the situation somewhat, there were concessions over pay, classification and over aspects of superannuation. In addition, in 1894, the eight-hour day was introduced into the dockyards, long before it

41. For details see Haas, *A Management Odyssey*, pp. 129–156.
42. Reports of Fane Committee on Dockyard Wages, 1893–1894, PRO ADM116/374.
43. Extracts of Director of Dockyard's Evidence Before the Royal Commission on Labour, Appendix A, May 1893, PRO ADM116/374.
44. Reports of Fane Committee, PRO ADM116/374.

was an agreed working period in private shipyards or elsewhere in British industry.[45] Whilst it appeared that the Admiralty were conceding to the demands in dockyardmen's petitions, there was often a price to pay. In the case of the introduction of a forty-eight-hour week, a number of privileges were withdrawn, such as a half day's holiday on the annual visitation of the Lords of the Admiralty, or when ships were launched. Women in the colour loft and the roperies also had their hours of work reduced, so that during the summer months they only worked for nine hours a day instead of twelve.[46]

There was also a massive expansion of the dockyard workforce from 1895 onwards, and Haas argues that there was thus a "long quiet" until 1912–1913.[47] Certainly numbers rose dramatically – from the 1895 figure of 19,000 to nearly 34,000 in 1905. However, this "long quiet" disguised many of the inherent tensions noted above. It also ignores the massive lay-off of hired men, begun in the autumn of 1905, which eventually saw 8,000 hired workers discharged (one-third of the total workforce). This action of a Conservative government had considerable political impact in the dockyard towns and contributed to the election of Liberal MPs in those constituencies (and a Liberal government nationally). It also meant that, when issues came to a head in the immediate prewar years, the challenges and the force of the arguments produced quite dramatic changes within dockyard labour relations.

PETITIONS: AN OUTMODED SYSTEM?

There were a number of ways in which dockyardmen were beginning to pressurize employers beyond the system of petitioning. In some senses this was again due to the wider processes of political development within Britain. The extension of the male franchise in 1867 and 1884/5 had given small, but significant, elements within the dockyard workforce a degree of political influence. Those who stood for dockyard constituencies had to take account both of the significance of the yards to the local economy and, now, the "dockies" vote.[48] By the late nineteenth century, the lobbying of dockyard MPs and their consequent representations in parliament were clear indications of the alternatives to conventional petitioning within the Admiralty framework.

There were also internal pressure groups being created, ones which linked across trades and the barriers of skill and sectionalism. In 1911, a

---

45. Haas, *A Management Odyssey*, pp. 160–167.
46. Introduction of Forty-Eight-Hour Week, 1894, PRO ADM116/382.
47. Haas, *A Management Odyssey*, p. 166.
48. K. Lunn, "Labour Culture in Dockyard Towns. A Study of Portsmouth, Plymouth and Chatham, 1900–1950", *Tijdschrift voor sociale geschiedenis*, 18 (1992), pp. 275–293.

Dockyard Grievances Committee was formed in Portsmouth from the local Trades Council, as the Admiral Superintendent of the yard was informed that, "The Dockyard Grievances Committee is representative of the organized men in the dockyard. The Portsmouth Trades Council has thirty-nine branches affiliated to it, twenty-six of which have members who are employed in the Dockyard".[49] Around the same time, a Chatham Dockyard Workers Committee had been formed. In an exchange with their Admiral Superintendent, this committee began to raise grievances directly with him. Most of them were dealt with in an uncontentious fashion. One issue, that of provision for workmen on the floating dock, seemed more complex, and the Committee were asked to refer it through the usual channels, i.e. a written petition from the workers concerned. The Admiral Superintendent's Secretary referred them to the existing regulations "complaints from the men must be made by them in this manner", and suggested that the Admiral Superintendent was "unable to take any notice of complaints raised by any outside agencies: but has made a special exception as regards your letter on this occasion".[50] This attempt to channel grievances back into the conventional petitioning mode met with a sharp response from the Committee. The secretary "respectfully" pointed out that it was hardly an "outside agency", since all its members were dockyard employees. It saw petitioning as relevant for individual cases, but clearly wanted a more collectivist agency for general grievances: "This method would prevent frivolous and vexatious matters troubling the Yard Officers while, inter alia, proving the need for investigation of any questions submitted through the Committee."[51] A curt response from the Admiral Superintendent, saying that all issues of principle affecting all the Royal Dockyards must be by petition to the Admiralty, indicated a closure of further debate: "I am to add that the Regulations promulgated by the Admiralty defining the method to be adopted by the Yard Workmen to secure redress of grievances are exhibited in prominent positions throughout the Yard."[52] The Committee then sought to broaden the discussion and seek clarification of its legitimacy by sending all the correspondence to the Admiralty in May 1913. The question of "outside agency" and alternatives to petitioning were clearly coming to a head by this time.

One of the major changes which reshaped the format of negotiation and, consequently, was instrumental in undermining the power of the petition,

---

49. G.W. Porter, President of Portsmouth Trades Council to Admiral Superintendent, Portsmouth Dockyard, 30 August 1911, PRO ADM116/1129A, cited in P. Galliver, "Trade Unionism in Portsmouth Dockyard, 1880–1914: Change and Continuity", in Lunn and Day, *History of Work*, p. 116.
50. C.R. Sayers, Secretary to the Admiralty Superintendent, Chatham Dockyard to P.W. Terry, Secretary of Chatham Dockyard Workers Committee, 3 January 1913, PRO ADM116/1216.
51. Terry to Sayers, 19 January 1913, PRO ADM116/1216.
52. Sayers to Terry, 22 January 1913, PRO ADM116/1216.

was the introduction of trade-union representation, albeit obliquely, into the petitioning process. In 1905, it was decided by the Admiralty that delegates from the various dockyards were allowed to travel to London, without loss of pay, in order to present their grievances. Each delegate had to be selected by the employees, usually two per trade, and these representatives had to attend the Admiral Superintendent's office in their respective dockyard in order to identify themselves. By this time it was clear that petitions were being used in a far more collaborative way by dockyardmen. The 1905 and 1906 petitions from Portsmouth, Chatham and Devonport outline almost exactly the same demands from each yard on specific issues, indicating a level of joint action and the desire to present a united front. The grievances in these petitions clustered around demands for increases in the rates of pay, but were accompanied by concerns about pensions, parity of pay within trades and payments to relatives on death.[53] The majority of the delegates elected were members of trade unions, although the Admiralty insisted that they were employed within the dockyards and trade unionists from outside could not act as workers' representatives.[54] Women colourmakers from Chatham Dockyard were also represented in the 1906 petitions, requesting higher rates of basic pay.[55] The signs were clearly there that the petitioning system was seen by dockyard workers as increasingly outmoded and ineffective and that direct workers' representation was the way forward, although the Admiralty insisted on maintaining it as a formal method of negotiation where they could continue to exert the state's authority.

TOWARDS THE WHITLEY SYSTEM: THE END OF PETITIONING?

What developed from this point was a sustained, and often quite fierce, campaign for more direct involvement of trade unions, whether or not delegates held positions within the dockyard, and for a more effective system of negotiating which ceased to rely upon the petition. Committees, such as those formed in Portsmouth and Chatham (as noted above) were part of that process, but it also involved activities which sought to challenge the legitimacy of the petition. A.G. Slaughter, an official of the Amalgamated Society of Engineers, wrote in 1913, "The style of application is slavish in the extreme, the form of the petition requiring the workmen to acknowledge themselves as 'the humble servants' of 'My Lords'. An emotion which they are far from feeling in these days of

53. Abstract of Petitions from Workmen, 1905 (Chatham, Portsmouth and Devonport Dockyards), PRO ADM116/374.
54. Regulations on Obtaining Grievances 1906, PRO ADM116/1029.
55. *Ibid.*

democratic control."[56] With a widening of the parliamentary franchise, there was no longer the need for a style of language which served to camouflage any overt political objective, as Zaret has pointed out existed in the earlier periods. One of the ways in which the framework of the petition could be challenged was by the "abuse" of the system. In the early years of the twentieth century, it becomes increasingly clear that the same petitions are being submitted every year, that arguments are being restated despite their rejection, and that the whole machinery of negotiation is becoming overwhelmed and hugely unproductive. The agreement to allow union officials as part of a delegation had, by 1911, caused the Admiralty to try and reform the system. The previous year, in the various deputations, John Jenkins, a shipwright official and former MP for Chatham,[57] described himself thus – "I am somewhat in the position of a Methodist preacher; I operate throughout the whole of the Dockyards and preach the same sermon wherever I go".[58] He represented many of the delegations to the Admiralty and, because the petitions were often virtually identical for each group of workers from each dockyard, repeated the points on each occasion. Essentially what was becoming more apparent was a resentment at the constant rejection of claims within the petitions, and also at the antiquity of the system itself. Speaking on behalf of the Portsmouth Dockyard shipwrights, Jenkins made this very clear.

> I should like to say at the outset that so far as our members are concerned they are keenly disappointed. Evidently for all practical purposes our petitions are useless. And although we have ventured to sign it again this year it is in the hope that you will give it more favourable consideration then hitherto.[59]

Elsewhere, he wondered at the point of petitioning, since little positive response ever seemed forthcoming and most petitions were returned bearing the Admiralty reply, "cannot be acceded to". It was this resentment, and its impact on negotiations, which caused doubts within the Admiralty about the viability of continuing. As Galliver has suggested, the "impending demise of the petitioning system was imminent".[60]

Eventually, in 1914, the Admiralty agreed that an annual London conference should be established as the main vehicle for the exchange of views and negotiations between dockyard workers and the employers. The delegations of dockyard worker representatives could constitute up to half nondockyardmen, that is, full-time trade-union officials. This effectively ended the petition and its concomitant apparatus, a process which seemed

56. *Portsmouth Evening News*, 26 February 1913.
57. For details see Lunn, "Labour Culture in Dockyard Towns", pp. 283–287.
58. Extracts from Minutes of 1910 Deputations, PRO ADM116/1179.
59. *Ibid.*
60. Galliver, "Trade Unionism in Portsmouth Dockyard", p. 120.

to be enhanced with the introduction of a more "democratic" system of state bargaining after the First World War.

THE LEGACY OF THE PETITION

The origins of the Whitley system go back to problems raised by the industrial unrest of the First World War, but also to some of the prewar pressures and conflicts. A committee, headed by J.H. Whitley, MP for Halifax, came up with a plan for joint councils of employers' associations and trade unions, with a committee structure which operated right down to factory level. Initially, its proposals were meant to refer to the private sector alone, but pressure from civil-service unions and industrial workers employed in the state sectors led to a second report in October 1917, which suggested that state and municipal authorities form joint councils.[61]

Initially, dockyard workers seemed to have been impressed by the Whitley system. In 1925, H. Berry, secretary of the trade union side of the Shipbuilding Trades Joint Council, publicly praised the new system,

> The day has passed away, I hope for ever, when Petitions to "My Lords" setting forth the burden of one's complaint and praying for redress thereof [...] it is not my purpose to say whether the Whitley Council is the best machine for improving "Rates and Conditions", but it has given the men, at least, a good opportunity of having their claims presented, listened to, and redressed in many cases.[62]

However, a closer evaluation might suggest that it took much longer for the impact of petitioning and its surrounding ideology to fade away. No significant study of industrial relations in the dockyards for this era exists as yet, but some tentative examination suggests a powerful echoing of previous centuries. Scanning the minutes of the committee proceedings in the later 1920s and 1930s, what comes across is the formality of proceedings, which in many ways reflected the old patterns of negotiation and of authority. The trade-union side would raise issues, ask for improvements to wages or conditions, and the employers' side, including Ministry of Labour officials, would make a consideration. This would often involve lengthy breaks between formal meetings, internal discussion and, on return, usually rejection of the trade-union requests. The system allowed for formal arbitration: the trade-union side could ask for issues to be sent to an Arbitration Court. However, very few decisions were in favour of the union argument. Ultimately the language and bearing of the employers' side seemed to symbolize an inheritance of petitioning, the

---

61. For details see, K. Lunn and A. Day, "Continuity and Change: Labour Relations in the Royal Dockyards, 1914–50" in Lunn and Day, *History of Work*, p. 133.
62. *The Dockyard Industrial Review*, 1(2), 2nd quarter, 1925.

refusal to negotiate directly around a table. Positions were stated, there was a brief discussion and responses were delivered as set pieces at the next meeting. Disagreements then went to arbitration. "Whatever the formal intentions of the JSTC and its wider framework of Whitleyism, it seems clear that old attitudes and entrenched positions were powerful factors in inter-war industrial relations."[63] Whilst Whitleyism may have provided a useful safety valve at a local level, and for a limited range of grievances about conditions, the essential points about pay and the nature of dockyard employment were left to the top-level committees. In these, it was apparent that real decision-making was still very much in the control of the Admiralty and other state agencies. The legacy of petitioning persisted well beyond its formal application.

CONCLUSIONS

At the end of the twentieth century, the Royal Dockyards had ceased to exist in their historically recognizable format. Privatization, the overall decline of British naval strength and the switch to "heritage" has seen dramatic physical and ideological shifts. Privatization has seen the effective end of the Whitley system and a move towards more direct union/management bargaining.

In looking back at the changing patterns of industrial relations over the centuries and the symbolic importance of the petition in that history, what becomes clear is the lack of any simplistic pattern. Notions of deference and defiance are woven throughout the whole gamut of labour relations in the Royal Dockyards. The conventional notion of servility and deference engendered and developed through the use of petitioning does, of course, have some validity. A great number of dockyard workers were unquestionably loyal to the Crown and to the state and accepted their authority and control, with the ultimate reward of job security and a pension. Alongside this, however, there are instances of more militant behaviour, of strikes and the slow growth of trade unionism, challenging what was seen by some workers as the heavy hand of the Admiralty and the British state. Above all, petitions demonstrate the many and varied aspects of dockyard workers' culture – the solidarity between trades but also divisions of status and skills resulting in the elitism of some workers, contrasted to the more egalitarian demands of some trade unionists. That history cannot be easily compartmentalized or chronologically divided. The impact of the petitioning system, even after its demise, has been identified and it was, arguably, its long history which has contributed to the particular nature of dockyard labour relations over the centuries.

---

63. Lunn and Day, "Continuity and Change", p. 134.

IRSH 46 (2001), Supplement, pp. 151–169 DOI: 10.1017/S0020859001000281
© 2001 Internationaal Instituut voor Sociale Geschiedenis

Petitions and the Social Context of Political Mobilization in the Revolution of 1848/49: A Microhistorical Actor-Centred Network Analysis

CAROLA LIPP AND LOTHAR KREMPEL

A great part of the political movement in the Revolution of 1848 took place in the form of group and mass petitions. The National Assembly in Frankfurt, the first national German parliament, received 17,000 petitions from more than three million people.[1] A great number of petitions, analysed by German scholars such as Best, dealt with the question of a liberal market economy, with problems resulting out of the developing process of industrialization, and with protective duties. The petitions expressed different group interests, articulated by craftsmen, merchants, entrepreneurs, and workers, who responded to current economic and social restraints. Another complex of petitions formulated requests regarding the constitution, the liberalization of the political system, or the organization of education, especially the separation of church and state. Another large mass of revolutionary petitions was addressed to the rulers or the ruling bodies of the different German states and was concerned with regional conflicts, and the adoption of ideas that were developed at national level.

Until now, these petitions have been analysed as the product of a collective body, and the signatories of these petitions have been identified through the names of the groups that were given at the head of the petitions. The assumption was that the information and social self-definition of the titles represented the actual social groups that issued these petitions. Due to the informational poverty of the sources, which usually only contained a handwritten name, surname, and locality, researchers were not able to reconstruct the social and cultural context of the petitioners. These petition lists mention occupations in only a few cases. Therefore, a differential social analysis was almost impossible, and it was taken for granted that there was a similarity between the named authorship and the social status of the signatories. A closer inspection of one of these

---

1. Heinrich Best, *Interessenpolitik und nationale Integration 1848/49. Handelspolitische Konflikte im frühindustriellen Deutschland* (Göttingen, 1980), p. 127; Joachim Heinrich Kumpf, *Petitionsrecht und öffentliche Meinung im Entstehungsprozeß der Paulskirchenverfassung 1848/49* (Frankfurt [etc.], 1983).

petitions reveals an astonishing configuration. A petition, headed *Gewerbeleute von Esslingen* (businessmen from Esslingen), that asked for protective duties for industrial textile products, was actually organized by the local entrepreneurs who signed at the top of the lists. But the identification of the other signatures shows that two-thirds of them were not from merchants but from workers, and an even narrower analysis makes clear that the petition must have been circulating in various production areas of the local industrial plants. Such a different perspective can only be made if the analysis is based on an identification of the historical actors.

In the case presented here, we have made a computer-based reconstitution of the entire population of the city of Esslingen, one of the rising industrial towns in the kingdom of Württemberg, with about 13,000 inhabitants in 1849.[2] The reconstitution is built on the individual social identification of each actor through the linkage of more than 150 sources.[3] With three textile firms and a plant for the production of railway engines and carriages, this middle-sized town was one of the most progressive industrial centres in Württemberg at that time. In 1850, we find that nearly 20 per cent of the household heads in the town were industrial workers. With 38 per cent of all household heads, craftsmen still represented the majority of the inhabitants. Although Esslingen became a Württembergian administration centre during the pre-Revolutionary period, known as the *Vormärz*, the town still lived on its past as a free *Reichsstadt* and contained within its community boundaries about 10 to 12 per cent agriculturally-based households, most of them small vintagers producing wine for the regional market. In its social spectrum Esslingen represented the typical mixture for the German southwest, a region with partible inheritance and small landholders, who were forced to take up artisanal or industrial occupations to supplement the income of the family.

The following analysis presents an exemplary microhistorical case study of the petition movement in Esslingen, and shows the political, social, and cultural networks in which the petition movement in this politically very active town was embedded. Eleven petitions[4] were analysed, which had

2. The project, financed by the Deutsche Forschungsgemeinschaft, is led by Professor Carola Lipp. Her assistant is Dr Jürgen Nemitz at the University of Göttingen. The network analysis was made by Dr Lothar Krempel and Michael Schnegg, Cologne.
3. To identify people socially the most important sources were inhabitant, tax and voting lists, town militia and civic guard registers, church registers, house assessment lists, and sources that linked the people to their actual workplace. On the political level, the records are based on the name lists of petitions, membership lists of associations, committees and communal institutions.
4. Addressee of five petitions: the Württembergian government and King; addressee of six petitions: The National Assembly in Frankfurt. The population of Esslingen wrote far more petitions but not all of the sources contained lists of names.

added name lists of different lengths.[5] Table 1 overleaf shows the issues that were formulated. Petitions were a form of political action which entailed low costs and normally few risks. The threshold of participation was rather low, but very often the signing of a petition marked the first step into political activity. Especially for people who felt marginalized, or were not prepared for long-term political involvement, petitions were an easy form of expressing their opinions and placing themselves in the realm of politics. As a quick way to mobilize the masses, petitions therefore were some of the most forceful, but often underrated, forms of revolutionary practice.

For historical research, the important aspect of petitions is that they represented actions in structured situations. Petitions during the Revolution were usually based on individual interaction and social contact, and they relied on indigenous networks and cultural organizations which contributed to the mobilization. They were also based on a long-term process of consensus formation during the *Vormärz*,[6] when most of the liberal ideologies and goals were formulated, the legitimation of the bureaucratic monarchical state was questioned, and nationalist ideas were developed. The discussions which took place in the pre-Revolutionary period produced a collective definition of the situation which led to activities.

Though Württemberg, since 1819, had been one of the rare German constitutional states with a near-parliamentary system, there was a lot of criticism of monarchical constitutional prerogatives, aristocratic privileges, and the authoritarian structure of bureaucratic administration. A central grievance was the repression of civil rights. The liberal movement in Württemberg which expressed these grievances dated back to the early 1830s, when the first liberal associations were founded. These associations were sometimes formed as cultural associations, such as musical and choral societies, which seemed to occupy themselves with entertainment, but actually formed a crypto-political framework for the modelling of political opinion. These early associations of the *Vormärz* were the core of the organizations that developed during the Revolution: especially the main political parties, and, in Württemberg, the constitutionalist and democratic organizations. As the political "diagnosis" was clear, liberals in southwest Germany held large meetings, even before the Revolution started, to

5. The 3,744 identified signatures represent 2,159 persons for whom we mostly have more information regarding their social position, their profession and, in many cases, their further political involvement. But not all of them were integrated in the political life of Esslingen. Therefore our network analyses contain only 1,986 petitioners that were linked to the organizational net.
6. Bert Klandermans, "The Formation and Mobilization of Consensus", in Bert Klandermans (ed.), *From Structure to Action: Comparing Social Movements Research Across Cultures*, *International Social Movement Research*, 1 (1988), pp. 174–196.

Table 1. Petitions with individual signatures in Esslingen 1848/49

	Petition	Date	Signatures	Identified	%
Phase 1 (T1)	Petition to the Conservative Government and King of Württemberg: demanding civil rights	28.2.1848	104	104	100
Phase 2 (T2)	Petition to the National Assembly: *Bruderbund*, re Constitution	29.5.1848	238	197	82.8
	Petition to the National Assembly: Catholics and religious freedom	9.7.1848	43	42	97.7
	Petition to the National Assembly: school–church relations	12.8.1848	232	232	100.0
	Petition to the National Assembly: artisanal requests	4.12.1848	245	244	99.6
	Petition to the National Assembly: businessmen	20.12.1848	248	241	97.6
	Petition to the National Assembly: duties on wine	23.12.1848	541	531	98.2
Phase 3 (T3)	Petition to the Liberal Government of Württemberg	9.3.1849	498	496	99.2
	Petition to the King of Württemberg: (National Constitution)	22.4.1849	1367	1233	90.2
	Petition to the Württembergian Minister of Justice: prisoners in Baden	25.7.1849	68	68	100.0
	Petition to the Württembergian Minister of Foreign Affairs: prisoners	30.8.1849	358	356	99.4
Total			3942	3744	95.0

discuss their demands, i.e. to formulate prospective challenges that were part of the later requests articulated in petitions at the beginning of the Revolution. On this level, people discussed grievances, shaped their political positions and adopted goals that were represented by the liberal movement.

The character of political developments during the *Vormärz* structured our analytical approach, which combines actor-centred perspectives with the structural view of network analyses, and uses techniques of visualizations of social relations and structures.[7] If political behaviour was embedded in the political culture and in the structure of everyday life of a city, there had to be a strong relationship between the organizational culture of the *Vormärz* and the political actions of people who were mobilized during the Revolution. Furthermore, we expect that political experiences during the *Vormärz* structured the forms of activities in 1848. And, indeed, usually the same strategies and measures observed in pre-Revolutionary times were reproduced during the Revolution. What differed was the acceleration of action, and the process of social diffusion and mass mobilization, which had its special political impact on an already ideologically destabilized system.

Petitions were one of the established political instruments used in local politics. Therefore, we have analysed the relationship between the actions taken during the *Vormärz* and in the petitions of 1848. We found that people who, (1) were active members in the local associations, (2) were used to petitioning, or (3) had electoral functions in the local community, were far more prone to participate in the Revolutionary movement than others (see Figure 1 overleaf).

This figure is based on membership data from more than twenty-five associations, the most important among them being the liberal Civil Society (*Bürgergesellschaft*) and several liberal choral societies founded between 1827 and 1847. As the most important cultural organizations in the town, these are one of the centres in our network analyses (see Figure 2).

We also looked at nine committees that organized local charities or local celebrations, and which played an important role in the configuration of the local elite. Next to the associations, a central function in the process of political formation in the *Vormärz* was performed by the local citizen initiatives. These activities (twenty-two analysed) usually consisted of

7. These techniques are based on force-directed placement algorithms, which can be extended to handle valued graphs and even two-mode data. Compared to the classical statistical approach which reduces information and eliminates small phenomena, these methods allow a reconstruction of the overall structure from relational information, while preserving information on how single elements are tied into the network. See Lothar Krempel, "Visualizing Networks with Spring Embedders: Two-mode and Valued Data", in American Statistical Association (ed.), *Proceedings of the Section of Statistical Graphics* (Alexandria, VA, 1999), pp. 36–45.

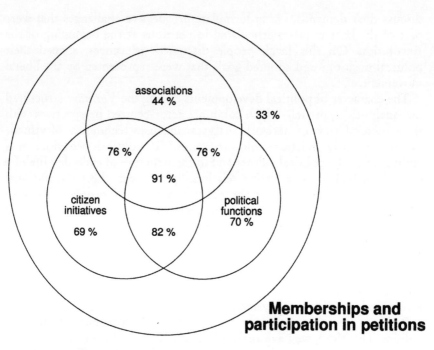

Figure 1. Participation in petitions and overlapping memberships
The highest participation rate (91 per cent) is found for those individuals who were connected to all three types of membership; 33 per cent of petitioners did not have any links to the organizational structure; 69 per cent of the actors who had links with citizen initiatives participated in the petition movement, while only 44 per cent of the members of associations signed petitions (N = 5103 male inhabitants of Esslingen).

petitions and were in some aspects models for later activities. The citizen initiatives which were analysed (called *Bürgerinitiativen* = BI) were normally concerned with neighbourhood problems or criticism of measures of the city executive. A fourth aspect of political activity that was important for political life in Esslingen was the membership of political institutions, such as the community council or citizens' committee. Other political functions included the secondary electors for the Württembergian parliament, titular offices in the local administration, and jurors. Finally, the members of political organizations that originated during the Revolution constituted another important group, integrated into the social network. With the foundation of these groups the network became polarized between the national and constitutional liberals on the one hand and the developing Democratic Party, that challenged the constitutional monarchy, on the other. These two organizations contributed to the left–right axis of the network, along which most of the events were organized.

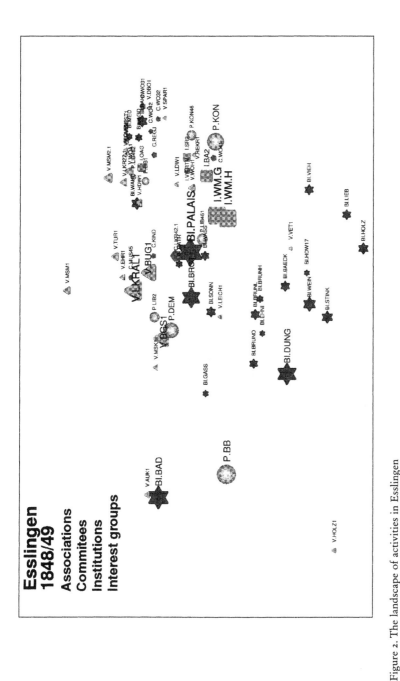

Figure 2. The landscape of activities in Esslingen
Political formations are marked with spheres and identify a left–right dimension in the layout: the *Bruderbund* (P.BB) on the left, the Democrats (P.DEM) in the middle and two constitutionalist factions at the right (P.KON), with several smaller liberal activities in between the latter two. Associations are marked as triangles, institutional memberships with squares and committees with pentacles. Citizen initiatives are shown as stars.

All groups had overlapping memberships, and some inhabitants of Esslingen were members of five to seven associations and took part in more than five local initiatives.

The network that was created through these multiple relations was rather complex and included more than ninety activities (see Figure 2). The large or small nodes in Figure 2 represent the size of the groups and the distances between the nodes reflect the degree of overlapping memberships. Organizations or groups that lie very closely together shared a great number of common participants. As a methodological constraint, the visualized networks contain only people who signed petitions and were involved in a second form of activity during the *Vormärz* or in the Revolution. The visualized network does not include people who were not integrated into the existing social structure of organizations and relations defined by the above mentioned groups. Among 5,097 male inhabitants of Esslingen older than 14 years of age in 1848, there were 2,184 signatories of petitions, but only 1,284 were identified as part of the cultural substructure, i.e. took part in one of the above-mentioned activities. This leaves 900 people who were obviously mobilized by the issues raised by the petition movement. On the other hand, there was a group of 702 persons who were members of different social organizations but did not sign a petition.

To observe the diffusion and acceleration of the mobilization process, we have structured the petition movement in three historical phases. The first phase is defined by the eve and the first days of the Revolutionary movement in February 1848 and two years before. It includes political factions of an election campaign of 1846 and the signatories of the first petition to the Württembergian sovereign, demanding basic civil liberties which were granted by the King in March 1848. This petition was primarily carried out by people who had already been engaged in former political activities during the election campaign of 1847, which had divided the entire population of Esslingen into two political camps.[8] The second phase was characterized by petitions addressed to the National Assembly in Frankfurt, elected in the national elections of May 1848. Until December 1848, when the new constitution was discussed, the people of Esslingen, like inhabitants of other towns in Germany, sent many petitions to different parliamentary commissions in Frankfurt.

The third phase of the petition movement in 1849 related to the internal affairs of Württemberg, the stabilization of the liberal government elected

---

8. For historical details please see Carola Lipp, "Zum Zusammenhang von lokaler Politik, Vereinswesen und Petitionsbewegung in der Revolution 1848. Eine Mikrostudie zu politischen Netzwerken und Formen der Massenmobilisierung in der politischen Kultur der Revolutionsjahre", *Esslinger Studien*, 36 (1997), pp. 211–269.

Petition activity over time

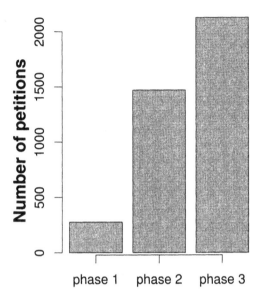

Figure 3. Historical phases of the petition movement

in March and the question of whether the King of Württemberg would accept the constitution written in Frankfurt. The Prussian King had already rejected a national constitution and the imperial crown offered by the Frankfurt parliament in March 1849. In Württemberg, the petitioners were more successful and, under pressure from the large petition movement, the Württembergian King accepted the *Reichsverfassung* and the provisional government in April 1849.

In this last phase of the German National Revolution more than half of the city's adult males were involved in the petition movement. Only a small group took part in all three phases; most of the people who left the petition movement at an earlier stage were intellectuals and state employees; others entered the movement in the second or even in the third phase.

When the Prussian army marched against Frankfurt in June 1849, the National Assembly fled to Württemberg, but was soon dissolved by the liberal government there which feared a war against Prussia. The last battles for the national constitution were fought by volunteers in Baden in June 1849. Therefore the petitions signed by the Esslinger inhabitants in July 1849 concerned the fate of local volunteers who went to Baden and took part in the military campaign for the national constitution.

The central questions of our analyses were: how was the disposition to sign petitions related to other forms of political involvement; who participated at what stage; how did the political consensus spread, and did it reach people who were marginal in the field of pre-Revolutionary politics of the *Vormärz*, or had little experience of petitioning? As our analysis focuses on the impact of network structures based on the above-mentioned membership in associations, institutions, and other groups, it concentrates on the core of people who participated in both types of actions. Opinion usually spreads through social contacts. The network structures resulting from the differing overlapping memberships should be an important indication of the diffusion of ideas and political initiatives. The exposure model we use in this study postulates that the disposition of an individual to engage in collective action is as great as the proportion of people who were already active in the person's environment. Depending on the place where an actor is positioned in the network of pre-Revolutionary activity, his multiplicative effect in the process of mobilization might be stronger or weaker and the actor himself might experience a drastic growth of activity in his personal life.

One would certainly expect a great intensity of contact among those people who were most active within the social and cultural life of Esslingen constituted by the different organizations, institutions, and cultural activities described above. Those who were not part of this structure seemed to be less likely to have a high degree of contacts and exposure to other people's opinions. Though this argument holds true in general, limited activity does not necessarily imply a low degree of contact. Consider the following case: an actor participates in only one event, but this event contains a large number of activists. The result will be a high degree of contacts. In other words: a high degree of participation is not a necessary condition for a high number of contacts.

The reasoning behind this argument is summarized in Figure 4, which differentiates between activists (A1 to A8) who had already become actively involved in the petition movement. Through a set of social organizations, events, and institutions, these activists are linked to others. Event E4 includes, for example, five activists whereas in the others only one or two activists of the petition movement are included. P marks people who were linked to certain groups within the structure but had not yet become active. There are great differences among these people: P5 is a member of one group, but has more contacts through his participation in E4 than, for example, P2 who is member of two groups (E1, E2) which have a fewer number of activists. In this figure P4 has the highest number of contacts.

Figures 5, 6 and 7, on pages 162–164, show the overall rise of contacts and how quickly the movement spread. There is an especially steep increase in the number of people who had many contacts.

Large circles mark the activities in Esslingen (compare Figure 2), while

Activists (A), Events (E) and Exposure of Contact for (P)

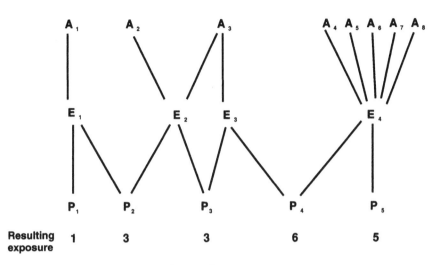

Figure 4. Activists, groups/events and personal contacts

small circles symbolize single individuals. The individual levels of exposure are coded with a scheme of grey shadings, as can be read from the legend in the lower right. The mark-up of the background with convex hulls identifies the area in the landscape in which we find all actors of a corresponding level of exposure. The most outer hull (rendered as the lightest grey line) shows the area covered by the least exposed individuals (code 1); the next, the area covered by the individuals exposed with the next level (code 2) etc.[9]

The analysis of the mobilization process can be described as a process of growing contact intensity between activists and inactive people. Contact intensity spreads with each phase of the petition movement. The distribution at the lower right bottom corner of each image and the different shades of grey and black show the degree of contact with other activists. Individual actors in the structure are shaded in accordance with the number of contacts made.

The mobilization process at the beginning of the Revolution started

9. A more refined graphic representation of the process described can be obtained from the coloured graphics available on: http://www.journals.cambridge.org/abstract S0020859001000281. These files are available for subscribers to the *International Review of Social History* only.

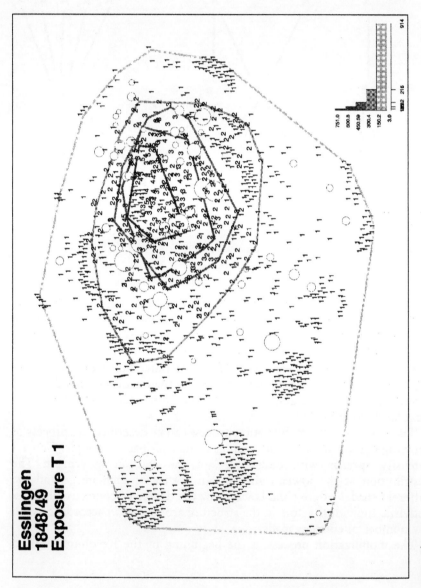

Esslingen
1848/49
Exposure T 1

Figure 5. Exposure Phase 1

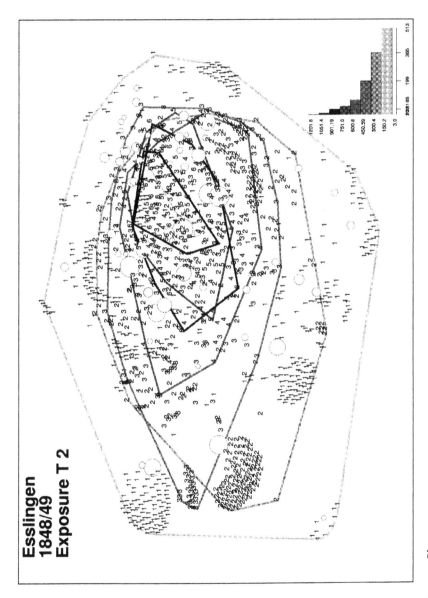

Figure 6. Exposure Phase 2

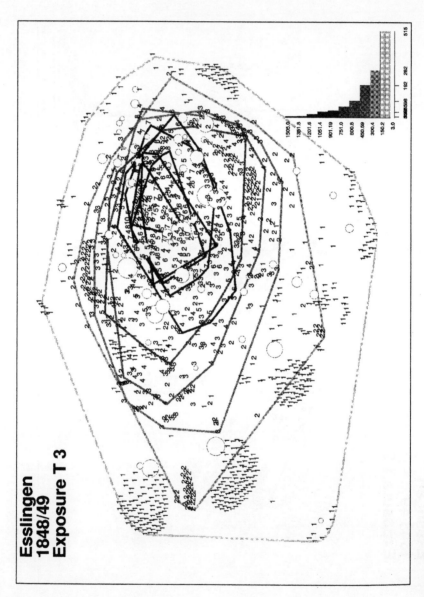

Figure 7. Exposure Phase 3

with a small number of people in the centre. Afterwards, in the second phase, contacts diffused rapidly from the centre of the social and cultural network structure to the periphery. The first phase is characterized by the activity of socially and politically highly integrated people, while in the second phase, the petition movement was joined by people who had far fewer contacts. How the intensity of contacts changed over the three periods becomes clear in Figures 5, 6 and 7. The images exhibit an overall rise of exposure and a steep increase of the spread for the most exposed actors. One can see the general tendency of the spreading of pressure from the centre of this system to its periphery.

A straightforward way to test the hypothesis of the relation between action and contacts is to correlate the degree of exposure/contacts with the degree of political action. The results show that there is a very high correlation of $r = 0.63$ for the first period of the movement. This correlation drops to $r = 0.27$ in the second phase. In the third stage of the movement it rises slightly to $r = 0.32$ because locally rooted people entered the movement. Most of the mobilization process therefore took place within the existing social and cultural substructure of city life.

This finding can be sustained if we look at the degree of political integration in the community. A strong indicator for local integration is represented by the right of citizenship, requiring, at that time, a household of one's own. For the citizen this right included the right to vote for the local council and the right to welfare support. Citizenship influenced the chances of people becoming members of the local political administration and electoral institutions. Noncitizens were not prevented from becoming members of free associations or neighbourhood activities. If we look at the three stages of the petition movement, it is not surprising that the number of people who have full citizens' rights in the town was highest in the first group (90 per cent) and lowest in the third group (57.6 per cent) thus indicating the different social positions in the town. The rate of people with citizenship was even lower among the 900 people who signed petitions and were not integrated in the organizational group structure shown in Figures 2, 5, 6, and 7.

The process of mobilization was strongly influenced by the social position of the participants. A statistical test of the relationship between the degree of enmeshment in the structure of social and political community life and the inclination to participate in the petition movement shows interesting differences between certain social groups. There is structured deviation from the general assumption that a high interrelation in the network structure leads to a high participation ratio. A comparison of the expected behaviour under the assumption of this model and the real level of participation reveals that the political behaviour of a group does not fit into the model in all cases.[10] The residuals from the regression

Table 2. *Political behaviour of groups in Phase 1*

Phase 1	Intensity	Activity	Residuals
Entrepreneurs/merchants	231.56	0.6	0.388
Craftsmen	138.49	0.19	−0.102
Educated bourgeois	120.56	0.18	0.006
Employees	106.25	0.12	−0.06
Vintagers	61.24	0.0	−0.065
Workers	48.92	0.02	0.148

analysis in Table 2 mark the difference between the expected behaviour based on integration into the structure and the actual behaviour. If the number of residuals approaches zero, or is relatively small, this means that observed group behaviour fits the model well.

There were groups, such as the industrial bourgeoisie and merchants, who were the most active during the first stage of mobilization. Out of this group (231 contacts per person in the first phase) there came many of the leading political figures of the democratic and liberal parties in the town. Esslingen underwent rapid industrial and social change at this time. Already in the *Vormärz*, new classes, such as entrepreneurs, formed the core of the liberal movement. This group, which had the largest social political and institutional experience, was economically emancipated and called for civil and economic rights. In respect to the overall level of activity and the intensity of contacts in town, this group was followed by the artisans (contact intensity in the first phase: 138) who, with regard to the entire mobilization process, were far more integrated into the social and political life of Esslingen than all other groups. In contrast, the educated bourgeoisie and academics started as a very active group at the beginning of the Revolution, but withdrew as soon as political splits became apparent. At the initial phase of the revolution, workers and vintagers participated only marginally in the petition movement. This changed rapidly in the second phase, when the negotiations in Frankfurt included a large number of different claims and requests, and when the newly written constitution opened up a new process of political bargaining.

During the second phase, the level of participation in the petition movement rose among all social groups, and contact intensity developed into a sort of spiral of mobilization. In this phase, vintagers and workers were the most active participants (activity level: 0.73 and 0.53). As the

10. Tables 2, 3, and 4 are based on the analysis of 1,986 individuals for which at least one link is reported to one of the activities, institutions or associations out of which 1,284 people have signed at least one of the petitions.

Table 3. *Political behaviour of groups in Phase 2*

Phase 2	Intensity	Activity	Residuals
Entrepreneurs/merchants	354.11	0.43	−0.314
Craftsmen	260.98	0.46	−0.114
Educated bourgeois	191.3	0.23	−0.388
Employees	180.56	0.25	−0.33
Vintagers	162.21	0.73	0.474
Workers	162.2	0.55	0.176

Table 4. *Political behaviour of groups in Phase 3*

Phase 3	Intensity	Activity	Residuals
Entrepreneurs/merchants	496.28	0.9	−0.058
Craftsmen	339.5	0.86	0.113
Educated bourgeois	271.63	0.52	−0.225
Employees	244.45	0.49	−0.22
Vintagers	180.93	0.71	0.158
Workers	179.39	0.51	−0.11

remainders show, this activity cannot be accounted for by the degree of integration into the social structure, but was obviously initiated by the political issues. The National Assembly attracted groups that were not, and felt themselves not, represented on the political level before 1848. The separate professional organization of these groups enhanced this process of self-organization and participation.

The third phase shows a further rise in the number of activities as well as on the level of exposure or contact intensity. Now the integrated and socially established groups of the merchants and industrial bourgeois, and even the academics, returned to the field of action and doubled their activity. The positive residuals indicate that only the vintagers and craftsmen were more active than would be expected in terms of their position in the network of political and social life, but that the educated bourgeoisie and employees were not as highly represented as would be expected, considering their role in the social network. In the third phase, the Esslinger inhabitants signed a mass petition which represented approximately the social strata of the whole city and, moreover, attracted a large number of vintagers and workers. Unlike other German states, the mass petitions of April 1848 in Württemberg were successful. The Württembergian King was one of the few rulers in Germany to accept the Frankfurt Constitution.

Looking at the distribution of professions in the network, it shows a centre with a slight tendency to the right (constitutional and conservative); to the upper right margin, there are the important committees, and welfare

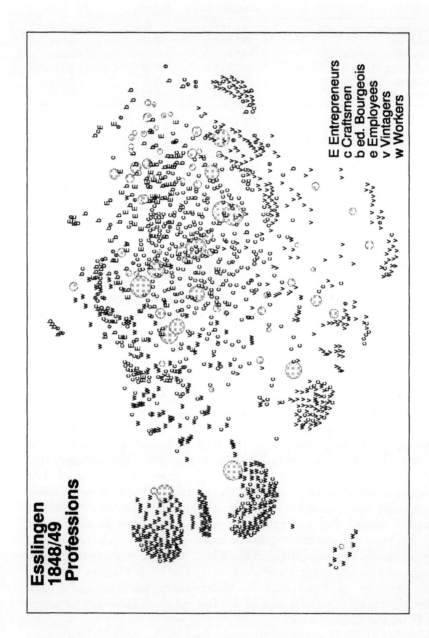

Figure 8. Individuals and their professions in the net of activities

activities. Within these groups the economic groups included the educated bourgeoisie. Their position is reflected in the leading role of these groups in the different organizations founded in pre-Revolutionary and Revolutionary times. In comparison, the workers and vintagers, as newly mobilized groups, were located at the periphery of the network structure. The workers were linked directly to the political factions on the left: radical democrats, and a more or less communist group called the *Bruderbund* (brotherhood), a sub-organization of the Democratic Party (see the "w" marks in the upper left margin of the network in Figure 8). The vintagers were grouped around the Constitutional Party, which had managed to recruit a great number of the small landowners for their partially conservative claims (see the "v" marks at the right bottom of the graph). Only a small number of vintagers were attracted to the Democratic Party or to substructures that were considered to belong to the democratic camp. What the figure also shows is the dominating position of artisans and craftsmen. This group participated not only because they were embedded in the structure of political life, but also because they really activated the masses; some of the artisans even managed to become speakers for and members of the leading boards of the revolutionary organizations.

The results of this study are twofold. On the one hand, it shows the mechanism of mobilization processes and multiplication of contacts that led to a rapid diffusion of the petition movement and to a spiral of mobilization. On the other hand, we tested a structural model and its deviations that were based on the assumption that a person was more easily mobilized if he had former political experience and, to a certain degree, was integrated into a given social, political and cultural network. The findings show that the impact of social integration into a community and its subcultures in the development of the petition movement during 1848/ 1849 was very strong and explains much of the phenomena. But there were obviously external stimuli that were related to the issues raised by the National Assembly and the process of national unification and liberalization which resulted in a fundamental and overall mobilization during the Revolution.

IRSH 46 (2001), Supplement, pp. 171–184 DOI: 10.1017/S0020859001000360
© 2001 Internationaal Instituut voor Sociale Geschiedenis

The Image of Jews in Byelorussia: Petitions as a Source for Popular Consciousness in the Early Twentieth Century

OLEG G. BUKHOVETS

The disintegration of the USSR, and of the communist system, in the last decade of the twentieth century, the rekindling of ethnic strife, and scholarly research into nationalism – all have renewed interest in the images that different ethnic and religious groups in eastern Europe have had of each other. In this context, the image of Jewishness has been of particular importance, both in political science and in history. An adequate analysis of ideas about Jewishness requires access to numerous mass sources. However, the number of sources available for this kind of enquiry is limited, compared, for instance, to the sources open for traditional Hebrew studies. This is especially true when we speak about the periods of autocracy and dictatorship. Both the Russian Empire and the USSR had – besides periods of overt anti-Semitism – a tradition of hidden anti-Semitism. The hidden and unofficial nature of this prejudice would not allow for mass opinion polls on anti-Semitism before the fall of the USSR.[1]

In the absence of other sources, the research presented here focuses on a well-known source of information on mass consciousness in the history of modern Russia and other Commonwealth of Independent States (CIS) countries, namely petitions. In St Petersburg and other CIS cities, the archives hold collections of petitions from all social strata, addressed to state bodies, newspapers, political parties and other organizations, and similar documents which express opinions: petitions (*nakazi*) of the electorate to the candidates running for the State Duma, sentences (*prigovori*) of meetings of peasants and the urban lower middle classes, resolutions of meetings and congresses.[2]

---

1. See, for example: L. Gudkov and A. Levinson, "Otnosheniya naseleniya SSSR k evreyam", *Vestnik evrejskogo universiteta v Moskve*, 1 (1992), pp. 6–41; "Izmenenija v otnoshenii k evrejam naselenija respublik na territorii byvshego SSSR", *Vestnik evrejskogo universiteta v Moskve*, 4 (1993), pp. 4–39; Ju S. Ermolaev, V.N. Karbalevich and V.N. Lomako, *Razvitie belorusskoj natsii. Anketa respublikanskogo oprosa.* (Minsk, 1992), pp. 5, 13–15.
2. O.G. Bukhovets, *Sotsial'nye konflicty I krestianskaja mentalnost v Rossijskoj imperii 20 veka: novye materially, metody, resultaty* (Moscow, 1996), pp. 63–79; *idem*, "Patterns of the Peasants' Political History in the Years of the 1905–1907 Russian Revolution", *Historical Social Research*, 16 (1991), pp. 60–73; *idem*, "The Political Consciousness of Russian Peasantry in the Revolution

Petitions were written in large numbers in the course of such major European upheavals as the French Revolution or the Revolution of 1848/ 49 in Germany. A number of them were submitted after the February Revolution in Russia in 1917. In 1989, while the First Congress of People's Deputies of the USSR was in session, it received some 300,000 letters and telegrams. A. de Tocqueville qualified the petitions of 1789 as "documents unique in history".[3] Historians of these and other upheavals have used petitions to monitor changes in public opinion.[4]

Soviet historical studies give a good example of how great the distance can be between what potentially can be derived from a source, the information that is consciously accepted by scholars, and, finally, the information that is extracted from them in reality. What the rigid system of ideological and methodological coordinates of Soviet political science would not recognize as topical and important was not recognized in the sources. That is why, although the petitions were analysed thoroughly in the Soviet period, this analysis was narrow and selective. The interest in petitions of the 1905–1907 and 1917 periods was mostly limited to the information on socioeconomic and political demands of peasants.[5] The emphasis was on "correct" elements of those demands, namely, those that corresponded to the views of Lenin, and the programme and tactics of the Bolshevik party. It will be clear that the potential value of a document is not exhausted by this kind of analysis. Numerous details in the documents, which reflect the concrete historical spectrum of social reality, were never explored in the historiography.

A less biased analysis of these petitions shows that they can, among other things, provide information on the attitude of the different nationalities, ethnic, and religious groups of the Russian Empire towards each other. This enables us to restore the images held of the typical German, Pole, Russian, Jew, or Catholic.[6]

That such possibilities were missed cannot be wholly attributed to the

---

of 1905–1907: Sources, Methods and Some Results", in M. Rothstein and D. Field (eds), *Quantitative Methods in Agrarian History* (Ames, 1993), pp. 209–226. The patriarchal nature of early twentieth-century Russian society vividly reveals itself in the fact that in all cases discussed here only males are considered.
3. A. de Tocqueville, *Staryj porjadok i revolutsiya* (Petrograd, 1918), p. 4.
4. François-Xavier Coquin and Céline Gervais-Francelle (eds), *1905. La première révolution Russe* (Paris, 1986), pp. 181–202; E. Champion *Franciya nakanune revolutcii po nakazam 1789 goda* (St Petersburg, 1906); H. Best "Analysis of Content and Context of Historical Documents. The case of Petitions to the Frankfurt National Assembly 1848/49", *Historic Social Research*, 4 (1980), pp. 244–266; E.A. Lukitskij "Krestianskie nakazy o zemle", *Istochnikovedenie istorii sovetskogo obtshestva*, 11 (1968), pp. 113, 114, 117, 161 and others.
5. Bukhovets, *Sotsial'nye konflicty*, pp. 117–136, and others.
6. Based on 4,000 of these documents, collected in dozens of central and local archives in Russia and other CIS countries; *ibid.* pp. 79–89.

imperatives of a dogmatic paradigm. However reductive the Soviet paradigm was, there were also more technical reasons, caused by the nature of the source itself. It is characterized by a very high density of information, even within individual documents. Furthermore, to derive additional information, the documents have to be analysed in series. Therefore, a method has been devised to extract information from the documents for further, formal analysis at a later stage.[7]

ATTITUDES TOWARDS JEWISHNESS

It seems opportune to analyse the information enclosed in petitions on the image of Jews, especially because the Revolution of 1905–1907 brought the issue of Jewishness to the fore. Even an initial analysis of the petitions concerned shows that the information that can be gleaned from them is, in essence, new. Even within the different territorial units of the Jewish Pale, we can see important differences in popular anti-Semitism. Byelorussia is an attractive area for this analysis. It is a substantial region of the European part of the Russian Empire. At the beginning of the twentieth century, 15 per cent of the population living within the present-day boundaries of the Republic of Byelorussia was Jewish.[8] This was four times the proportion of Jews in the general population of the country, and twice the proportion in the Ukraine, which was considered a "Jewish" region. The Jewish presence in industry and trade, on the labour market and in land leasing, among craftsmen, and in other spheres of daily life, was quite substantial. In Byelorussia, Jews made up 54 per cent of the urban population and owned half of all factories and plants. Half the intellectuals were Jewish, and even 84.5 per cent of the merchants.[9] This large Jewish presence makes Byelorussia an excellent candidate for an analysis of popular ideas on Jewishness.

For this analysis, 662 Byelorussian petitions connected with the 1905–1907 Revolution were analysed.[10] These dealt with numerous topics. The

7. See the literature mentioned in note 2.
8. The share of the Jewish population in the five Byelorussian *goubernii* (non-Byelorussian *ouyezds* included) is a little lower: 13. 8 per cent; *Narysy Gistopyi Belarusi u 2–h chastkah*, ch. 1 (Minsk, 1994), p. 333.
9. Z. V. Shybeka *Garady Belarusi 60 gady* (Minsk, 1997), pp. 260, 265; *Narysy Gistoryi Belarusi*, ch. 1, p. 341.
10. Out of 673 petitions identified. Most of these were found in 15 funds of the Russian State Historic Archive (RGIA) in St. Peterburg. Others came from the State Archive of the Russian Federation (GARF) and the national archives of Byelorussia, Lithuania and the Ukraine, out of document collections and other publications. The complex of petitions under consideration covers 37 districts (*ouyezds*) of the Vilnyus, Viitebsk, Grodno, Minsk and Mogilyev regions (*goubernii*) that are included in the present-day territory of Byelorussia and the Byelorussian party of the Novoaleksandrovsk district of the Koven region. An important share of the petitions comes not from separate villages but from groups of villages. More than a 100 documents were

200 petitions of the Samara and Voronej regions alone discussed 177 different topics, 113 of which were mentioned in three or more petitions.[11] However, only 69 documents (or 10.4 per cent) touched upon, or mentioned, Jewishness. This is an important result by itself. That 90 per cent of the petitions are indifferent to the Jewish subject is not due to any special characteristic of the source. Petitions as a source were not "deaf". They could "hear" very well, but only when there was something to register. Percentages like these reflect the mentality of the authors of petitions and this allows us to draw relevant conclusions from the analysis that follows.

The 69 petitions that do mention Jewishness, do not differ in other aspects from the petitions that are indifferent to the subject. Still, given the Jewish presence in Byelorussia, the authors of these others petitions must have had contacts with Jews as well.

Let us take as an example the petition of the peasants of the villages Mouudriki, Guirino, Kletchino, and Aksanovks of the Vitebsk district, dated June 1906. It is addressed to the State Duma of Russia. The authors of the petition complain that their interests are neglected by merchants who cut down wood. These merchants' names are quoted as Mendel' Rarbinovitch, Shaya Shmerlin, and others. Nowhere in the nine-page-long petition is it mentioned that the merchants in question were Jewish. The same applies to an earlier petition to the Minister of Land Cultivation and State Property.[12]

Different approaches to Jewishness are visible in the petitions of peasants from neighbouring villages. The petitions of the Ozer'ye and Tcherepy villages, of the small rural district (*volost*) of Nutchiporovitch in the Mogilyev region, are dated on the same day, 19 January 1906, and deal with the same issue, namely the refusal of Ms Krivosheina to sell a part of her woods. The peasants from Tcherepy accuse the land owner of preferring to deal with Jewish timber traders, but the inhabitants of the other village never mention this.[13] The same can be said of the petitions of the neighbouring villages of the Oloutsha *oblast* in the Brest district, written in March–April 1906.[14] These examples show that the petitions lend themselves to an analysis of subtle differences in opinion between groups of people in a similar position.

approved by *volost'* and parishes (both Orthodox and Catholic) The final work to determine the exact number of villages is still to be carried out. The estimated number is 2,000–3,000 settlements. The research strategy is described in Bukhovets, *Sotsial'nye konflicty*, pp. 79–89.
11. *Ibid.* pp. 363–367.
12. Russian State Historic Archive (St Petersburg) (RGIA) Fund 1278–The State Duma, op. 1 (1st convene), d. 291, l. 221–227.
13. RGIA Fund 1412 – His Royal Majesty's Office for the Registration of Petitions Addressed to his Royal Majesty, op. 242, d. 1196, l. 1, d. 1197, l. 1.
14. *Ibid.*, d. 615 l. 1–2.

Apart from the sixty-nine documents which touch upon Jewishness directly, there is another group of petitions which mention this topic in an indirect way. This is true for a group of nine documents with a conservative political orientation.[15] These are characterized by the use of terms such as "aliens", and "heterodox", in an obviously negative sense, combined with the use of phrases such as "we, ethnic Russians", "we, ethnic Byelorussians" or "we, ethnic Russian peasants". For instance, the parishioners of the church of St Nicholas in the village of Tcherkessy (Disnen district, Vilno region), in their telegram dated October 1906, appeal to Emperor Nicholas II in Tsarskoye Selo "not to let us, Ethnic Russians, and our Orthodox Church die in this western part of the Empire under the pressure of the aliens".[16] We can safely assume that the authors of this group of documents included Jews when they referred to "aliens".

The other extreme is represented by fifteen petitions of a radical, antigovernmental orientation. In these documents, the words "Jews" or "Jewish" are not directly present either, but the opinion is voiced that equal rights should be granted in Russia to all citizens, regardless of nationality and religion.[17] "Our plea to you, Your Majesty", wrote the peasants of the Selyshshe *volost* in the district of Gorodok, region of Vibetsk, "is both for ourselves and for the others: make us equal before the law. Let there be no people in your great country, who are deprived of all rights by birth."[18] This position or demand makes these petitions comparable to the sixty-nine which do mention Jewishness explicitly. There are many more petitions which directly or indirectly express ideas in support of equality, but, to meet the strict conditions laid down for our analysis, only these fifteen will be included in the group of documents discussed.

If we add nine conservative and fifteen left-wing and liberal petitions which mention Jewishness implicitly to the sixty-nine which do so explicitly, the total number grows to ninety-three documents. They come from thirty-one Byelorussian districts, were written by the peasants of

---

15. *Ibid.,* Fund 91 – Free Economic Society; op. 1, d. 837, l. 83–84; Fund 1282 – The Office of the Minister of the Interior, op. 3, d. 684, l. 59; Fund 1291 – The Zemsky Department of the Ministry of the Interior op. 122–1906, d. 15, l. 117; d. 24, l. 225, 237–238, d. 27, l. 117, d. 62, l. 96; Fund 1327 – The Special Office for the Elections to the State Duma and the State Council of Russia, op. 2, d. 59, l. 17, 25, 37.

16. *Ibid.,* f. 1327, op. 2, d. 59, l. 37.

17. The State Archive of the Russian Federation (Moscow) (GARF) Fund 102 – The Police Department – The Special Department, DP–oo, 1905, d. 999, part 45, l. 200–202, RGIA f. 91, op. 1, d. 837, l. 19–20, 33–34, 40–41, 45, 96, 99, 109, 172–173; Fund 396 – Department of State Land Properties, op. 3, d. 42, l. 28; Fund 1276 – The Council of Ministers, op. 1, d. 22, l. 158–159; F. 1278, op. 1 (1st convene) d. 236, l. 133–134; d. 270, l. 50–52; (2nd convene) d. 759, l. 167; *Vtoroy period revolutii. 1906–1907* (Moscow, 1963), pp. 507–510.

18. RGIA f. 1276, op. 1, d. 22, l. 159.

ninety-eight villages, three agricultural cooperatives, two peasants' groups and two peasants' organizations, twenty-nine rural communities (which in Byelorussia on average counted two to three villages), eight *volosts* and six parishes.

THE VARIETIES OF ATTITUDES

Let us now consider the typology of the sixty-nine documents which refer to Jewishness directly, and see precisely which attitudes are reflected. It is of particular importance to recognize the qualitative differences in the various attitudes. As the total group of documents is relatively small, we shall have only a few petitions to represent some of the attitudes. However, it must be kept in mind that these small numbers probably represent the attitudes of large groups over the whole of Russia. Studying the documents allows us to single out seven different types of attitudes. They are described here from "left to right".

The first type is found in five documents. Their authors see Jews as a social and ethno-confessional group to which they clearly have a positive and sympathetic attitude.[19] Thus the peasants of Monastyrshsina, a small village in the Mstislav district of the Mogilyev region, describe the local Jews as their direct competitors, but also mention with sympathy that they "do not possess land and also need to feed their families".[20] In late June 1906, the peasants of Lazorevtsy, a village in the Novo-Bykhove *volost* of the Mstislav district in the Mogilyev region, sent a petition to a left-wing member of the State Duma, Bouslov. In it they state that the forced concentration of Jews ("landless and jobless people") in the western regions of the Empire is harming both the Jews and the local population. The recommend eliminating the Jewish Pale and granting Jews freedom of movement. They expect that, in that case, Jews will not have to "exploit people with a low level of knowledge", but "will be able to take up their own businesses".[21] A petition of a group of peasants' representatives of the Grodno district to the State Duma is of great interest. These peasants had struck a deal with urban Jewish representatives to employ a mutually advantageous tactic at the 1907 elections for the second Duma. This enraged the city authorities, who wanted to promote a deal between peasants and the district's landowners. The peasants described the pressure by the Orthodox clergy and the police to accept the coalition with the

---

19. *Ibid.*, f. 91, op. 1, d. 838. l. 10, 35–37; f. 1278, op. 1 (2nd convene); d. 750, sh. 98–100, f. 1291, op. 63–1907, d. 1, l. 281–282, f. 1327, op. 1 (2nd convene), d. 10, l. 63.
20. *Ibid.*, f. 91, op. 1, d. 837, l. 10.
21. *Ibid.*, l. 37.

landowners as an "act of violence against our personality, consciousness and religious feelings".[22]

The second group is formed by eight documents, the authors of which use the term "Jew" only to qualify a social and ethnoconfessional group. Their attitude is purely neutral.[23] For example, in November 1905, the residents of Skilled', a small settlement in the Grodno district, in their petition to the Tsar, write that their pasture, small as it is, is a "mutual property with all Jews and other inhabitants of that place".[24] In October 1906, in a lengthy appeal to the Minister of the Interior of the Russian Empire, the peasants of Tourov, a small settlement in the Mozyr district of the Minsk region, mention in passing that they "buy manure from the Jews".[25] And the parishioners of the Orthodox parish of Meleshkovici in the diocese of Minsk, in a complaint about their local priest addressed to the Holy Synod, accuse him, among other things, of having sold illegally materials designated for the construction of the Church "to local peasants and a Jew Yeleska Rozenman".[26]

The third group of petitions is the most numerous one. It includes twenty-three documents, or one-third of our group of sixty-nine. They use the designation "Jew" or "Jewish" as a synonym for "rich".[27] The peasants of Dragoun, a rural community in the Bykhov district of the Mogilyev region, for example, write that their own hayfields are not enough and they have to "spend all we have buying from the Jewish leaseholders".[28] The residents of the Yakoubovitchi and Krasnoye settlements of the Bershtovo *volost*, in the Grodno district and region, wrote an appeal to the first Duma on 4 December 1905, complaining of the high prices of timber. As a result, so they wrote, only "merchants and Jews can afford to buy it while a poor peasant [...] has to buy from a Jew and pay big money".[29] It is obvious that the attitude in all these documents is hostile, but it is not verbalized as anti-Semitic hostility. To the authors of the petitions, it is not the nationality or the confession that matters, but the fact that the specific Jews who are

22. *Ibid.*, f. 1327, op. 1 (2nd convene), d. 10, l. 63.

23. *Ibid.*, f. 91, op. 1, d. 837, l. 112; f. 796, op. 188, d. 7185, l. 1; f. 1291, op. 63–1906, d. 228, l. 269–276, 319–320; f. 1412, op. 242, d. 615, l. 1; d. 625, l. 1–3; d. 1150, l. 2–3; d. 1159, l. 1–5.

24. *Ibid.*, f. 1412, op. 242, d. 625 l. 1.

25. *Ibid.*, f. 1291, op. 63–1906, d. 228, l. 274.

26. *Ibid.*, Fund 796 – The Secretariat of the Synod, op. 188, d 7185, l. 1.

27. The State Historic Archive of Lithuania (GIA Litvi), f. 445, op.1, d. 4483, l. 76; RGIA, f. 91, op. 1, d.. 837, l. 15–16, 17–18, 42, 62–63, 64, 100, 103, 130–132, 161, 166; f. 1278, op. 1 (1st. convene), d. 244, l. 285–286; d. 268, l. 224–225; d. 277, l. 59–60; d. 282, l. 49–50; d. 291, l. 212–213; (2nd. convene), d. 779, l. 74–75, 76–77, 79–81; d. 785, l. 44–46, f. 1291, op. 63–1905, d. 450, l. 256; op. 63–1906, d. 230, l. 400–401; op. 73–1906, d. 724, l. 356, 359; f. 1412, op. 242, d. 1195, l. 1; d. 1197, l. 1.

28. RGIA, f. 91, jg. 1, d. 837, l. 64.

29. *Ibid.*, f. 1278, op. 1 (1st convene) d. 277, l. 59.

mentioned are rich. To quote another example from this group, the residents of Kolotovo, a village in the Mstislav district in the region of Mogilyev, in their report to the Duma, accuse the forester of having sold "the woods to the Jews which provided profit both for the Jews and for himself".[30]

The fourth is one of the smallest, with only four documents. They express a moderate negative attitude towards Jews.[31] For example, the parishioners of the Kokhanovitcy church in the Drissi district of the Vitebsk region write, in their appeal to the Holy Synod, that local Jews use the indecent behaviour of a local priest to mock the local Orthodox residents.[32] The residents of four villages – Zapolye, Lesnaya, Zjouky and Krasnaya in the Korelitchi *volost*, in the district of Novogroud in the Minsk region – sent an appeal to the Chairman of the Duma, dated 21 June 1906, on their lawsuit with their landlord, the Count of Pouttkamer, about a piece of land. Several courts had decided in favour of the count, but, according to the peasants, this was because the two witnesses of the count "were the Jews who had and still have close contacts with the count".[33] The negative attitude audible in these petitions is limited to the action of the particular Jews mentioned. In the last case, the dependence of the two witnesses on the count is mentioned to explain their behaviour.

The fifth group comprises fourteen petitions which show a clearly hostile attitude towards Jews.[34] But again, in this category, their complaints are concrete and specific, without any hint of anti-Semitic ideologies. The accusations levelled against Jews never exceed local boundaries. For example, the residents of Milashevo village, in the *volost* of Drouya (Disna district, Vilno region), in their petition of June 1907 to the Holy Senate, write that the Jews Stoutchinsky and Taubman, having acquired the big Drouya estate, "began to exploit the population of a huge region".[35] Furthermore, in thirteen of these fourteen cases the word "Jew" is a synonym to the words "rich", "successful", or "tricky competitor", who can come to an understanding not only with the local authorities, but also with the landlords, can use the elected government of rural communities, or can seduce the peasants. Thus, the residents of the three

---

30. *Ibid.*, d. 244, l. 285.
31. *Ibid.*, f. 91 op. 1, d. 837, l. 154–155; f. 796, op. 187, d. 737, l. 1–2, op. 188, d. 7212, l. 1–2; f. 1278, op. 1 (1st convene) d. 250, l. 154–155.
32. *Ibid.*, f. 796, op. 187, d. 737, l. 1; op. 188, l. 7212, l. 1.
33. *Ibid.*, f. 1278, op. 1 (1st convene), d. 250, l. 155.
34. *Ibid.*, f. 396 op. 3, d. 482, l. 24; f. 1278, op. 1 (1st convene), d. 244, l. 101–103; d. 287, l. 109; d. 293, l. 10–152; (2nd convene) d. 799, l. 15–16, 173–175; f. 1327, op. 2, d. 59, l. 18; Fund 1344 – The Second (Peasant) Department of the Senate, op. 203, d. 953. l. 2–3; f. 1412, op. 242, d. 614, l. 2–3; d. 1077, l. 2–5; d. 1125, l. 18–21, d. 1158, l. 2–3; d. 1207 l. 2–3; d. 1222, l. 1–2.
35. *Ibid.*, f. 1344, op. d. 953, l. 2.

rural communities if the Narovlyany *volost* in the Retchitsa district of the Minsk region insisted in their petition of March 1906, that from the Jewish landholders they "often hear bad news and they are also guilty of robbery".[36] The telegram to the Chairman of the first Duma signed by the peasants of the village of Thchernyany in the distric of Brest accused the Jews, Vinograd and Liftshits, the *de facto* owners of the neighbouring estate, of bribing the court and grasping the ownership of the local pasture.[37]

The sixth type is represented by eleven petitions. These offer a theoretical basis for legal and political discrimination against Jews.[38] Even so, within this group the arguments sometimes have a liberal ring to them. The peasants of the Minsk region and the urban lower-middle class inhabitants of the Retchitsa district write: "we believe that the time is not yet ripe to give equal rights to Jews because we are not educated enough as to coexist peacefully with Jews who are mentally developed and well educated in all spheres".[39]

The other petitions of this type taken together make up a sort of "saga" about the struggle of peasants with Jews for land and forests. The petitions call upon the authorities to introduce limitations for Jews in the fields of economy, law, and culture. Take, for example, the resolution of the united rural assembly of the Zabolotye and Gautzevitchi villages of the Soly *volost*, in the Oshmyany district of Vilno region, of 19 December 1905, asking "to protect the local population from rich private owners and merchants, especially Jews, and not give the latter any privileges as compared to Christians".[40] The peasants of the village Dvoretz, in the *volost* Tikhinitchi, in the Rogatchev district of the Mogilyev region, insisted that they had a "moral right" to possess the estate of the same name (Dvoretz) as they used to be serfs on this estate. They were deeply convinced that the current leaseholder Josil' Slavin "as a Jew" had no right to hold the lease at all.[41] The residents of Garvel' village in the *volost* Zaslavl', in the district of Minsk, who petitioned the first Duma in May 1906, argued that Jews could be allowed to lease land, but only small plots. They should, however, be forbidden to buy land or trade horses as "they are all connected with thieves".[42]

The ideology of integral anti-Semitism is represented by a group of four

36. *Ibid.*, f. 1412, op. 242, d. 1158, l. 2.
37. *Ibid.*, f. 1278, op. 1 (1st convene), d. 287, l. 109.
38. *Ibid.*, f. 91, op. 1, d. 837, l. 152–153; f. 1278, op. 1 (1st convene), d. 264, l. 17–20; d. 288, l. 253–256; (2nd convene), d. 756, l. 26–27; d. 757, l. 1417; d. 787, l. 342–34; f. 1412, op. 242, d. 134, l.8–10, 13–16, 19–22, 25–28; d.1225, l. 2–3.
39. *Ibid.*, f. 1278, op. 1 (2nd convene); d. 787, l. 342.
40. *Ibid.*, f. 1412, op. 242, d. 134, l. 21.
41. *Ibid.*, d. 1225, l. 3.
42. *Ibid.*, f. 1278, op. 1, (1st convene), d. 288, l. 256.

petitions that make up the seventh type. Their authors do not care whether the Jews are rich or poor, left- or right-oriented. They consider Jews to be "parasitic aliens" who seek to "destroy the state", to establish a republican government, and to elect Grishka Roubinstain or Moska Vinaver as president.[43] "If they do not like Russia, let them go and live in any Republic where they will have the right to rule the country", and "down with the pro-Jewish and heterodox Duma", as representatives of "For the Faith, the Tsar and the Fatherland", a circle of peasants in the Grodn'o region, claiming to have 1,256 members, wrote on 8 July 1906.[44] The petition the elected representatives of the peasants of the village of Yanovo in the Stolbouny *volost* of the Gomel' district sent, in September 1905, to the chairman of the Special Council is characterized by extreme intolerance. It characterizes the whole revolutionary movement as a conspiracy of "the criminal Jewish Bund [...] that excites the illiterate masses everywhere to grasp power". The authors of the petition call upon the government to deny to Jews the right to lease land, as "the majority of the estates is now in the hands of Jews who [...] exploit the people so severely that even serfdom seems to be Heaven".[45] The petition of Poly-anovitchi village in the Novo-Bykhov *volost*, in the region of Mogilyev, reads that Jews "should not be allowed to work in the field of education and should be sent to live in Palestine so as not to disturb and provoke Russia".[46] Anti-Semitism here is but a form of hatred of everything "alien and heterodox", or is comparable to a negative attitude "to the Poles, the Tartars and to Finland".[47] The peasants of "For the Faith, the Tsar and the Fatherland", and of Polyanovitchi village, also oppose the equality of women, and the last document condemns intellectuals as "mean, villainous and bad for peasants".

43. *Ibid.*, f. 91, op. 1, d. 837, l. 23–29; f. 396, op. 3, d. 1117, l. 159–160; Fund 1212 – A Special Council on the Measures to Support Peasants' Land ownership, op. 1, d. 2, l. 446–447; f. 1278, op. 1, (1st convene), d. 145, l. 239–240. Grishka Roubinstain: in all probability the authors mean Dmitry L'vovich Roubinshtain, a Jewish public activist, (1876–?), who was later close to Grigory Raspoutin. After Raspoutin's death in 1916 he was arrested and accused of speculations. After he was released he immigrated and his further biography – even the date of his death – is unknown. By Moska Vinaver the authors mean Maksim Moiseevich Vinaver (1862/63–1926), a well-known Jewish lawyer and deputy of the State Duma of Russia. A leader of the Cadet party, he was a theoretician of liberalism and founded several organizations to acquire civil rights for Jews in Russia.
44. In a petition addressed to Mouromtsev, the chairman of the State Duma, Count Geiden, a Duma Deputy, and Tchemodourov, a State Council member; *ibid.*, f. 1278, op. 1 (1st convene), d. 145, l. 238–240.
45. *Ibid*, f. 1212, op. 1, d. 2, l. 446–447.
46. *Ibid.*, f. 91, op. 1, d. 837, l. 29.
47. The second quotation is from the petition of Polyanovitchi village quoted before; *ibid.*, f. 91, op. 1, d. 837, l. 2526.

The core image of a Jew as understood by the authors of the sixty-nine petitions was thus one of a "rich", "wealthy", or "successful" person. In forty-nine documents (71 per cent) out of the sixty-nine, Jews are leaseholders, merchants, timer producers, or top managers. In this context, the word "Jew" is used only in the documents with a negative connotation, the petitions of groups 4–7. Only eight out of the thirty-three petitions in these groups fail to associate "Jewish" with "rich". In the petitions of the complementary and neutral groups, only in one case can the word "Jew" be interpreted as meaning rich. Given the real situation of most of the Jewish population, the petitions which equate "Jewish" and "rich" cannot be seen as an actual representative image of Jews as a social and ethno-confessional community.

But even in the petitions which associate Jews exclusively with the rich and wealthy, they are not the prime target for invective. In seventeen out of the thirty-three petitions concerned, the main targets for accusation are landlords. In three other documents the priests and hierarchs of the Orthodox Church are criticized, and in two more, accusations are levelled as much against the separatist attempts of Poland, Lithuania, and other parts of the Empire as against Jews. In other petitions, accusations are made as much against landlords, or an Orthodox monastery, as against Jews. Only in eight out of the thirty-three documents in the most negative groups, are Jews the main target for the peasants' invectives. In this context, it is worthwhile to consider again the third group of documents, in which the words "Jew" and "Jewish" are synonyms for "rich and "wealthy". In twenty out of twenty-three documents of this type, the main target of criticism is the landlords, and, in two other cases, the main criticism is directed against civil servants.

As was mentioned before, we can also take into consideration fifteen petitions for equality and nine petitions against aliens, which are concerned with Jewishness implicitly. This brings the total of documents in our analysis up to ninety-three. Of these, twenty documents (fifteen of the "for equality" set and five petitions in the first group), which together make up 21.5 per cent of the total, show a positive attitude towards Jews. The eight documents in the second group (8.6 per cent of the total) have a neutral attitude. The authors of the twenty-three petitions in the third group (24.7 per cent) show an indifferent attitude. The small fourth group exhibits a moderately negative attitude towards Jews. The petitions of the fifth, sixth, and seventh groups, and of the set against aliens, demonstrate an openly negative attitude. No more than thirty-eight documents (40.9 per cent of the total) fall within these groups.

Compared with much historical research in this slippery field, which is so full of stereotypes and prejudices, these results are relatively clear. Contrary to what would have been expected on the basis of the existing literature, the general level of anti-Semitic feeling, as expressed in petitions, is low. Even in the petitions that voice a position on Jews, only 45.2 per cent (forty-two documents) are moderately or openly negative. And this result was obtained in the part of the Russian Empire with the highest density of Jews. Even the negative attitudes are rather moderate. Anti-Jewish feelings crop up in the shadow of a much stronger negative attitude toward landlords. Among the aliens mentioned in these petitions, together with Jews, as those who cannot be treated as one of "ours", are also Catholics, Polish, Lithuanians and Latvians.[48] For example, the Orthodox peasants of the village of Tserkoviye of the Merkoulovitchy *volost*, in the district of Rogatchev in the Mogilyev region, when pressing charges against a certain Shklyarevitch, among other arguments mentioned the fact that he was an Old Believer.[49] In the same way, when the opposite side in a dispute happened to be Jewish, this fact was mentioned to "strengthen" the position of the accusing party.

THE SILENT MAJORITY

The high concentration of Jews among the Byelorussian population in the epoch under analysis would seem to offer a potential for anti-Jewish feelings. The analysis shows that this potential was not realized. Of the petitions identified in the course of this research project, 86 per cent do not refer to Jews. How do we interpret this? It cannot be the case that the nature of the source did not allow Jews to be mentioned. As we saw, hundreds of subjects were touched upon. The documents represent all thirty-eight districts of Byelorussia without exception, and in two-thirds of the cases each district is represented by dozens of villages. The petitioners, coming from all parts of Byelorussia, must have noticed the strong presence of Jews in most spheres of life, and especially among those engaged in intellectual activities, merchants, and the urban population.[50] If they must have been aware of the Jewish presence, this was clearly not very important for the majority of those writing petitions. We can thus use the sources as an *argumentum ex silentio*: the attitude to Jews of the authors of petitions that do not mention Jewishness was probably indifferent or neutral.

There are some additional arguments for this position. Of the whole collection of 662 petitions, 54 contain some information about the identity

---

48. RGIA, f. 396, op. 4, d. 13, l. 200; f. 1278, op. 1 (1st convene), d. 145, l. 240; f. 1282, op. 3, d. 684, l. 59; f. 1291, op. 63–1905, d. 450, l. 233; op. 122–1906, d. 62, l. 96; f. 1327, op. 2, d. 59, l. 17, 18, 25, 37; f. 1412, op. 242, d. 1158, l. 2; d. 1225, l. 3 etc.
49. *Ibid.*, f. 1278, op. 1, (1st convene), d. 279, l. 64.
50. Shybeka, *Garady Belarusi* p. 265; P.A. Grigorieva and M.Ju. Martynova, "Mezhetnicheskie otnosheniya I natsional'naja politika Belorussii", *Novye slavyanskie diaspory* (Moscow 1996), p. 142; V.P. Panjutich *Social'no-economicheskoe razvitie belorusskoj derevni v 1861–1900 gg.* (Minsk, 1990), p. 361.

of the people who wrote them for the illiterate peasants ("from their words" as the documents put it), edited the final version and, in some cases, signed the documents for those unable to do so. In 18 of the 54 cases, the scribes were local, or – more rarely – immigrant Jews.[51] Jewish scribes were not only employed when a left-wing petition was to be written. Only three of the petitions put down by Jews were of an antigovernmental orientation, two more were apolitical, and the other thirteen were quite pro-tzarist. This is direct proof to the fact that when the peasants selected the scribes and editors for their petitions, they were not influenced by religious and racial prejudices.

Further support for the proposed interpretation of the silence of the majority of the petitions can be gleaned from the historic context. The high density of the Jewish population in Byelorussia went hand in hand with a high level of religious and ethnic tolerance of the population, for Eastern Europe, including a tolerance of Jews. Anti-Semitism was mild, compared with other regions of the Jewish Pale, not very aggressive and not uncompromising.[52] This seems to be continuous factor in Byelorussian history: it is true for the periods of the Great Lithuanian Principality and the Retch Pospolitaya periods as well as for modern history, especially for such critical periods as those of the pogroms in the Russian Empire in the second half of the nineteenth and the early twentieth centuries, the 1905–1907 Revolution, the October Revolution, the Civil War, the Nazi occupation of 1941–1944, the disintegration of the Soviet Union, and the establishment of the independent Byelorussian state. There may be a connection here with the national consciousness of Byelorussians, which is not very manifest and not intensely held. This holds true to the present day.

In conclusion, we can state that we found both nonverbalized and verbalized traces of attitudes towards Jews in petitions, and that these have allowed us to map attitudes towards Jews better than before. To sum up: of the petitions that explicitly mention Jews, less than half do so in a clearly negative way. This negative attitude is overshadowed by a stronger negative attitude towards landlords. Even in the turbulent period of the 1905–1907 Revolution, Orthodox Byelorussians were much more tolerant

51. The Central State Historic Archive of the Ukraine (Kiev) (CGIA of Ukraine), Fund 317 – The District Court, op. 1, d. 3657, l. 1–2; Fund 318 – The District Court Procurator. op. 1, d. 891, l. 19; RGIA f. 396, op. 3, d. 488, l. 268; f. 1291, op. 63–1905, d. 450, l. 235; op. 122–1905, d. 101, l. 106; f. 1412, op. 242, d. 1081, l. 2; d. 1082, l. 2; d. 1086, l. 3; d. 1115, l. 2, 4; d. 123, l. 2; d. 1130, l. 2; d. 1132, l. 2; d. 1138, l. 4; d. 1140, l. 2, 5; d. 1180, l. 2.
52. The main results of this study can be found in O.G. Bukhovets "Evrei v narodnom soznanii (opyt izucheniya na primere Belorussii v 20 v.)", *pravo na svobody*. The papers of an international conference 29–30 October 1998, "Istoriya bor'by za svobody v 17–20 vv." (k 50-letiju odobreniya General'noj Assambleej OON Vseobtshej deklaratsii prav cheloveka) (Moscow, 2000), pp. 93–99, 102–104.

of Jews than of landlords with whom they shared their ethnic and religious background. The variety of attitudes that come out of the petitions is striking. They force us to adjust radically previous ideas on feelings about Jews and Jewishness in early twentieth-century Byelorussia.

IRSH 46 (2001), Supplement, pp. 185–207 DOI: 10.1017/S0020859001000372
© 2001 Internationaal Instituut voor Sociale Geschiedenis

"Begging the Sages of the Party-State": Citizenship and Government in Transition in Nationalist China, 1927–1937*

REBECCA NEDOSTUP AND LIANG HONG-MING

The premise of the Nationalist government at Nanjing (1927–1937) rested on a precarious balance of democracy and paternalism. The Nationalists drew their power from China's citizens, but they also subjected them to a regimen of training and control. Petitions from the "Nanjing decade" highlight the resulting tensions between government and the governed. Citizens from all walks of life accepted the ruling party's invitation to participate in the construction of the republic. Yet they also used petitions to seek redress when they believed the Nationalists had fallen short of their obligations. These documents mark a turbulent period of transition from imperial rule to representative democracy. They also characterize an era when new political ideas, new media, and new social organizations helped people take an old device and transform it into a useful weapon for asserting their rights as modern citizens.

TUTELARY GOVERNMENT AND THE EVOLUTION OF THE MODERN PETITION

The final Chinese dynasty had been overthrown in 1911 because it was unresponsive to the changing opinions of its subjects. The imperial government had maintained a tradition of court memorials circulated between local and higher officials, all the way up to the Emperor.[1] But this

* The materials used in this article were gathered with support from the Center for Chinese Studies (Taipei, Taiwan), the Fulbright Foundation, the Chiang-Ching Kuo Foundation, the Committee on Scholarly Communication with China, and the American Council of Learned Societies. Chinese terms are transcribed with the *pinyin* system of romanization, except in cases where another transcription is more familiarly used (Sun Yat-sen, Chiang Kai-shek) or employed by the original source (Kuomintang, Taipei.)
1. Silas H.L. Wu, *Communication and Imperial Control in China: Evolution of the Palace Memorial System 1693–1735* (Cambridge, MA, 1970); Jonathan K. Ocko, *Bureaucratic Reform in Provincial China: Ting Jih-ch'ang in Restoration Kiangsu, 1867–1870* (Cambridge, MA, 1983), pp. 68–72. A thorough account of the details of the Qing administrative process can also be found in Beatrice S. Bartlett, *Monarchs and Ministers: the Grand Council in Mid-Ch'ing China, 1723–1820* (Berkeley, CA, 1991).

system was increasingly taxed as the Qing government faced complex foreign and domestic crises, and in its final years the Qing dealt poorly with such challenges. The Chinese republic was founded on the idea that, by contrast, the new form of government would represent and be responsive to the will of the people. The promise of the republic was quickly thwarted, however. The revolutionary Sun Yat-sen was celebrated as its founder, and then unceremoniously chased from power. In the end, the 1911 revolution essentially replaced an ineffective imperial dynasty with an equally ineffective military dictatorship.[2]

Sun Yat-sen and his followers migrated south, where they retooled the organization and ideology of Sun's Nationalist Party (Kuomintang, or KMT). Sun eventually accepted Soviet advice and restructured the Kuomintang along the Leninist model. Having absorbed members of the Chinese Communist Party into the KMT ranks, the party leadership created political departments that would lead their companion government bureaucracies. Yet along with the notion that the "nation was ruled through the party", Kuomintang ideologues declaimed Sun Yat-sen's Three Principles of the People, which consisted of pledges to realize nationalism, democracy, and an assured livelihood for the Chinese people. By 1925 the KMT was ready to claim its place as the ruling party of China. That year, however, Sun Yat-sen died without designating an heir. Immediately, the leader and his writings became the symbols of legitimacy for any would-be successor. Invoking the final instructions of the dead Premier, Chiang Kai-shek and other party leaders launched the Northern Expedition to reunify China.

When the Kuomintang finally swept to power in 1927, appeals to Sun Yat-sen's image barely concealed a party and government rife with divisions and conflicts. On the other hand, any would-be successor to Sun found parts of his legacy inescapable. First, despite the fact that, upon reaching Nanjing, Chiang Kai-shek had purged the KMT of its communist members, the new government was to be led by the Kuomintang in the same manner as the Soviet government was led by the Russian Communist Party. Second, the participatory democracy promised by the Kuomintang would not occur until the party and the government ensured that the citizens had successfully undergone the Period of Political Tutelage. This was to be a period where Chinese citizens would be purified from all qualities deemed backward and feudal, and taught knowledge essential for them to take their places in a modern economy, culture, and polity.[3]

Still, the Kuomintang presented Chinese citizens with an opportunity to refashion their relationship with political authority. The party promised a

2. Ch'ien Tuan-sheng, *The Government and Politics of China, 1912–1949* (Stanford, CA, 1950, repr. 1970), pp.61–80.
3. *Ibid.*, pp. 81–149.

revolution that would realize the Three Principles and eventually lead to representative democracy. Such a promise spurred people both near and far from centers of power to rework the traditional mechanisms of supplication and protest. Well-connected Buddhists and party elders as well as lone schoolteachers and dispossessed fortune-tellers adopted the rituals of the imperial system by taking up the petition as the main conduit from ruled to ruler. But they did so to take advantage of Nationalist offers of rights and freedoms. Petitioners quickly caught on to the Nationalist political structure and vocabulary, presenting their requests in the language of the party's leaders. The petitioners' attention to language demonstrates that a wide range of people invested faith in the Nationalist political program, for reasons both ideal and practical. It also shows how the Kuomintang successfully publicized many of its revolutionary and governmental principles. The gap between principle and practice, however, proved to be the Nationalists' undoing.

THE VERY HUMBLE SCHOOLTEACHER, WANG MINGDING

The Leninist legacy in the Kuomintang included a party hierarchy in which delegates from all over China would meet annually for a national congress to set party policies. Party leaders saw these congresses as opportunities to ratify their pre-existing positions. Yet dissident party members, local delegates, and outside interest groups such as merchants, doctors, and teachers used the party congress as an occasion to petition the leadership for a redress of grievances. One such petitioner, an undistinguished schoolteacher in the province of Jiangsu, handwrote a proposal imploring the party to reform the education system fundamentally in order to preserve the Nationalist revolution. This book-length petition, like many of its kind, was dutifully received and cataloged by the party secretariat, and then languished in bureaucratic limbo. The petition demonstrates how a loyal cadre managed to criticize the party's policies while couching the petition in the political language of the party's leaders.

In 1934, on the occasion of the Kuomintang's long delayed Fifth National Congress, a party member from Jiangsu Province named Wang Mingding copied more than 200 pages of his proposal on education reform, entitled "My Humble Opinion on Revolutionizing Education", and submitted it as a petition. The congress, pressed for time, barely had the patience to process the proposals submitted by party leaders, and did not take up Wang's manuscript. But his petition is a good example of the many similar proposals submitted by political nobodies from the localities who took to heart the party's call for all citizens to contribute to the Chinese republic. The Kuomintang, after all, had made education reform their top priority since coming to power, and promised radical and important changes. Wang's petition shows that in 1934, after nearly seven years of KMT power, many rank-and-file party members were unimpressed with the party's progress, and were more than ready to compare the party's performance with its promises.

In this lengthy manuscript, Wang proposed many provocative remedies to reverse the crisis in Chinese education. He proposed an early dual track for vocational and regular education, steering 80 per cent of children towards the former. Wang asserted that the party must truly exert its will upon every aspect of Chinese education. The most useful feature of Wang's proposals is how he went about expressing his assessment, as a party member, of why Chinese education was in such dire straits.

After apologizing for his lack of insight and wisdom, Wang introduced his proposal by saying,

> [...] [now] our nation is in great crisis, the state of the people's livelihood is less stable, and the corruption and poison in education increases by the day. Whether it's in the newspapers or magazines, or in speeches of notable people, the phrase "Failure of Education" frequently appears. And no matter where [one looks], those who have received education [in China] frequently complain that "schooling has ruined me". A generation of "to graduate is to be unemployed" university students are looking lost and aimless at the crossroads, at a loss for an answer.[4]

Wang continued with a devastating shot, "luckily education in China has yet to be universal. If it were, would not China immediately become the 'nation of the unemployed'?"[5]

His explanation was simple. The party's tutelage was in name only, not in substance, or in spirit.

> Ever since our party finished the Northern Expedition, we have only applied the label of the party onto the existing education system [...]. Whether it is "Party Doctrine Education", "Partification of Education", or "Civics Education", these are merely changes in the title. Where is the application of the party's spirit in the promotion of education? What has been accomplished with the frequent changes in the name of the education program? The current situation is that after our victory non-revolutionary elements have, using guile and trickery, come under the banner of our party, added a title of party member [to themselves], and counted themselves as true revolutionaries.[6]

Returning to his view that the cause of the failure of Chinese education was

---

4. Wang Mingding, "My Humble Opinion on Revolutionizing Education" (1934), a petition submitted to the Fifth National Congress of the Chinese Nationalist Party (Kuomintang); no pagination; Archives of the Commission on Historical Affairs of the Kuomintang, Taipei, Taiwan [hereafter, KMT].

5. *Ibid.*

6. *Ibid.*

the lack of party supervision, Wang succinctly outlined the relationship between the state and the people.

> The people's understanding of the nation is very weak and superficial. They always relegate the important issues of the nation to very few bureaucrats and politicians [...]. After our party came to power and promoted mass movements, many people started to participate in politics. Yet they are adversely affected by the spirit of liberalism. They therefore lack a sense of responsibility. From now on the phrase "responsibility" must replace the phrase "freedom". As a son you must be filial and care for your parents – you have the responsibility of a son, not freedom. As a citizen you must be loyal to the nation – you have the responsibility to the nation, not freedom.[7]

Wang continued, "Based on [my] analysis, a revolution in education should infuse the masses with the Three Principles of the People. In other words, its goal is to Kuomintangize the Chinese people."[8] What Wang proposed here would have found little dissent among most Kuomintang leaders, except for the fact that for seven years the party had claimed the revolution was completed. In a very careful way, Wang's petition laid out the case for why the 1927 revolution was as much a failure as the 1911 one.

From there, Wang proceeded to outline the root causes of the problems of the Chinese education system, citing the promotion of materialism, bureaucratism, and unprofessionalism. Wang pointed out that, far from the universal education the Kuomintang promised in 1928, in 1934 the tuition fees for elementary school, much less middle or higher education, were within the reach of only the wealthiest minority in China. The present education system, Wang concludes, "is not education for the common people, but can be properly seen as 'education for the rich'".[9] Even more devastating, the prohibitive cost of education had attracted students who graduated with an attitude of entitlement. These students were not conscious of their responsibilities as citizens as defined by the Kuomintang. Here, Wang was repeating a well-circulated, and probably exaggerated, caricature of Chinese students in the 1930s. Drawn from the wealthiest minority, these students refused practical learning, and were unwilling to enter into practical careers after they graduated. "Most of our students today wear fancy Western suits, and are arrogant and without respect for others", Wang complained.

> They see themselves as superior to others, their hands are unwilling to take on anything difficult, and their feet too precious to travel far. Their fathers and elder brothers might have gathered their family's wealth with hard work and perseverance, and due to the climate of the times, allowed their sons and brothers into [modern day] schools. How are they to know that [when the

7. *Ibid.*
8. *Ibid.*
9. *Ibid.*

students] graduate and return to their homes, often they disdain and look down upon their own families, and are arrogant and rude towards their fathers and elder brothers.[10]

On the problem of bureaucratism, Wang repeated a second common caricature of modern students. Kuomintang governance had, according to Wang, failed to resolve the legacy of the dynastic examination system, in which education was equated with a job as a government bureaucrat. "To Become a High Official and to Get Wealthy" was the catchphrase. Wang painted a vivid picture of this problem, but, like many who bemoaned the desire of the educated to seek government jobs, his conclusion was terribly simplistic. For Wang, students refused to apply their specialty towards the good of the nation. "Those who study agriculture want to enter into government service", Wang said, "and those who study industry also want to enter into government service. What they study they do not apply, what they end up doing has nothing to do with their studies. To find those who study agriculture or industry working in their field of specialty is rare."[11]

Wang's proposed solution was also widely advocated by people of very different political allegiances during the period. The government should drastically increase enrollment in vocational education, so that more graduates would apply their knowledge in professions that would benefit China. This would cut the unemployment rate as well. What Wang, and the many Kuomintang members who shared this idea, failed to account for was that maybe these students were not applying what they learned because there were no more jobs for agricultural, industrial, or engineering students.

Students were not only arrogant, unfilial, and incapable of hard work or work suited to their training. They were, for Wang, society's dead weight.

From elementary school to college [a student] has about twenty years to become "lazy in four limbs and unable to distinguish among the five grains", and to reinforce their lazy characteristics and become incapable of enduring hardship and poverty [...]. [These students] have become nothing better than wandering vagrants. Their status as wandering vagrant varies by their level of education. Sigh! What School! What Education! Nothing but production centers for wandering vagrants![12]

Wang's proposal was not taken up by the congress, which was busy with the task of reunifying the party in the face of increasing tension with the Japanese. In a way, it was a most unrealistic petition, given the length of his manuscript and Wang's lack of standing or powerful personal backing in the party. On the other hand, his approach was not at all atypical. Often, a

10. *Ibid.*
11. *Ibid.*
12. *Ibid.*

member of the Kuomintang would take the occasion of the national congress to take a shot in the dark, hoping for the unlikely chance that his petition would be noticed by a key party leader. Wang's petition is also representative of the fact that, even as the party leaders continued their incessant plea for steadfast unity, and even as the party sought to quiet dissent, critics of the Kuomintang often adopted the language of the party to express harsh, albeit properly couched, criticism.

FREEDOMS PROMISED AND FREEDOMS CLAIMED

Harsh criticism came from outside the party ranks as well. The Kuomintang's extensive program of social reform frequently drew the public's ire, with one of the thorniest problems being the issue of religion. Party charters and draft constitutions affirmed freedom of belief as a basic right. At the same time, however, politicians across the political spectrum believed that "superstition" posed a grave threat to the strength of the nation and its citizens. The precise demarcation of the line between the two plagued the Kuomintang. Efforts to restrict practice and nationalize monastic property were met by angry protests from established Buddhists and leaders of new sects alike. In the crucible of the Nationalist campaigns against superstition, Buddhists forged a potent weapon in the petition. Their skilled deployment of the language of citizens' rights and government responsibility prompted the KMT to rethink the costs of attacking Chinese religion.

Since the beginnings of constitutionalism in the late Qing, drafters of national laws had scrupled to include freedom of religion among the rights guaranteed to Chinese citizens. The Nationalists did not diverge from this path. The platform of the KMT First National Congress (31 January 1924), for example, had promised that the party would "assure people have complete freedom and right of assembly, association, speech, press, residence and belief".[13] But a second line of thought ran through the minds of many KMT members, particularly during the era of tutelary government. This stipulated that such freedoms were not "complete", but were granted "except in accordance with law".[14]

Thus a contradiction was generated. The party in power granted freedoms, but chose to curtail them as needed. The more abstract moral teachings of religion, combined with a proper sense of scientific progress, might contribute to the particularly Chinese essence that would form the core of the new nation. But the wrong kinds of religious practice would

13. *Zhongguo Guomindang dangzhang zhenggang ji*, in *Geming wenxian*, unfinished multi-volume series, 70 (Taipei, 1976), p. 384.
14. Such language appeared, for example, in the "5.5" Draft Constitution of 5 May 1936. Duan Xiaohu, *Jindai Zhongguo xianfa shi* (Shanghai, 1997), appendix.

not only complicate the KMT's job of governance, but actually threaten the nation's very existence. The persistent belief in supernatural authority, the Minister of Interior wrote in 1928, had tarnished more than 4,000 years of Chinese civilization: "In this era of constantly new culture and advanced science, we must reform these sorts of vulgar customs. If we do not, not only will it obstruct the knowledge of the people, but it really will arouse the laughter of other countries."[15] Nationalist leaders also considered superstition an obstacle to their own leadership, and to the unfolding of the era of tutelary government. Party propaganda officers noted that "The premier [Sun] has said, 'without washing away the old filth, we cannot carry out the new rule' and also, 'if one wants to save China, one first has to revive China's ability to believe in itself.' This is the most practical reason why we want to destroy superstition."[16]

But the Nationalists found it difficult to draw a clean line between religion and superstition, because this was a distinction in many ways irrelevant to the main of religious practice in China. Though Buddhists, Daoists, and Confucians certainly created and asserted canonical orthodoxy within their own teachings, the concept of "religion" as a discrete category did not appear in China until the late nineteenth century, as did the neologisms "science" and "superstition." Everyday lay practice was, and still is, functionalist in approach, centered around the concept of *ling*, or efficacy, which engendered a resolute syncretism. As local KMT party cadres and enterprising middle-school teachers set about dismantling temples and shrines that were deemed superstitious, however, clarifying the legitimacy of religious practices suddenly became less a matter of semantics than of sheer survival.

At the first signs of the antisuperstition campaign, religious leaders began petitioning individuals and institutions in the central party and government at a fast and furious rate. In their appeals, prominent Buddhist monks tacitly accepted the KMT regime's goal of combating superstition while striving to defend their own existence. "Right now," the educator and reformer Taixu wrote to the central government in 1929, "in this period when the Nationalist revolution has not yet succeeded, and all places are under tutelary rule, of course China's religion also follows the trend of revolution".[17] Rather than accepting the methods of the KMT activists, however, he outlined his own ideas for the reform and renewal of Chinese Buddhism. The previous year, Taixu's colleagues and rivals Dixian and Yuanying had already petitioned Nanjing with their plans "to

---

15. Minister of Interior Xue Dubi to National Government, 20 October 1928, Academia Historica, Taipei, Taiwan [hereafter AH], National Government files, reel 259, pp. 1455–1459.
16. *Pochu mixin xuanchuan dagang* (Nanjing, 1929), KMT 436.24, p. 2.
17. Venerable Taixu, "Fosi guanli tiaoli zhi jianyi", in *idem* (ed.), *Haichaoyin wenku*, 34 parts in 26 vols (Taipei, 1975), vol. 6, pp. 80–91, 80.

put the monastic system in order and gradually erase superstition".[18] The two acknowledged prevalent criticisms of the wastefulness of popular religious practices by proposing that a "superstition tax" be levied on the fees that clergy charged for performing rites for the dead, and by pledging to monitor monasteries more closely. In return for these changes, they demanded the right to form groups "with a pure and unadulterated [religious] purpose".[19] Dixian and Yuanying noted that the Nationalists encouraged other types of regulated social organization – business associations, for example, or women's groups – as a means of ordering society and preparing citizens for representative rule. Buddhists, they held, should be permitted the same right of association. Not only would their particular reformist stance serve the party-state, but also they would pledge not to tolerate any (counter-revolutionary) political activity within their groups. Pointing out that local Buddhist societies had made cash donations to the new national treasury, Dixian coyly added, "we ask ourselves, this isn't completely without advantage to the party-state, is it?".[20]

Other, less powerful, clergy also espoused the Nationalist cause to their own advantage. Keduan was a monk seeking government accreditation for his Buddhist academy in Yangzhou, Jiangsu province. In his 1927 petition to the education authorities he claimed that his "seminary for the citizen-monk" would allow "the Chinese *sangha* to realize the Three People's Principles and also promote Buddhism".[21] He proposed to instruct his students as much in Sun Yat-sen's ideology, the KMT's charter and platform, and the founding principles of the Republic as in the Buddhist canon. In return, the central authorities praised Keduan's curriculum as containing nothing but "the promotion of science [...] and the tenets of pure, orthodox Buddhism". Therefore, the academy could receive protection, since "freedom of religion is [indeed] a principle under the law".[22]

It is important to recognize the political context of such promises. In pledging to teach party ideology, Keduan was adopting the propaganda techniques the KMT had used during the Northern Expedition, and anticipated the push for "partified" education that Wang Mingding commented on several years later. When they claimed the "pure and

18. Executive Council on Education to National Government, 13 September 1927, AH National Government files, reel 214, pp. 1567–1572.
19. *Ibid.*
20. *Ibid.*
21. Keduan, President of the Huayan Chinese Buddhist Academy, to the Executive Council on Education, National Government, 3 July 1927, Second Historical Archives, Nanjing, China [hereafter SHA], 5:2264.
22. Advisory Office [of the Executive Council on Education], "Report of the review of the Huayan Chinese Buddhist Academy's request for accreditation", n.d., SHA 5:2264.

unadulterated purpose" of their Buddhist group, Dixian and Yuanying alluded to the general KMT clampdown on popular organizations that had followed the communist purge, and more specifically to the party's pursuit of new sects and secret societies, which had occasionally fostered anti-Nationalist sentiment and outright rebellion. Finally, in deploying the vocabulary of revolution and tutelage, Taixu not only acknowledged the Nationalist regime's authority over religious practitioners, as over all citizens, but also argued for the active role of religion in creating the new Chinese nation.

To note the monks' adept allusions to current political concerns, however, is not to argue that they simply toadied to the new government out of crass self-preservation. Many Buddhists, lay and clergy alike, had supported the revolution from its earliest days.[23] The most powerful argument against the portrayal of religious leaders as political sycophants, though, lies in the fact that they also skillfully employed Nationalist ideology to criticize the party's own actions. Their greatest challenge came with the movement among party cadres and government leaders to seize temple lands. The physical battle took place in the towns and villages where the Nationalists asserted power – sometimes quite literally, with temple managers, monks, and enraged locals coming to blows with KMT cadres and enterprising reformers. The ideological battle, however, evolved through petitions and the press.

Buddhists saw the proposal of a young college professor and KMT member, Tai Shuangqiu, to the 1928 First National Conference on Education as the opening salvo in this battle. Pondering the problem of financing education during an era of serious fiscal deficit, Tai estimated that "the worth of temple property throughout the country must be 10 billion [silver dollars] at least". "How is it not regrettable", he lamented, "that such a big chunk of assets should have fallen into the hands of monks and nuns?".[24] He urged the government to confiscate all but a tiny portion of the nation's temples, and the lands that supported them, and turn the proceeds over to education. Most of the clergy would be laicized, sent to "common peoples' factories" to learn productive trades. Religious freedom may have been guaranteed, Tai argued, but it simply did not apply to this issue of property. No freedom could supersede the ruling ideology of a nation, and China's present ideology, the Three Principles, called for the

---

23. Holmes Welch, *The Buddhist Revival in China* (Cambridge, MA, 1968), pp. 1–22.
24. Nanjing Special Municipality Bureau of Education, "Quan guo miaochan ying you guojia lifa qingli chongzuo quan guo jiaoyu jijin an", [proposal that temple property throughout the country should be organized according to national law to provide capital for education], Zhonghua minguo Daxue yuan (ed.), *Quan guo jiaoyu huiyi baogao* (Nanjing, 1928) part 2, pp. 4–6; reprinted in Shen Yunlong (ed.), *Jindai Zhongguo shiliao congkan xubian* no. 43 (Taipei, 1977).

equal distribution of land. In violating this ideal, he concluded, land-holding monasteries differed little from any other big landlord or powerful capitalist.[25]

Tai's proposal ended up in the newspapers, and the story quickly found its way into the pages of *Haichaoyin*, the major Buddhist monthly. The then Minister of Interior's own ideas about abolishing all but a select few temples, the sort that would "concentrate the people's belief on the former sages and saints of old", also quickly made the rounds in the summer of 1928.[26] Besieged by the protest that resulted, government officials backed away from complete nationalization. They nonetheless passed regulations that gave political authorities majority or even complete control over the management of temple properties. The rules also subjected temples to confiscation if the monks violated their vows or "contravened party rule".[27] In response, Taixu and others took a two-pronged approach to fashioning the content of their petitions. One method was, once again, to affirm the KMT's antisuperstition stance. In a response to Tai that he submitted to the national government and published in the Buddhist press, Taixu admitted that over the centuries, the mixture of canonical Buddhism and local popular religion had caused people, some of them monks, to "create superstitions about spirits and ghosts bringing disaster or luck as a tool to fool the ignorant".[28] In their own appeals to the government, Dixian, Yuanying, and other monastic leaders sought to distinguish their great institutions from run-of-the-mill "illicit shrines" or local temples.[29] While distancing themselves from the bulk of everyday religious practice in China, the Buddhist leaders pledged to reform their own religion. To do so, however, the government had to allow them to control and manage their own property.

Thus the second line of argument was to assert full citizens' rights for Buddhists and other followers of true "religion". To begin, the Buddhists argued for their property rights by modifying the tenets of the monastic system to fit a modern vocabulary. In separately authored appeals, Taixu and his colleague Changxing both stated that, since the traditional principle held that the major monasteries and their branches were not owned by individuals but by the *sangha* as a whole, in legal terms each site

---

25. *Ibid.*

26. Minutes of the fourth internal meeting of the Ministry of the Interior, National Government, 7 April 1928, *Neizheng gongbao* 1:1 (May 1928), vol. 5, pp. 6–7.

27. "Simiao guanli tiaoli" [Rules for the Management of Temples], promulgated by the Ministry of Interior 25 January 1929, SHA 2:1039.

28. [Taixu], "Duiyu Tai Shuangqiu miaochan xingxue yundong de xiuzheng", *Haichaoyin wenku*, vol. 6, pp. 66–69, 67. See Venerable Yinshun, *Taixu fashi nianpu*, pp. 137–138 for attribution of this editorial to Taixu.

29. Jiangsu-Zhejiang Buddhist Federation to Executive Yuan 20 March 1929 and 14 May 1929; Dacan, abbot of Puyuan, Putuoshan, Zhejiang Province, to Executive Yuan, 5 June 1929; Buddhist Association of China to Executive Yuan, 6 June 1929, SHA 2:1039.

belonged to a "corporate owner". It was neither public land nor individually owned. Therefore, the government should allow the clergy to exercise its property rights and afford its members survival under Sun's Principle of Livelihood.[30] The monks argued that associations of Buddhists, now transformed from mere groupings of the faithful into corporate entities, did not differ from any other civic or financial association. Moreover, Taixu pledged that, left to manage themselves, monasteries would run their own programs of social services, including schools open to all. Thus, he aimed to place Buddhists and their property firmly inside an everyday social and civic framework.

Buddhist leaders also pointed out to the government that, according to the nondiscrimination principles found in the various draft constitutions and party platforms, monks and priests were to enjoy the same protections as ordinary citizens. When the Ministry of Interior attempted to pass the provision allowing local governments to seize temples based on the behavior of individual monks, for example, Dixian cried foul. In his protest, the monk implied that the government was not all that it seemed. "Now, when officials commit crimes", he acidly remarked, "one doesn't hear of his office being abolished, or his entire household punished".[31] Meanwhile, the Beiping Buddhist Popular Education Federation forwarded a document in which they employed an even harsher analogy:

> How is this different from the way the English have treated the Indians during the past twenty or thirty years, or the Japanese the Koreans? How is it different from the way the Americans treated black slaves for more than a century? In the same fashion, descendants of the Yellow Emperor are being treated as if they were conquered foreigners. It is truly reprehensible.[32]

Even monks who possessed fewer political connections than the likes of Taixu readily employed nationalism, and Nationalism, in their defense. A collection of more conservative Jiangsu abbots wrote to complain, "monks are citizens of the Republic of China as well. They too live under the flag with the blue sky and white sun. Why then this unfair discrimination?".[33]

By late 1929, the Nanjing government backed off its more radical plans. KMT propaganda units continued to agitate against superstition, but the discord and fighting temple seizures had caused led them to use greater caution. Though this local chaos was the primary factor behind the center's

30. Taixu, "Duiyu Tai Shuangqiu", pp. 67–68. Changxing, "Simiao guanli tiaoli yu zongjiao weiyuanhui", *Haochaoyin wenku*, vol. 6, pp. 76–79, 78.
31. Jiangsu-Zhejiang Buddhist Federation to Executive Yuan, 20 March 1929.
32. Juexian, Chairman of the Beiping China Buddhist Popular Education Federation, *et al.* to National Government Chairman Jiang, 17 April 1929, AH National Government files reel 323, p. 1869.
33. Yinbing, Abbot of Jiangtian Monastery, Jinshan, Zhenjiang, et al to Executive Yuan Chairman Tan, 2 May 1929, SHA 2:1039.

reining in of widespread temple seizures, the Buddhist protests played no small role. The success of such petitions shows in the revised regulations governing temple property. By New Year's Day, 1930, the Ministry of Interior had drawn up new rules that freed temples from the most overt government control, although they still subjected them to a system of registration, approval and scrutiny.[34] Meanwhile, Taixu and his colleagues, driven by government challenges, finally overcame internal dissension and formed the Buddhist Association of China, the first enduring national Buddhist organization.[35] Its members' preferred weapon remained the petition.

That habit was learned during the early years of the Nanjing regime, when administrative processes were disorganized and court systems erratic. Even as these systems smoothed out during the 1930s, Buddhists continued to employ the petition to try to leapfrog the bureaucratic mire. Sometimes the Buddhist Association used petitions to bring the central government's attention to crimes of seizure and discrimination happening far from the capital, as when it complained that local efforts to develop tourism at the prominent pilgrimage site of Emeishan, in Sichuan province, were displacing and dispossessing monks.[36] Other times, the issue lay closer to home, and petitions proved useful to individual monks when the decisions made by local authorities weren't going the temple's way. For example, the monk Miaokong of the Baiyi Priory in Nanjing appealed to the central party and government for help in defending his temple property from "local bullies" using it to house a city fire brigade.[37] Frustrated by delays on the municipal level, Miaokong sent a deluge of petitions to an incredible array of party and government institutions: first to the Ministry of Interior, then to the Military Affairs Commission, finally culminating in a printed appeal addressed to Chiang Kai-shek, the KMT Central Committee, the national government and more than fifteen other ministries and offices.[38] He also got the Buddhist Association of China to write to central government on his behalf.[39]

By this time – 1937 – the legal apparatus around the capital was fairly well-established. Local courts were in operation, and the central

34. "Jiandu simiao tiaoli" [Regulations for the Oversight of Temples] promulgated by the National Government 7 December 1929, in Lifa yuan bianyi chu (ed.), *Zhonghuo minguo fagui huibian* (Shanghai, 1934), 13 vols, vol. 4, pp. 814–815.

35. Chinese Buddhist Association to Ministry of Interior, 12 July 1937, AH 129:1802.

36. Miaokong to Nanjing Municipal Government, 25 July 1936; Nanjing Federation of District Fire Brigades to Nanjing Municipal Government, 20 October 1936; Miaokong to Nanjing Municipal Government, July 1937, Nanjing Municipal Archives [hereafter NMA] 1–1:1313.

37. Miaokong to Military Affairs Commission, 15 June 1937; Miaokong to KMT Central Committee *et al.*, 9 June 1937, NMA 1–1:1313.

38. Taixu *et al.*, Directors of Buddhist Association of China to Nanjing Municipal Government and Ministry of Interior, 24 March 1937, NMA 1–1:1313.

39. *Ibid.*

government had even set up an administrative court designed to take in complaints against ministerial decisions. The Nationalists did a much poorer job of advertising these developments, however, than they earlier had done for their ideology and for their major political institutions and leaders. Furthermore, they provided little assurance that such a framework stood free of corruption, nor did they vouch the same for local governments. Miaokong may have felt safer appealing directly to the top. But he was also following a well-established pattern of petitioning the highest KMT authorities to protest the loss of property rights. The phrases the Buddhist Association leaders used on his behalf – "please follow the law and investigate this matter", they asked the Ministry of Interior, "so as to protect religion, and to value property rights"[40] – were ones they had rolled out on behalf of many dozens of other temples around the country since 1929.

The success of their appeals was not assured, but central government officials could not fail to notice that the Buddhists would not shrink from asserting their constitutional rights. Once threatened with virtual extinction, now the Buddhists claimed a national organization that had come up with a proven method of keeping their concerns in the regime's sight. They possessed little outright political power. The fact remains, however, that while City God temples, shrines to the God of Wealth, and other sites of Chinese popular religion continued to come under attack in the 1930s, mostly with little defense on any but the local level, problems at Buddhist temples like Miaokong's got national attention. Sometimes they ended up resolved in the clergy's favor to boot. In the petition, Buddhists found a new way of making their grievances public, often circulating the texts to government newspapers like the *Central Daily News*, and private ones such as Shanghai's *Shen bao* and Tianjin's *Dagong bao*, as well as publishing them in their own periodicals. They also found a way of answering Nationalist charges about the excess and unseemliness of religious practice by first defending their own patriotic and reformist credentials, and then demanding that the KMT live up to its own promises and obligations. Though Taixu and his colleagues stood among the most skillful at wielding this two-pronged weapon, they were not alone among the targets of the antisuperstition campaigns. Some of the most surprising uses of Nationalist ideology against the regime came from persons much weaker than Buddhist monks.

"IMPOVERISHED LITTLE PEOPLE, CRIPPLED AND FRAIL"

The Nationalists' disputes with fortune-tellers, and other fixtures of popular religious culture, also illuminate the increased expectations of

40. *Ibid.*

government from its citizens during the Nanjing decade. Threatened by KMT activism, blind soothsayers mobilized in protest. In defense of their "traditional" employment, however, they employed up-to-date methods, forming a professional association, and printing and circulating their pleas to the government. In citing Nationalist principles, the fortune-tellers not only strove to hold the KMT to its economic promises, but also hoped to shame the central authorities into restraining activist local governments. Even a group ostensibly on the outermost margins of economic and political power, then, saw the opportunities afforded by the tool of the petition.

Like the Buddhists and their temples, fortune-tellers formed a primary target of the antisuperstition campaigns. Politicians deemed the public's reliance on diviners and popular healers unseemly behavior for the citizens of a modern, scientific nation. In addition, they claimed that the money people spent on hiring such charlatans constituted a drain on the national economy that could only further contribute to China's impoverishment. Just as other "evil habits", such as prostitution and opium, generated their own economic circles, superstition supported a world of mediums and geomancers, makers of spirit money and firecrackers, and monks and priests who made a living from funerary rites. The Nationalists recognized that this economy had to be broken if habits were ever to be improved.

Thus, not long after Chiang Kai-shek declared the new capital at Nanjing, the city's mayor, Liu Jiwen, declared all fortune-tellers, whether they relied on hexagrams, astrology, physiognomy, or other methods to make their prognostications, as "the worst blot on a revolutionary capital". He ordered them all to find new occupations by 1 September 1928. Soon the Ministry of Interior issued a nationwide seven-point plan banning many kinds of religious paraprofessionals. Included were people who predicted the future according to the *Yijing* or divination sticks, or who took guidance from the stars or the client's physiognomy. Spirit mediums and geomancers were also prohibited from conducting business. The Ministry called on local public security bureaus to clean the nation's streets of such people within three months.[41]

Police were also to spearhead a propaganda campaign, reminding people that "the future and fortune of humankind rested entirely on their own efforts".[42] An example of the sort of material they were supposed to use can be found in a KMT "Song for Destroying Superstition", published in 1930. The chant uses rationalism to attack each superstitious practice and

---

41. "Feichu bushi xingxiang wuxi kanyu banfa" [Method for abolishing diviners, physiognomers, mediums and geomancers], promulgated 22 September 1928, *Fagui huibian*, vol. 4, pp. 794–795.
42. *Ibid.*

question the authority of each type of diviner. For instance, it mocks the practice of reading facial features to tell a person's fortune:

> The cause of being poor
> Rests with one's own hard work
> Dying young or old
> Depends on public health
> The job you choose to do
> Relies on your own brains
> All these kinds of things
> Have what to do with a face?[43]

A 1931 reading primer for adults similarly mocks belief in predestination:

> Reckoning your stems and branches, assessing what is your fate [...]
> This sort of enterprise is really most crude.
> Fortune must be sought after, and advantage should be struggled for.
> That is "fate", that is "luck".[44]

Encouraged by rhymes such as these, then, the diviners' customers were to learn faith in individual human will. Until that mental transformation took place, however, local government officials were required to go after supply as well as demand.

Overall, the program posed a tall order for city and county authorities. Those diviners who had not found new work on their own after three months were to be steered into local factories, or, if factories did not exist, "work appropriate to their responsibilities". Relief houses were to absorb the "aged and crippled" who could not find other jobs.[45] Though the Nationalists formed ambitious plans to expand the country's relief system, however, financial limitations and a growing refugee problem left few resources to provide for out-of-work fortune-tellers.

The Nationalists then found themselves facing another obstacle from a less expected quarter: the diviners themselves. KMT officials, particularly those in the party's Department of Propaganda, spoke of mediums, fortune-tellers and geomancers much as they did of Buddhist and Daoist clergy – as con artists who perpetrated ignorance. Yet despite claiming that such people possessed "a broad influence, enough to ruin families and destroy the country",[46] and "constituted the greatest obstacle to social evolution",[47] officials never regarded them as an organized social force. Though the collective harm they did was alleged to be great, in the

---

43. *Pochu mixin ge* (Hangzhou, 1930), KMT 436:173, p. 8.
44. Zhang Xiaoming (ed.), *Minzhong shizi keben* [People's literacy primer] (Shanghai, 1931), part 1, p. 23.
45. "Feichu bushi".
46. "Qudi mixin", *Nanjing shehui tekan*, 3 (1932), pp. 204–206, 204.
47. *Pochu mixin xuanchuan dagang*, pp. 10–11.

governmental mind diviners and *fengshui* experts were detached individuals on the margins of society. They possessed no learning, no skills, and no support other than the public's mistaken belief in their abilities. Who could be a more powerless figure than a blind fortune-teller?

Party leaders may have been surprised then, as they began to receive a steady stream of protests against the ban on diviners. In one case, a collection of Shanghai diviners, geomancers, and physiognomists recruited prominent businessman, Buddhist, and Chiang Kai-shek ally, Wang Yiting, into their corner. Wang used his position as chairman of the Shanghai Federation of Charitable Organizations to lobby the government against increasing the already staggering number of unemployed in the city and the country as a whole.[48] Diviner, Zhang Zhengming, and forty-five colleagues had begged for his help, noting that members of their profession were either physically handicapped, of great age, or extremely poor. They even acknowledged the distastefulness of their profession, pleading that "although our lives are insect-like, we have nothing else to rely on".[49]

Even with this admission, however, the Shanghai diviners also pursued a rhetorical strategy similar to that which Buddhist leaders had used: heap greater blame on a third party. The "other" in this case was the spirit medium. The diviners argued that their form of fatalism was in fact safer for social harmony than the practice of spirit-channeling, which bore connections to the apocalyptic sects that had caused so many problems for Chinese governments in the past century. "We show people how to encourage good luck and avoid bad", they stated,

> Isn't this really "aiding the masses"? If you wish for the signs of good fortune, you must not forget good acts; if you want to avoid bad luck, you oughtn't to create evil. You must wait for the cause, and the effect will follow; if there is no cause, there will be no effect. This is not like the way spirit mediums stir up the masses.[50]

Finally, the diviners referred to the Three Principles of the People. They begged the government to show them mercy so as to "settle peoples' livelihoods".[51] Despite such arguments, and despite Wang Yiting's patronage, the diviners' pleas fell on deaf ears. The Ministry of Interior went ahead with its plans to enact the ban.[52] But this petition was soon followed by others, and the ban became harder and harder to carry out.

48. Wang Zhen [Wang Yiting], Chairman, Shanghai Federation of Charitable Organizations, to National Government, 25 October 1928; AH National Government files reel 324, pp. 2409–2412.
49. *Ibid.*, p. 2409.
50. *Ibid.*
51. Zhang Zhengming *et al.* to National Government, 25 October 1928, AH National Government files reel 324, pp. 2413–2419, 2419.
52. Ministry of Interior to Office of Civil Service, National Government, 10 November 1928; AH National Government files reel 324, pp. 2427–2428.

The next month, an even more surprising protest arrived in central government offices. It came in the form of an appeal printed and submitted by a group calling itself the "Shanghai Association of Blind Gentlemen". The members of the group did not identify themselves except as "impoverished little people, crippled and frail".[53] Yet their approach showed a certain amount of political sophistication. Not only was their petition typeset and printed, rather than the standard handwritten communication, it was accompanied by an appeal they called, in the manner of Nationalist Party congresses, a "proclamation" (*xuanyan*) Furthermore, by writing under the name of something called a "public association" (*gonghui*), a term usually used for commercial groups, the blind diviners rhetorically linked themselves to all the other professional associations and unions in the city. Indeed, the rhetorical connection soon became a real one. One month later the Shanghai General Chamber of Commerce itself would petition the center on the diviners' behalf.[54]

Beyond this stroke of genius in naming, the language of the petition and proclamation reveals a fairly thorough absorption of the ideology of the Nationalist Party and the concept of tutelary government, mixed as it was with leftover conventions of the imperial state. Lacing the language of humble memorials to the Emperor with the vocabulary of modern politics, the diviners wrote, "on bended knee we beg the sages of the party-state, and the good people of society, to permit some help for our benighted and dark lives".[55] Born into poverty (for the blind children of the rich, they noted, need not learn to provide for themselves), they had chosen their field through necessity, and gained expertise in it only through lengthy study. The party-state had an obligation to recognize such efforts, and provide for an alternative.

> We humbly note that the Three Principles of the People emphasizes the people's livelihood above all. Furthermore, party ideology has specified that poor people must be the first to be helped. Blind fortune-tellers are both poor and crippled – among the impoverished they have the fewest opportunities. Only this beggar-like enterprise gives them a chance to earn a little rice. The day that they do not have this chance is the day they go hungry.[56]

The diviners gently pointed out that the new regime hardly had sufficient resources to provide for this new group of indigents, as was its obligation. "Now is only the beginning of the construction of the party-state", they pointed out, and "the execution of relief for the crippled is proceeding

---

53. Shanghai Association of Blind Gentlemen to Executive Yuan, December 1928, SHA 2:1032.
54. Shanghai Special Municipality General Chamber of Commerce to Executive Yuan, 8 January 1928, SHA 2:1032.
55. Shanghai Association of Blind Gentlemen.
56. *Ibid.*

none too speedily".[57] Under such circumstances, how could the Nationalists ask them to give up their only livelihood? Finally, though, the diviners were careful to combine any oblique criticism with an affirmation of the regime's goals. Ultimately they requested that "the government on the one hand use the power of education to destroy superstition, and on the other plan a way for the country's millions of blind masters to survive. That way we may reap the benefits of education, as well as help it to advance".[58]

In one sense the message was that the diviners were pitiful creatures who needed the government's help. This image was driven home by the line drawing that decorated the proclamation, showing a fortune-teller in long gown and cap, a lute on his back, walking stick in one hand and cymbal in the other, but most strikingly with a face composed of sunken cheeks and blank eyes. The contrast with the more literary, better-connected type of geomancer, for example, was notable. Even before the establishment of the Nanjing regime, published *fengshui* experts, as members of the literate elite, had already recognized a threat from government officials and cultural reformers. Rather than embrace the cause of combating superstition, however, geomancers tended to defend themselves as proud heirs to the best of Chinese culture. In a 1925 preface to *fengshui* text, *The Shen School of the Mystic Void*, for example, Gu Shibai called geomancers "China's national essence" and demanded that their long history be continued unbroken.[59] The blind diviners, by contrast, threw themselves at the government's feet. But they also made a second message clear: the proclamation of a new regime, with new ideals of universal education and social justice, generated an expectation among citizens that those promises would be fulfilled.

The Shanghai blind fortune-tellers' adept employment of Nationalist ideology, mixed in with the remnants of classical education and imperial etiquette, leads one to wonder just how marginalized they were. Certainly the various types of professionals lumped under the Nationalist ban did not constitute a single unified social group, however KMT officials may have considered them. Richard Smith's study of divination during the Qing, for example, shows that fortune-tellers might be imperial degree holders who provided private consultations for wealthy families, or they could be men (more rarely women) trained specifically for their profession, and who wandered cities and towns or set up in street stalls.[60] Some diviners – the ones who performed character analysis (*chaizi*), for

57. *Ibid.*
58. *Ibid.*
59. Gu Shibai, preface to Shen Zhureng, *Shenshi xuankong xue*, in *idem*, *Zengguang Shenshi xuankong xue*, Jiang Zhiyi and Wang Zexian (eds) (Suzhou, 1933; repr. Taipei, 1977), pt 1, p. 16.
60. Richard J. Smith, *Fortune-tellers and Philosophers: Divination in Traditional Chinese Society* (Boulder, CO, 1991), pp. 205–206.

example – also provided general letter-writing services for the public. The blind and illiterate fortune-tellers, on the other hand, learned their methods by rote memorization.

It was the itinerants and the publicly visible street merchants who concerned Nationalist officials. Though many of these were poor and some illiterate, however, they did not necessarily lack social ties, as the KMT had implied. As part of its plan to enforce the ban on diviners, the Nanjing Municipal Bureau of Social Affairs happened to perform a survey that offers a rare glimpse of the social makeup of urban fortune-tellers. Among blind and sighted diviners, the vast majority were not refugees from elsewhere, but counted themselves as natives of Nanjing and nearby counties.[61] The proportion of natives among fortune-tellers in fact exceeded that among Nanjing residents as a whole.[62] Neither did fortune-tellers live a solitary existence. The vast majority of both blind and sighted fortune-tellers in Nanjing had families, supporting households of an average of four and five persons, respectively.[63] The image of stable households is consistent with portraits of diviners painted by outside observers, such as the nineteenth-century missionary John Nevius, who described blind fortune-tellers as fixtures in their neighborhoods, taking advantage of their itinerant occupation to deliver gossip as well as prognostications to local households.[64]

Questions remain, however, about the extent of formal social organization among diviners and geomancers. In other words, was the "Shanghai Association of Blind Gentlemen" formed solely to respond to the Nationalist threat, or did it reflect a pre-existing professional organization? Certainly, traditional business confederations existed among the less socially and politically savory occupations. Beggars, for example, were known to divide up many Chinese cities into territories governed by specific groups.[65] Whether or not fortune-tellers ever made similar territorial arrangements, the groups that made their case to the central government were of a rather different flavor than beggar rings. The latter were more commonly referred to, by themselves and others, as "gangs" (*bang*) – the kind of "second-tier social group", in Chi Zihua's phrase, that despite its visibility in the social landscape, did not fit into the realm of legitimated organizations (*tuanti*) that could demand official government

61. *Nanjing shehui tekan*, 3 (1932), unpaginated chart following p. 204.
62. Ye Chucang and Liu Yizheng (eds), *Shoudu zhi* (Nanjing, 1935; repr. Nanjing, 1985), p. 503.
63. *Nanjing shehui tekan*, 3 (1932), unpaginated chart following p. 204.
64. John Nevius, *China and the Chinese* (New York, 1869), cited in Richard J. Smith, *Fortunetellers*, pp. 205–206.
65. Hanchao Lu, "Becoming Urban: Mendicancy and Vagrants in Modern Shanghai", *Journal of Social History*, 33 (1999), pp. 7–37, 21–25.

attention.[66] By calling their groups "associations" or "societies", the fortune-tellers clearly sought to move up to that more exalted plane. In that sense whether or not such groups existed beyond the leaders who spoke for them was immaterial: the government took notice anyhow. The soothsayers aimed for broad publicity as well. The Shanghai blind diviners, by printing up a proclamation, demonstrated that they knew well the 1928 methods for bringing grievances before the literate public of a large city.

Two years after the passage of the ban on diviners and mediums, long after the three-month deadline had come and gone, even fervent party activists lamented the situation. "We originally thought", admitted cadres in the Department of Propaganda,

> [...] that it would not be difficult to use political force to eradicate this kind of pest quickly. But it turned out the infection had gone very deep. [Such practices] had gradually turned into a profession. If we wiped it all out at once, with great severity, we could not avoid adding to social strife.[67]

Though the Department claimed to be moving forward with a gradualist program of reform in the ban's stead, in truth the regime had been frightened away by the specter of unrest. Blind fortune-tellers turned out to have social networks, and many of them turned out to have absorbed the regime's lessons on party ideology. By combining arguments based in party ideology with the trappings of social organizations, the seemingly dispossessed diviners forced the government to see them in a new light. In doing so, they rewrote the Nationalist conception of the economic and political roles of superstitious ritual, and reminded KMT politicians that their promises could come back to haunt them.

THE FRUITS OF NATIONALISM

In the twenty-five years since the publication of *The Abortive Revolution*, Lloyd Eastman's influential assessment of the Nanjing decade of Nationalist rule, the prevailing opinion on KMT politics and government has been that it failed due to extreme factionalism within the party, an inability to combat corruption, and ultimately a failure to capture the public's faith. The very shapelessness of Sun Yat-sen's writings, combined with the propensity of KMT leaders to use them mainly as weapons in the battle for inheriting his personal authority, has led many historians to de-emphasize the Nationalist ideological program. Eastman admitted that "although ideology held little meaning for most of China's political actors,

---

66. Chi Zihua, *Zhongguo jindai liumin* (Hangzhou, 1996), p. 115. Outside the realm of the petitions and formal channels, of course, *bang* of all sorts did demand government attention by more forcible means.
67. *Pochu mixin xuanchuan dagang*, p. 10.

they by no means ignored it". But he judged that in the end "these ideological polemics and doctrinal explications were little more than froth covering the struggle for office and political power".[68] In recent years, historians have, however, greatly added to our understanding of the workings of some of the political institutions of the time, reminding us, for instance, that the KMT party and the KMT government were not interchangeable entities with identical concerns. Yet these studies have largely confined themselves to the workings of one locality (most frequently Shanghai) or one institution.[69] Now that scholars such as John Fitzgerald have begun to examine the broader roles of Nationalist propaganda and political activism during the party's years of exile from national power,[70] there is ample room to investigate further how they might have functioned after the party asserted rule over the nation as a whole.

Petitions such as Wang Mingding's, and the Shanghai blind fortune-tellers', open up new interpretations of the ways citizens conceived of their relationship to the government in the 1920s and 1930s. Even in 1934, when Chiang Kai-shek was completing his assertion of power over his party and government rivals, and stirring up fierce debates about the role of dictatorship in the new China, low-ranking KMT members such as Wang continued to see an opportunity in a party congress. Wang viewed the congress not simply as a chance for him to rubber-stamp the preformed decisions of the central leadership, but as a time to make his contribution to the building of the Chinese nation. Though he saw failure and missed opportunities in the education system as it had evolved under the Nationalists, he did not finger party ideals as the culprit, but rather the failure to realize them. His appeal, "Where is the application of the party's spirit in the promotion of education?" does not seem mere "froth" hiding an ambition to maneuver within the realms of party power – the fate of his petition speaks to his meager chances in that regard – but rather shows that, though KMT leaders may have acquired a patina of cynicism about ideology, the rank and file could still take it very seriously.

Similarly, the Buddhists and the diviners resorted to petitions to save their own skins, but the way in which they used them demonstrates that

68. Lloyd E. Eastman, *The Abortive Revolution: China under Nationalist Rule, 1927–1937* (Cambridge, MA, 1974, 1990), p. 306.

69. For an assessment of the state of the field, see Julia C. Strauss, "The Evolution of Republican Government", in Frederic Wakeman, Jr and Richard Louis Edmonds (eds), *Reappraising Republican China* (Oxford [etc.], 2000), pp. 75–97. Notable local studies include Christian Henriot, *Shanghai 1927–1937: Municipal Power, Locality And Modernization*, trans. Noel Castelino (Berkeley, CA, 1993) and Frederic Wakeman, Jr, *Policing Shanghai, 1927–1937* (Berkeley, CA, 1995). A third model is the diplomatic history exemplified by William C. Kirby, *Germany and Republican China* (Stanford, CA, 1984).

70. John Fitzgerald, *Awakening China: Politics, Culture and Class in the Nationalist Revolution* (Stanford, CA, 1996).

they had received the full complement of Nationalist propaganda, and had absorbed it well enough to turn it against its authors. Accepting the KMT's antisuperstition program, perhaps sincerely in the case of reformist monks like Taixu, and with resignation in the case of the Shanghai fortune-tellers, the petitioners refused to accede to the deprivation of their rights in its name. Tutelage, they pointed out, carried both power and obligation. They allowed that in the interests of building a strong nation the party and government might need to reform Chinese culture and society. But, according to the principles of Sun Yat-sen, they also had to provide for every citizen of that nation. The petitions written by religious professionals and paraprofessionals may show some lingering characteristics of the imperial memorial, most obviously in the language used by the blind fortune-tellers. They are also filled, however, with the vocabulary of nationalism and revolution, and the technique of political savvy.

The very existence of these petitions in such great numbers points to a weakness of political institutions, or perhaps more accurately, to the public's distrust of them and dissatisfaction with the way they worked. The Buddhist Association of China and its branch members preferred to plead cases of temple seizures directly to the top as well as through the courts and local administrations. The length and passion of Wang Mingding's party congress submission hints that he may have found only frustration in his attempts to instill change in his home county. Yet the petitions also bespeak a wish to become part of the Chinese revolution. The staple of the imperial meritocracy had been that learned men might present to the Emperor their humble opinions on the state of the country. In some ways these petitions carry a hint of that tradition. But their authors composed and presented them based on the very new idea that the government not only ruled society, it represented it, and took its authority not from Heaven but from China's citizens. It turned out that the Nationalists imparted these ideas very well, so much so that even the most disenfranchised individuals could complicate the Kuomintang vision of a tutelary regime.

IRSH 46 (2001), Supplement, pp. 209–234 DOI: 10.1017/S0020859001000384
© 2001 Internationaal Instituut voor Sociale Geschiedenis

Private Matters: Family and Race and the Post-World-War-II Translation of "American"*

NANCY K. OTA

The US Constitution preserves the right of the people to petition the government for redress of grievances.[1] This right allows individuals to request private legislation from Congress and, as such, private bill petitions involve individual claims or pleas for relief for a specified person, or persons. Private petitions to Congress fall into two principal categories: claims against the US government (e.g., claims stemming from automobile accidents with government vehicles) and relief from immigration and naturalization laws. Although private laws concerning immigration and naturalization have influenced later public legislation by highlighting areas in need of reform,[2] the private laws have limited application. Other than serving as precedent for subsequent private legislation for similarly situated individuals making requests for enactment of private laws, the laws do not benefit anyone other than the named beneficiaries of the bills.

In the immigration and naturalization context, a private bill petition is the last resort to avoiding consequences required by the law, such as exclusion or deportation from the United States or denial of US citizenship. In order to receive consideration of her petition, the beneficiary of the bill must overcome at least the two threshold requirements of: (1) unusual hardship that would result from application of the existing law, and (2) lack of remedy under existing law. Assuming the petitioner can meet these requirements, she must then convince her Representative to introduce a bill that describes circumstances that persuade the House and Senate committees to report the bill favorably, and ultimately to convince Congress and the President that her particular situation merits circumventing the law. Consequently, the petitions typically depict poignant stories detailing personal relationships, political and social upheaval, harsh economic realities, or heroic feats.

This article examines the contents of private bill petitions for relief from immigration laws presented in the House and Senate reports during the

---

* Thanks to Ann Horowitz and Lauren E. Willis and special thanks to Laura J. Shore.
1. US Constitutional amendment 1.
2. Bernadette Maguire, *Immigration: Public Legislation and Private Bills* (Lanham, MD, 1997), p. 5.

period following World War II, focusing primarily on bills introduced
during the 81st Congress (1949–1951).[3] While this Congress was not the
most generous with respect to private bills, it met at the beginning of a ten-
year period when Congress would consider and enact over half of the
private laws for all of the first 100 congressional sessions.[4] This time period
also marks a turning point for immigration and naturalization law. That
is, the House and Senate Judiciary Committees would begin seriously
grappling with the racist exclusion provisions in the law. By approving
many of the petitions considered here, Congress had to ignore the law that
prohibited certain immigration on the basis of race. More generally, the
private bill decisions that Congress made in the postwar period reveal the
evolution in immigration policy that softened the restrictionist attitude
present in the law, and encouraged the changes to the structure and
procedure of immigration law.

The aim of the petitions is membership in the American community,
initially by physical entry into the US and, only in some cases, by
naturalization to American citizenship. Thus petitions also embody ideals
of who belongs or what it means to be an American, a concept distinct
from formal citizenship because it encompasses a broader set of people.
Each petition presented an opportunity for Congress to determine
whether a specific individual met those ideals while, at the same time,
the petitions gave Congress a glimpse at the variability that the notion
"American" can accommodate. And, since race-based exclusion featured
prominently in US immigration law, Congress was forced to reformulate
an ideology of "American" that was not so obviously racist.

The narratives contained in the successful petitions portend the current
"colorblind" race ideology, and take advantage of the discourse that
highlights conformity to another American norm – the nuclear family.
The dominant race ideology that developed in US law after World War II
makes race irrelevant in legal decision-making, by relying on the idea that
the formal equality of races, expressed as race neutrality, maintains
substantive equality. This shift in thinking, which began in the 1950s,
required undoing legally-sanctioned social arrangements of the prior 170
years. Convincing Congress that race neutrality, not race separation, is
consistent with American ideals meant shifting the collective notion of
belonging to America by highlighting a common humanity that over-
powered racial differences. Petitioners, ineligible for membership in the
American community, could individually take advantage of the changing

3. The petitions examined in this article consist of private bills reported out of the House or
Senate Judiciary Committee. These bills already enjoyed the success of passing a committee
hearing and therefore one cannot assume that all private petitions presented to members of
Congress contained similar information. With the exception of three bills cited at notes 22, 29,
and 44, all of the private bills discussed in this article were enacted into private law.
4. Maguire, *Immigration: Public Legislation*, pp. 69–71.

tide by portraying themselves as a member of a nuclear family, or an antifascist or anticommunist hero.

This article will discuss the legal and procedural background to the petitions process in the US, and then examine the narratives presented in the petitions to Congress. I will discuss the ways that the petitioners, and their legislative sponsors, neutralized legal impediments to entry into the American community in the petitions. I track two principle strands of attack on these legal bars to entry: the conventional nuclear family, and the heroic enforcer of democracy. Remarkably, both these attacks helped to render legal race restrictions irrelevant and were tools that also helped to transform perceptions of race, which at the time worked a radical transformation in the American legal system. At the same time, they helped fix as "natural" a particular configuration of family in American law and society. As American society has increasingly embraced diversity, this narrow notion of family has been a barrier to distribution of legal and social benefits in the US. Thus, the private petitions discussed here illustrate the way that appeals for legal change work like a double-edged sword, to broaden racial diversity and to narrow the legal conception of family.

THE LAWS

In her study of private immigration bills, Bernadette Maguire identifies three broad categories of law that define private petitions for relief from immigration law: naturalization, quotas, and exclusion.[5] In addition to these three categories, petitioners have also sought private bills to avoid deportation. The first use of private petitions in 1839 addressed the rules governing naturalization. Private bills granting US citizenship occur with the least amount of frequency, but during the post-World-War-II period, several petitioners sought to reinstate citizenship lost as a result of long-term residence abroad, or voting in foreign elections. Other petitioners affected by citizenship and naturalization laws sought private laws to get around quirky application of citizenship rules.[6] Petitioners more frequently petitioned for private law to overcome immigration restrictions. Congress began establishing restrictive measures during the first quarter of the twentieth century. These restrictions took the form of quotas or limitations on the number of visas available, and exclusions or outright bans on entry of people with certain health problems, criminal records, or

---

5. *Ibid.*
6. The statutes governing the *jus sanguinis* transmission of US citizenship have undergone a number of amendments and some of these changes did not apply retroactively. As a result, similarly situated citizens born on either side of an amendment date would have a different rule apply to their children born outside of the US.

with a particular nationality or ancestry.[7] In the post-World-War-II period, thousands of petitioners sought relief from long waits for visas. Many other petitioners were attempting to enter or prevent their ouster from the US, notwithstanding the fact that they had committed crimes, or were racially ineligible for permanent residence. For example, AM and RA petitioned Congress for relief after they were ordered to be deported for practicing prostitution,[8] and AMR requested relief from the law that prevented her admittance into the US because she had admitted to shoplifting less than $50-worth of merchandise from a Woolworth store.[9]

The principal hindrance to massive immigration to the US was the quota system. This scheme, first implemented in 1921, limited the total number of visas to 150,000, and allocated those visas by national origin, based on a formula that favored people from northern European countries over people from southern and eastern European countries, while disfavoring immigration from Africa and Asia.[10] In 1924, Congress refined the quota system in order to control the racial composition of the American population, by maintaining the proportions present in the US in 1920.[11] Within a country quota, the scheme established a preference system that favored close family members. But for the exception of a narrowly defined class of nonquota family members, even those immigrants with family ties to US citizens were subject to annual numerical limitations. This restriction frequently affected children adopted by citizens and resident aliens, like JH, an eleven-year-old orphan who was adopted by an aunt. JH had no other impediments to his entry besides the fact that his relationship with his aunt/adoptive mother was not among the law's preferred categories that would exempt him from the quota.[12] The net effect of the quota system was to restrict entry severely, even in cases where the restrictions forced the separation of close family members. Furthermore, the low quotas had the negative effect of hindering the entry of war refugees and those people fleeing countries coming under the domination of the Soviet Union.

Immigration laws also defined whole classes of people that Congress did not want in the US. Among the grounds for exclusion were: prostitution, or coming for purpose of prostitution; mental health problems; contagious diseases; poverty, or propensity to become poor; commission of a felony,

7. Act of 5 February 1917, 39 Stat. 874, Sect. 3 and 19. This Act was the first of a series of statutes to implement restrictions on immigration that had a significant impact on the net flow of immigrants to the US.

8. H.Rep. 81-239 (1949).

9. H.Rep. 81-136 (1949).

10. Act of May 19, 1921, 42 Stat. 5, (1921).

11. The House Report states that the quota "is used in an effort to preserve, as nearly as possible, the racial status quo in the United States. It is hoped to guarantee, as best we can at this late date, racial homogeneity in the United States." H.Rep. 68-350, p. 16.

12. H.Rep. 81-2128 (1950).

or a crime of moral turpitude; believing in the practice of polygamy; supporting anarchy, or other systems that do not believe in democratic principles; and entering as coolie laborers. Similarly, an immigrant who demonstrated undesirable characteristics after entry often faced deportation. The grounds for deportation overlapped the grounds for exclusion, and allowed the government to expel persons who committed acts subsequent to their arrival in the US that would have been grounds for exclusion. In addition, deportation laws enabled the government to expel individuals who had violated the immigration laws.[13]

The other significant category of excluded people was that pertaining to "alien[s] ineligible to citizenship". Until 1943, this provision of The Act of 1917 prohibited immigration of people from the so-called "barred triangle", more simply defined as Asia. In the postwar period, the scope of this exclusion narrowed somewhat with the repeal of the Chinese Exclusion Acts and The Act of July 2, 1946 that removed people from the Philippine Islands and India from the "Asiatic barred zone". However, very low quotas for China, the Philippines, and India and the application of quotas based on ancestry, instead of on national origin, tempered any increase in immigration from these Asian countries that might have occurred with the relaxation of the bans on Asian immigration.[14] Ironically, applying the Asian country quotas on the basis of national origin and ancestry made the law overinclusive, which meant that non-Asians could be subject to its limitations on entry. One example of the overinclusiveness was AGW, a white man who was born to Norwegian missionaries while they were in the Philippines, and therefore subject to Philippine quota. In his petition, he argued that he should not be chargeable to the quota of only 105 people per year because his inclusion would defeat the purpose of the race-based restriction.[15]

In the postwar period, the US would see the beginning of a steady increase in the number of immigrants over the relatively low numbers of people allowed in since 1930.[16] World War II resulted in the displacement of countless numbers of people throughout the world, and disabled many people from maintaining livelihoods. Many of those seeking entry into the US simply wanted to seek a better life. Others sought a safe home. And many others wanted to join family members already in the US. Among those seeking family reunification were relatives of, and orphans adopted

13. This right to expel aliens continues in the present immigration law. Immigration and Nationality Act, §237, 8 USC, §1227.
14. Act of December 17, 1943, 57 Stat. 600 and Act of July 2, 1946, 60 Stat. 416.
15. H.Rep. 81-1725 (1950).
16. Total immigration to the US in the ten-year period beginning in 1931 and ending in 1940 was 528,000. Since 649,000 people left the US during this same period, the US experienced a net loss of population due to immigration of 121,000. Immigration and Naturalization Service, *Annual Report* (1998), available at: <http://www.ins.usdoj.gov/graphics/aboutins/statistics/300.htm.>

by, American citizens or permanent residents, and people with new ties to American citizens or permanent residents. This last category arose because of the large number of military enlisted, commissioned, and civilian personnel who were part of postwar US military occupation campaigns. During the occupations they established relationships with local people that often led to marriage and/or children. Consequently, over 100,000 war brides entered the US by the end of 1948, as did thousands of alien children of members of the US armed forces, and children that US citizens adopted. Many citizen couples had to use the petitions process to bring their children home.[17]

Immigration laws, however, were hindering the resettlement of refugees, restricting the numbers of those wanting a better life, and dividing families. Congress was in the process of studying reforms, but in the meantime, in order to address some of the problems that prospective immigrants faced, it began enacting temporary remedies. Most significantly, Congress passed the Displaced Persons Act in 1948, which was the first body of US law specifically to address the admission of persons fleeing from persecution.[18] Until then, an executive order authorized preferential use of quotas for people from countries in the American Zones of central and eastern Europe. The Act only covered specific refugees and left others desirous of entry into the US unable to move. Massive migration and limited quotas meant that many people whose lives were disrupted by the war had to find alternate means of entry. Thus, countless people reached US soil as temporary visitors, or without proper documents, and subsequently turned to the petitions process in order to secure permanent visas.

Indeed, during the 80th Congress (1947–1948), the number of private bills introduced rose from 423 in the previous Congress to 1,157. Through the 85th Congress (1957–1958), Congress would enact over 4,000 of the more than 21,000 bills introduced over the twelve-year period beginning with the 80th Congress. These figures compare dramatically with the prior ten years, when Congress enacted less than 300 of the roughly 4,000 bills introduced.[19] The large increase in the numbers of bills introduced, and private laws enacted, is at least partly explained by the increase in unlawful immigration into the US in the postwar period.[20] As the number of aliens without proper documentation in the US increased, the number of people who needed relief from quota restrictions, inadmissibility rules, and deportation criteria likewise increased.

17. For example, the WFKs adopted a child while they were living overseas as a result of Mr K's military assignment; H.Rep. 81-1037 (1949).
18. The Displaced Persons Act of 25 June 1948 made available 220,000 visas without regard to quota; 62 Stat. 1009. Congress increased this number to 341,000 in June 1950; 64 Stat. 219.
19. Maguire, *Immigration: Public Legislation*, p. 24.
20. *Ibid.*

Additionally, in the five years following World War II, Congress enacted the so-called War Brides and GI Fiancées Acts, which enabled approximately 123,000 spouses, children, and prospective spouses to enter the US from 1945 to 1948, without having to wait for visa availability.[21] Passed in 1945, the War Brides Act provided nonquota immigration that waived physical and mental health exclusions for spouses and children of current members and veterans of the US armed forces. This initial act did not waive other exclusionary provisions of the law. Spouses who did not fit the profile of someone with good moral character were prevented from entering to join their families. For example SN was refused entry to join her citizen husband after she was convicted of an act of disloyalty in her home country for allegedly collaborating with the Nazis.[22] And spouses and children from Asia were still barred from entry under the anti-Asian provisions of the 1917 immigration act. But in the wake of the attack against Hitler's racism, the US had to face up to charges of hypocrisy because of the racist official policy towards its own citizens of Japanese ancestry, African-American military personnel, and other migrants from Asia.

In July 1947, Congress amended the War Brides Act to address explicit race discrimination. The amendment made Asian spouses, but not children, of active and honorably discharged members of the armed forces eligible for nonquota admission.[23] The Act added a new section to the War Brides Act that stated, "The alien spouse of an American citizen by a marriage occurring before thirty days after the enactment of this Act, shall not be considered as inadmissible because of race, if otherwise admissible under this Act." For the many GIs and veterans who could not obtain permission to marry prior to the enactment of the amendment, the act provided a short thirty-day window in which to arrange a wedding. In those cases where the GI had returned to the US, the likelihood of arranging a marriage overseas was slim. Additionally, many GIs and civilian employees of the military in Asia were denied permission to marry prior to the amendment because immigration law barred entry of their spouses to the US. When the War Brides Act expired in December 1948, citizen spouses who had not yet begun the process of seeking admission for their noncitizen spouses or fiancées had to wait for visa eligibility under the quota system. Finally, in August 1950, Congress made all spouses and minor children of service members eligible to immigrate under nonquota status, so long as the marriage occurred before 19 March 1952.[24]

---

21. The War Brides Act is otherwise known as the Act of December 28, 1945; 59 Stat. 659. The Veterans' Alien Fiancées or Fiancés Act was the Act of June 29, 1946; 60 Stat. 339.
22. H.Rep. 81-1625 (1950).
23. Act of July 22, 1947; 61 Stat. 401.
24. Act of August 19, 1950; 65 Stat. 464.

The combined effect of the Acts, and their amendments, was to facilitate the immigration of mostly women and children from Europe during the five years immediately after the war. Hundreds of wives, fiancées, and noncitizen children of Asian descent, or who were ineligible for admission because of past crimes, had to use the private petitions process because Congress had not extended the benefits of the various War Brides Acts to them. Even after the Act of 19 March 1952, eliminating the racial exclusion for spouses and children, and the major reforms of the McCarran–Walter Act later that year, fiancées and adopted children of Asian descent still fell under the limited quota numbers allotted to Asian countries.[25]

THE PETITIONS

The 81st Congress enacted 507 private laws. About half of these laws concerned relief from quota restrictions, 43 per cent concerned admission restrictions, and the remainder concerned citizenship/naturalization questions.[26] The petitioners seeking quota relief included those people who were facing long waits for visas to become available and people who wanted to avoid deportation for overstaying visitors' visas. When their country quota was oversubscribed, the petitioners reasoned that it would be fair to allow them to jump to the front of the visa line because of family ties to an American citizen or resident, their unique occupational skills, or other sympathetic reasons. For those people who wanted to circumvent the bars to their entry or to prevent deportation for criminal offenses, the petitions questioned unjust racial exclusion or excessive consequences for minor criminal offenses. Although the nominal beneficiaries of the bills were the immigrants who were relieved from the effects of the law, quite often the principal beneficiaries were American spouses, relatives, or employers. The petitions thus reflect a mixed portrayal of both immigrants and Americans claiming they deserved the special dispensations of law requested in the petitions. The contents of the petitions paint a picture of Americans who deserve better treatment under the law, and aliens who deserve to be American (and in many ways, there is nothing humble about these requests).

The private petitions that were reported out of the Judiciary committees during the 81st Congress also reflect the effectiveness of the law in minimizing or preventing immigration from certain countries. The most frequently represented national origin of beneficiaries of private bills was

25. McCarran–Walter Act, June 27, 1952; 66 Stat 163.
26. Maguire, *Immigration: Public Legislation*, p. 102.

Japan, followed by Italy, China, Germany, and Greece.²⁷ The bills benefiting people from Japan overwhelmingly concerned war brides or fiancées seeking admission without regard to the racial exclusion policy. The petitions from other countries were more evenly distributed across gender lines and were spread amongst deportation and admissions concerns.

Following the initial request from the petitioner, and in order to provide a full account of the circumstances to the Senate or House Judiciary Committees, the sponsors often requested specific information from the petitioners, and, in turn, petitioners sent their representatives a variety of supporting information depending on their level of sophistication. Some petitioners responded to the Representative's request with a handwritten letter or note, while others had lawyers prepare memorandums. Additionally, the Subcommittee chairman usually requested an advisory opinion from the Department of Justice (which included the Immigration and Naturalization Service – INS) or Department of State (which included the overseas consular offices). Assuming the committee found the petition meritorious, it would "report out" the bill. This process meant that a selection of the documents was compiled into the reports to accompany the bills when they came up for vote. The Senate or House Report was generally composed of: the report from the INS; a letter from either the sponsoring member of Congress and/or the petitioner or beneficiary of the bill, describing the reasons the beneficiary merited special dispensation; letters of support from family, friends, employers, and community leaders; and other documentary evidence to support the petition. The sponsoring Representative had some discretion regarding what would ultimately get to the Committee, and would be available to include in the Committee report. In a typical case involving racial exclusion of the Japanese wife of a US citizen, the subcommittee received a history of the case composed by the sponsoring member of Congress; a copy of the petitioning citizen's honorable discharge, and a copy of a statement regarding his military service from the President; a copy of the petitioning citizen's enlistment record, and report of separation from the military; affidavits attesting to the petitioning citizen's character; and affidavits attesting to the fact that the couple married under Japanese law.²⁸

Other items most frequently found in the reports were letters from other supporters. Family members often wrote to encourage enactment in support of the uncle, aunt, son, daughter, niece, or nephew making the request. Some petitioners enlisted the support of influential members of

27. This accounting is based on the distribution among the roughly 600 private bills I examined from the 81st Congress. Beneficiaries from Japan represented approximately one-third of the total.
28. H.Rep. 81-1492 (1950).

their community – such as high-ranking military officers, employers, clergy, elected officials, police chiefs, lawyers, and judges. In some cases, the petitioner and beneficiary's plight had achieved some notoriety. In these instances, ordinary citizens with, at most, minor connection, if any, to the parties occasionally wrote letters to support the petitions. This additional encouragement put pressure on the individual Representative sponsoring the bill, such that he or she saw to it that the Committee reported the bill out for a vote. A celebrated case was that of Ellen Knauff, a war bride who was detained on Ellis Island without the opportunity of a hearing because the Attorney General viewed her as a risk to national security. As her case dragged on, the public began urging she be allowed to stay in the US.[29]

Thus, any petition reported out of Committee underwent at least two levels of review before presentation to the House or Senate. First, the petitioners had to make a credible claim to a Senator or Congressperson. And second, that Representative had to present a supportable claim to the Judiciary Committee. Assuming this initial screening process weeded out weak claims, the numbers of actual petitions filed with a member of Congress is not reflected by the number of bills introduced.

Given the variety of documentation that comprised a petition, what kind of story did these reports tell? In some cases of family unification, only the most cold-hearted person would have been able to deny the requests. For example, PMH was the two-year-old stepson of an honorably discharged veteran who had married the child's mother in Cyprus. The citizen had established a relationship with the boy when he was four months old, and married the child's mother just before his first birthday. His mother was approved to enter on a nonquota basis, but without the bill, the child would have to stay behind, because the quota for visas was oversubscribed by several years.[30] Similarly, a number of other petitions sought relief from oversubscribed quotas that applied to orphans adopted by American citizens.[31] A and C, twin sisters orphaned when their mother died in 1948, petitioned for relief from the preference system that prevented their immigration to live with their sister who was their only living relative. When a newspaper ran an account of their plight, Congressman Allen was flooded with letters urging passage of the bill.[32] These cases, and many others, were easy decisions for Congress to make

---

29. Knauff's bill failed but she was eventually admitted by order of the Board of Immigration Appeals when it overturned the INS Board of Special Inquiry decision to exclude her as a threat to national security. Charles D. Weisselberg, "The Exclusion and Detention of Aliens: Lessons From the Lives of Ellen Knauff and Ignatz Mezei", *University of Pennsylvania Law Review*, 143, (1995), pp. 958–964 .
30. H.Rep. 81-1712 (1950).
31. H.Rep. 81-1813 (1950).
32. H.Rep. 81-2475 (1950).

because they united children with families. Furthermore, with a connection to an American family, Congress believed that these children deserved the advantage of growing up in the US, where they would develop an attachment to superior American values.

Not all petitions were so clearly justifiable. F and MM petitioned Congressman Allen of California in order to avoid deportation to China for overstaying a temporary visa. F and MM's petition attempted to win support for a permanent visa by portraying the family as "desirable immigrants". What qualified this Chinese family, with no living connection to the US, for this status? According to the petition, the family lived by American ideals and customs taught to them by their spouse and father, Mr M, who was tortured to death by the Japanese, having received his college education in America at Yale. Furthermore, following Mr M's death, Mrs M provided heroic services to the American war effort by taking part in guerilla warfare against the Japanese. In the past year, the family had resided in the US, and they proved to be exemplary citizens who owned their own home and small business. Moreover, their home in China was in communist hands and their return would be risky, since Mr M had supported the Nationalist Chinese.[33] The M family presented what many petitioners believed to be requisite characteristics of a meritorious petition: a clear tie to American ideals, or evidence of personal sacrifice for Americans or American ideals, and evidence of extreme hardship if the bill was not passed. The M family demonstrated its tie to American ideals by its effort to support American war efforts against the Japanese, the way the family suffered extreme personal loss, their participation in the local community, and the fact that they acted like Americans. Allowing them to stay seemed like a small price when the alternative was the specter of the anti-American evil – communism. Simply fleeing communism, or the harsh economic circumstances that resulted from the war, the petition was less likely to be reported out of the subcommittee. Members of Congress had to be able to view the M family as members of the American community.

In contrast, WH, who met his fiancée while stationed in Japan, petitioned Congressman Lesinski of Michigan to obtain visas for his fiancée and son so that they could join him in the US. WH could easily make the hardship claim that the law was forcing his separation from his family. In fact, when he asked his commander for permission to marry MH, he was refused because of immigration restrictions. He later attempted to secure a visitor's visa for his fiancée and the consulate told him that she was not admissible, whether or not married to an American citizen. Furthermore, the consul explained that "the present policy of the Occupation authorities does not permit foreign travel for personal reasons

33. H.Rep. 81-217 (1949).

by Japanese nationals, and it is extremely doubtful whether a Japanese passport would be issued for even a temporary visit to the United States". The law stymied any attempt to unite WH with his family. But, rather than explaining why MH and his son, AH, belonged in the American community, WH's petition to Congressman Lesinski discusses his military record and his ability to support his family with the assistance of his mother.[34] Apart from the names of his fiancée and son, the petition provides no further information that would enable Congress to make a determination whether or not either one belongs in America. The presumption underlying the petition is that a citizen is free to choose his or her family, and to have the family living in the US, if they so desire.

Similarly, other petitions seem to discuss everything but the beneficiary, under the assumption that the reason for enactment – usually the beneficiary's occupation – is obvious. Congressman Reed of New York managed to guide a bill to enactment for a petitioner who overstayed a visitor's visa from Italy by discussing prior legislation for someone else. He did not compare the petitioner to that individual, except to say that both were medical doctors. Furthermore, Reed devoted two paragraphs to a description of the history of the educational institutions in Italy that the beneficiary attended. Congress approved the petition, knowing little more about the petitioner than he "likes this country, its form of government and institutions, as well as our professional methods and techniques, rather than return to Italy, a country which he considers now is far behind the United States politically, economically, and otherwise".[35]

As these examples show, four general types of justification show up in these private bill petitions. The least controversial justification is the type that confers nonquota status to children who will live with a citizen or alien resident, like a blood-related child, whether or not the blood connection exists. This justification simply relies on a natural state – child with parents. The second type of justification is that based on the merit of an immigrant's past conduct, from which Congress can infer a commitment to the American ideals of democracy. The third type is based on the entitlement that arises out of US citizenship of a close family member. The fourth type relates to the economic benefit for the US, or for someone living in the US, that the alien's admission confers. These four types of justifications are not mutually exclusive. And, unless a petitioner was relying on the second type of justification, the petitioners ordinarily based their claims on family relationships.

34. H.Rep. 81-1484 (1950).
35. H.Rep. 81-1583 (1950).

DEFINING "AMERICAN" THROUGH FAMILY

A closer look at the contents of private bill petitions discloses much more than the basic requests, and their justifications for relief from immigration law. Immigration law contributes to the definition of the national community in part by specifying who does not belong in the community. Because the bills involve people legitimately excluded from the US, they are, by definition, people who do not belong in the community. So, what characteristics of American-ness do the beneficiaries emphasize in order to de-emphasize their difference? Many of the petitions stress a notion of family that conforms to that of the heteropatriarchal nuclear family. A credible claim of membership in a traditional family could neutralize the legal impediment to entry, whether that impediment was prior illegal activity, prior status as an enemy, poverty, or race.

First, what role does the concept of nuclear family play? The answer depends, in part, on facts that portray a traditional family by white middle-class standards. In the post-World-War-II US, that model was a family with a male-headed household in which the wife does not need to work, presumably enabling her to take care of the home and children. This image of family was one with which members of Congress voting on the bills could easily identify, but it was not descriptive of all families, and in particular of all families of color. Continuing legal, social, and economic discrimination based on race often made it impossible to maintain a traditional family, let alone one that one person could support financially. Moreover, many members in Congress did not think that such discrimination was unwarranted. But, once Congress visualizes a petitioner's case as one involving a nuclear family, the white middle-class family becomes the standard by which the legislators measure the degree of unfairness in the application of the law. Because it can evoke an empathic response, presentations of family in the petitions attempt to portray the normative American family, by emphasizing conventional gender roles, cultural conformity, and economic self-reliance.

The return of millions of men to the US labor market during the postwar period forced a renegotiation of gender roles that had been redefined during the war. Government policies encouraged women to return to their roles as wives and mothers in order to allow men to resume their roles; in other words, policies endorsed a patriarchal family structure. Petitioners participated in the renegotiation of acceptable gender roles by relying on the resilience of those traditions. Thus, a male beneficiary of a petition could benefit where his deportation would result in the loss of support for a family. For example, SM first entered the US illegally by misrepresenting that he was a permanent resident. A few years after this entry, he was deported to Greece. He returned the following year, falsely claiming he was a resident, and the consulate permitted him to re-enter on a permanent visa. SM grounded his petition to stay in the US, in spite of his fraud-based second entry, on the fact that he was the sole support for his alien resident wife and three citizen children. The Board of Immigration Appeals supported his petition because he was gainfully employed and, apart from the perjury, had no additional blemishes on his record.[36] In another case, GW had a bewildering series of name changes and aliases that resulted in considerable confusion over his identity and origin, and this confusion was compounded by the fact that he had little or no documentation of his various identities. Nonetheless, his petition to avoid deportation to Germany was successful, in large part because he claimed that his deportation would result in undue hardship on his wife and daughter.[37]

When a male alien was found to lack good moral character, perhaps due to the fact that he committed crimes making him deportable, he became ineligible for suspension of deportation and was left to seek a petition for relief. In spite of this character flaw, he could assert that the law interfered with his fulfillment of his patriarchal obligation by demonstrating the economic and emotional hardship on family members that his deportation would cause. In many instances, their appreciation for this sense of responsibility pushed Congress towards leniency.[38] FG was a long-term resident who entered illegally from Italy with other family members when he was a child. He was arrested and convicted several times, as a minor and as an adult, for offenses including theft, driving without a license, and grand larceny. After he was ordered deported, he fled, and was later arrested and detained for parole violation. Under the circumstances, the Department of Justice could not recommend his petition, but his bill nevertheless passed. FG's sponsor received a handwritten letter from FG's wife who pleaded for his release and stated that she was certain he would be a good husband and father. She wrote, "Our son is going to be five years old in April. He needs his father very much. That's all he talks about his is [sic] father."[39] Although FG had not yet acted in a way that would lead anyone to conclude he would be an upstanding family man, this emotional appeal from his wife vividly linked him to the conventional role. Likewise, Congress exempted LE from the law after he was ordered deported following his conviction for aiding in drug smuggling – he could not avoid deportation after failing to receive a pardon for that crime. In his petition, he successfully argued that he would not be able to earn enough in Italy to

36. H.Rep. 81-1896 (1950).
37. H.Rep. 81-2400 (1950).
38. Hardship constitutes a justification for providing administrative relief from deportation or waiving disqualification for admission in the current statute, which authorizes the Attorney General to provide such relief; Immigration and Nationality Act, §240A(b)(1)(D), 8 USC, §1229b and §212(h)(1)(B), 8 USC, §1182.
39. H.Rep. 81-1764 (1950).

support his wife and niece who would remain in the US and who depended on him.[40]

Other men made use of the patriarchal role to bolster support for petitions for family members stuck outside of the US. KH petitioned his Representative for a bill to allow his fiancée and son to join him in the US from Germany where the quota was oversubscribed. He could have avoided the process if he went to Germany and married his fiancée, but he could not afford to do so.[41] Likewise, after returning to the US and securing employment, SC was in a position to support the family he abandoned in Italy. The family was impoverished; in fact, his four-year-old child had been living in a convent. Because he had not married OD, she and the child were not eligible for a nonquota visa and would have to wait years.[42] The bills granted in these cases endorsed the idea of male responsibility for the family's support and family unification with the patriarch.

The notion of male responsibility for family support even worked to dispel fear of possible homosexuality. PC petitioned to avoid deportation on the grounds that prior to his entry into the US from Ireland he was convicted of attempted buggery and was diagnosed with psychopathic inferiority. Friends of his from his church attested to his reputation as a good father, husband, and provider, and thereby helped him remain in the country.[43] At least one interpretation of his successful petition is that his assumption of a conventional family role negated his connection to homosexuality, a status that was criminally punishable, socially unacceptable, and a basis for exclusion.

Was gender-role conformity important for women who were negatively affected by immigration laws? SL, a native of Poland who had become a naturalized citizen of Canada and subsequently lost her Canadian citizenship by living in the US, and was therefore stateless, was attempting to avoid deportation to Poland. She had entered the US illegally in 1937, and this offense apparently was the only affirmative act that made her deportable. Her husband abandoned her in Buffalo, New York with her youngest child, a US citizen by birth. She had two other children who were living in an orphanage in Newark, New Jersey. SL worked as a machine operator earning $50 per week. Although a number of supporters attested to her good moral character, her petition stalled in the Senate sub-committee.[44] Barring other circumstances omitted from the report, SL had

40. H.Rep. 81-473 (1949).
41. H.Rep. 81-1998 (1950).
42. H.Rep. 81-2632 (1950).
43. H.Rep. 81-1751 (1950).
44. H.Rep. 81-26 (1949). The bill passed the House, then stalled in the Senate. From the legislative record, one cannot discern whether or not she was deported. It is possible that she remained in the US, if so one possible explanation that SL's petition did not get out of the Senate

not offended immigration laws any worse than the aliens SM, GW, and FG, described above, whose petitions were granted. Is it then possible that the Senate Committee thought that, without the support of her husband, she was at risk of becoming a public charge, or that her position as the family's economic provider made her ill-suited for membership of the American community? Indeed, the fact that two of her children were living in an orphanage might have suggested that she was incapable of taking care of her family financially and that she had abandoned her proper maternal role. But, deporting her to a country from which she fled and renounced citizenship seems cruel when her only infraction was to enter the US illegally. SL's situation is puzzling, especially because she had been a long-term resident in the US. Taking the bare facts presented in the petition, her request is similar to the other petitioners described above, except for the fact that SL's circumstances do not fit within the traditional notion of family. She has no husband who can take care of her and the children, and since she is working and has had to give up the care of two of her children, she does not fit the model of a good mother.

In contrast to SL, AIF was a war bride from Ireland who was barred from entry because of her criminal past over the fifteen years preceding her entry. Before her marriage in 1945 to HF, a US citizen, she was convicted of larceny, prostitution, drunkenness, indecent behavior, and conspiracy to commit robbery. According to the Attorney General's office, she was "regarded by local authorities as being of unqualifiedly bad character". In spite of these disqualifications, her petition succeeded because her American husband claimed to have reformed her and was committed to supporting her financially. Thus, in the US, she would assume a proper role as a housewife.[45]

In addition to overcoming bars to entry based on immigration or criminal violations, petitioners relied on the idea of male breadwinner to persuade Congress to enact bills that overcame race-based restrictions. AC, a British subject from Jamaica, had previously entered temporarily under special legislation to perform farm work, and while he was in the US he married FF. They had two children before he was required to return to Jamaica. AC was unable to return to the US because he was of Chinese ancestry and therefore was ineligible to enter under the provision granting nonquota status to spouses of citizens. Instead, he had to wait for a visa to become available under the heavily oversubscribed quota for Chinese. AC was a successful petitioner, in part because of the fact that he would assume a traditional role as head of household. Mrs C had four children from a previous marriage and was struggling to take care of the family; AC could

committee is that the INS reconsidered, and she was adjusted as a Canadian instead of having to wait for a visa to become available under the Polish quota.
45. H.Rep. 81-1696 (1950).

not earn enough in Jamaica to adequately care for the family, and the petition presented evidence that she had received welfare. Moreover, if AC were allowed to immigrate, his former employer would hire him permanently.[46] His ability to assume the role of patriarch meant that his family would not have to rely on government assistance for its survival. Significantly, approval of his bill also tacitly approved an interracial marriage, a relationship that was still illegal in nearly half of the US.[47]

Women excluded by their race were also able to make successful claims for family unity by emphasizing their traditional position in the nuclear family. One war bride from Japan, MN, had skills that enabled her to work as typist in Osaka. But, highlighted on her petition was the fact that to prepare her for life in the US, she agreed to take sewing lessons.[48] She offered this evidence to support the notion that she was going to assume a role of homemaker in the US.

The petitions that sought to overcome racial restrictions also illustrate a complicated relationship between culture and family. The family is a site of cultural assimilation and the individual's family role is a determining factor of cultural assimilation. Many of the racially ineligible war brides indicated their assimilability by demonstrating their adaptation to American-style homemaking. MM was a Japanese fiancée of an honorably discharged veteran. She, like many other war brides from occupied Japan, received on-the-job training in "American ways" by working as a domestic worker in the homes of officers and missionaries. Additionally, in homes, and at war brides' schools run by the Red Cross in cooperation with the Army, the Japanese wives of soldiers learned how to use a vacuum cleaner, toaster, coffee maker, sandwich grill, to bake pies, to use cosmetics, to walk in high-heeled shoes, and to care for a baby.[49] The missionary who employed MM wrote in her support, "She has grasped countless ideas that we feel are necessary in looking toward a future home in America as an American homemaker." Her future husband also reported that the missionaries informed him that "she has done well with them and has learned many modern methods of cooking".[50]

A number of petitions emphasized the beneficiary's efforts at cultural assimilation through language lessons and religious conversion. Military officials who had the obligation to deny permission to soldiers wanting

46. H.Rep. 81-2507 (1950).
47. David H. Fowler, *Northern Attitudes Towards Interracial Marriage: Legislation and Public Opinion in the Middle Atlantic and the States of the Old Northwest, 1780–1930* (New York, 1987), pp. 339–439.
48. H.Rep. 81-1714 (1950)
49. Motion Picture NWDNM(m)-111-LC-30177; "Japanese War Brides School, Tokyo, Japan", June 1952; Record Group 111; National Archives Motion Picture, Sound, and Video Branch (College Park).
50. H.Rep. 81-1587 (1950).

to marry Japanese women often did so on the basis of potential marital difficulties arising from language and religious differences. A petitioner could provide evidence of a sound marital relationship, and one where the man was in control, when he could demonstrate his wife's willingness to learn English. For example, RK explained to Congressman Wilson of Texas, "She could only speak a few words of English when I first met her, so most of our conversation came out of an English–Japanese dictionary. However, she now has a good working knowledge of English and is improving every day."[51] The accusations of heathenism so prominent in the anti-Chinese/Asian rhetoric in the latter half of the nineteenth century, and continuing through the war, created a setting in which American-ness could be established by religious conversion.[52] Many supporters lauded the fact that the beneficiary had adopted Western religion, hinting that conversion also strengthened marriage. LJ glorified his wife's commitment to Christianity and how her commitment had renewed his faith. In his letter to Congressman O'Konski to obtain a bill for his wife he asked, "What more [...] could America desire in a prospective citizen than one who has done so much to inspire one of her citizens and soldiers toward higher ideals and to better himself and be an asset to his country?" He describes KJ as an

> [...] outstanding girl of the highest ideals and principles, having been raised a Christian girl and a regular attendant at a Christian Church since childhood, always maintaining a most strict and serious view of the church and its teachings, always eager to learn more of the Christian way of life and live her own life accordingly.[53]

Similarly, TR's parents wrote in support of the petition for his Japanese fiancée, stressing, "One reason we particularly like this girl is that she is studying to become a Catholic, and our son had fallen away from the church; now she has him returning to the church, for which we are ever grateful to her."[54] Many other war bride petitions attest to the beneficiaries' good moral character based on their having adopted Christianity.[55] In these cases involving cultural conformity exhibited through language training and religious conversion, the petitions present women as devoted homemakers, perhaps to dispel any stereotypical perceptions of Asian women and of how they might raise the next generation.

51. H.Rep. 81-2101 (1950).
52. Motion Picture NWDNM(m)-111-LC-30178; "Japanese War Brides School, Tokyo, Japan", June 1952; Record Group 111; National Archives Motion Picture, Sound, and Video Branch (College Park).
53. H.Rep. 81-2652 (1950).
54. H.Rep. 81-1942 (1950).
55. See, e.g., H.Rep. 81-1491 (1950); H.Rep. 81-2455 (1950); H.Rep. 81-2505 (1950).

Family relationships were important to gain preferences under the immigration laws, but were not required. Additionally, a family relationship alone would not guarantee entry into the American community, especially where the party seeking to join the community was disqualified by race or past illegal activity. However, the petitions discussed in this section illustrate that chances for membership in the American community were enhanced by membership in a particular kind of family, that is, a heterosexual, nuclear family. And, a petitioner could boost his or her chances by highlighting the ways that the petitioner would functionally and culturally fit into his or her appropriate role. This sort of belonging to a nuclear family made many of the petitioners seem more like acceptable Americans. Plus, the presence of a nuclear family enabled the government to assume that the individual admitted would not be an economic burden on the government. The family stands in to resolve financial concerns and renders racial difference invisible and as a result, banishment from the US seemed too harsh and resulted in bestowal of the immigration benefits sought.

THE HERO'S REWARD

Difference formed the basis for the negative consequences required by immigration law, and when petitioners did not have a family relationship to erase their difference, they attempted to hide the issue of their foreignness by highlighting extraordinary deeds that qualified the aliens as acceptable members of the American community. The petitioners appealed to Congress's postwar sense of American superiority and hostility toward growing totalitarian regimes. The political atmosphere in the US was one in which American democracy was pitted against creeping communism and created faith in those who would protect American democratic ideals. Petitioners created their sense of worthiness by stressing past military deeds or dangerous actions that assisted US military efforts. The petitions based on these heroic deeds fall into three categories that incrementally expand the benefit. The narrowest group of claimants is that which seeks a direct benefit; the next category extends the benefit to the close relatives of people who demonstrated worthy conduct; and related to those bills are the petitions that claim entitlement to the private bills for a foreign relative because the American earned it. Put another way, the latter two categories bestow the immigration benefit to another person in the first instance to show appreciation for worthy conduct, and in the second instance because the petitioner expects it as a reward.

As Congress acted favorably for the M family, discussed earlier, so it acted similarly on numerous petitions for foreigners who risked their lives in support of the US. Other examples include WO's petition, which sought to get around the residence requirement for naturalization in order to qualify him for employment with the US military. He was a Polish citizen who rendered meritorious service to the US government, in part as Commander-in-Chief of the Polish armies in England, whence he had fled.[56] And MSH provided assistance to American POWs and, upon being caught by the Japanese, was "subjected to extreme cruelty". In support of her petition to avoid deportation a supporter wrote, "her past experience in the Philippines has given her a greater appreciation of the values of Americanism and the ideals for which this country stands, preparing her to be a far more valuable citizen than most of us who have been fortunate to have American birthright".[57] Likewise, FL was a long-term resident from Germany who had been ordered deported for larceny and petitioned Congress for relief from deportation. During the war, FL had been arrested as an enemy alien. According to the commander of the internment camp, he volunteered to work on the construction of US Army target ranges, was repeatedly given jobs of trust and responsibility involving the protection of ammunition cars, and was marked as a traitor by other internees, who stoned his hut and threatened him with death for his pro-American activities.[58]

Petitioners did not have to risk their lives to demonstrate their attachment to American ideals. Like SSS, other petitioners established their credentials merely by exhibiting a strong work ethic. She had entered the US to study and, even though unauthorized to work, she got a job in a clinical laboratory. Co-workers and other members of her community who supported her petition wrote of her industriousness, loyalty to her employers, and conscientious work habits. The supporters presented these qualities as key characteristics of an American citizen.[59] Individual merit was at the center of these petitions, but the goodwill created by the aliens' meritorious conduct did not extend any further than that individual beneficiary.

However, Congress also extended the benefits to relatives of US citizens who likewise demonstrated attachment to American principles of freedom and democracy through honorable military service. Many of these petitions barely mention the beneficiary, and instead focus on the US citizen who would also benefit from a favorable disposition of the private bill. And even though time constraints and long distance likely contributed to the absence of information about the alien, Congress nevertheless enacted bills based solely on the reputation of a US citizen. One of these petitions indicates only that YT "is the Japanese wife of" RT "an American

56. H.Rep. 81-550 (1949).
57. H.Rep. 81-1825 (1950).
58. H.Rep. 81-476 (1949).
59. H.Rep. 81-702 (1949).

citizen and honorably discharged veteran of World War II". Letters of
support from two of his friends attest to his "good qualities" but say
nothing about her qualities.[60] Congressman Willis of Louisiana sponsored
a petition for NH. In the report, he mentions the beneficiary's name and
the fact that she is married to TJH, with whom he is acquainted by way of
TJH's parents. The strength of character in this petition belongs to TJH's
father who Willis describes as a veteran of World War I and an active
participant in local civic functions.[61] DO petitioned for an entry visa for
his fiancée through a lawyer who wrote,

> While I do not know this young man personally, we served in the Intelligence
> Service in Alaska together during the same period. My interest in the case stems
> from the fact that I commanded several hundred Nisei interpreters, interrogators
> and translators and would like to repay in a small way the devotion which they
> showed their country during the war.[62]

These and other petitioners benefited from the desire of the subcommittee
to expedite the petitions for war brides and fiancées in a way that enabled
the aliens to rely on their association with another person's reputation.
This reliance made the enactment of these bills more like rewards for
meritorious service to the country and ignored the character of the
beneficiaries of the bills.[63]

In the process of approving many of these bills, the petitioners and
Congress ignored the facts that the beneficiaries were hindered by a legal
rule defining them as outsiders. But, other petitioners challenged the rules
that, for most of US history, have made gender and race central to
determining citizenship in the US.[64] These petitioners used their status as
deserving war heroes to question the hypocrisy of American immigration
policies. The petitions expressed shock at the blunt racism and evoked a
sense of entitlement to better treatment. In one case, WH, a corporal
stationed with the Army occupation forces in Japan, expressed this
conviction in his petition for his wife and son who were barred from entry.

> I am placed in this position because the immigration laws of the United States,
> which permit the entry of wives of Americans from almost every other country,
> exclude Japanese wives on a purely discriminatory basis, simply because they are
> Japanese. In recent years, the oriental exclusion laws have been changed to admit
> Chinese, Indians, and Filipinos to the United States, and to continue to apply this
> racially discriminatory law to Japanese causes the United States and its

60. H.Rep. 81-1824 (1950).
61. H.Rep. 81-1591 (1950).
62. H.Rep. 81-2413 (1950).
63. H.Rep. 81-1678 (1950).
64. Ian F. Haney López, *White by Law: The Legal Construction of Race* (New York, 1996), pp. 37–47.

conception of democracy to lose stature in the eyes of the Japanese people, to whom we are supposedly teaching democracy.[65]

Corporal RF also wanted his wife and son to move to the US with him when he returned from duty in Japan. He provided some indication of the reaction to regulations that prevented him from bringing his family home when he wrote, "My three sisters are getting pretty mad about the way the Army is doing this and the way I look at it my citizen's rights are to let me marry who I want to."[66] DO summed up the liberal, colorblind ideology he felt was being trampled upon when he stated, "I realize that I will have problems and difficulties that would not arise if I married an American girl. I can only say that all I have is my faith and trust in God, myself, and people who believe that an individual is an individual regardless of color."[67]

Veterans like DO expanded the way the deserving war-hero justification worked. They were able both to make a claim for an immigration benefit for their family members and to criticize the government's practice of unequal treatment. However, the criticism had its own problems. Ironically, at the same time that he expresses this ideology, DO's statement reflects an underlying presumption about the race of "American girls". DO and others betray the underlying racist presumptions in the process of expressing their dismay or frustration with the discriminatory rules. Although the petitioners' confrontation with discrimination that results in their indignation over the law's mistreatment of people uncovered the privileging of their whiteness, the petitioners presuppose the standard of comparison against which the beneficiaries should be measured is racially white and culturally Western. One petitioner pointed out his wife's "Caucasian appearance" and use of a European last name in an effort to distinguish her from among the racially ineligible.[68] Others offered a similar sentiment. An army officer and his wife adopted a five-month-old baby and, as if to reinforce the strength of their bond with the child, state that "she has no facial or physical oriental characteristics and persons who do not know her background believe that she is our own flesh and blood".[69] Another petition illustrates the illogicality of the race exclusion, but instead of countering the underlying presumption about Asian racial inferiority, suggests that someone can overcome that inferiority. GP, who was a French citizen born in China to a French father and Japanese mother, was not allowed into the country with her husband and child on account of her race. Her sponsor argued "Mrs P is considered an Asiatic by birth, yet

65. H.Rep. 81-2648 (1950).
66. H.Rep. 81-2549 (1950).
67. H.Rep. 81-1630 (1950).
68. H.Rep. 81-1938 (1950).
69. H.Rep. 81-1850 (1950).

her paternal ancestry, education, customs, habits, domicile, citizenship and her entire background are all French."[70]

That these petitions try to discount the beneficiaries' race is not to say that the petitioners harbor intolerance or ill will towards people because of race, rather their statements reflect a presumption of a standard of white racial superiority. Indeed supporters of the petitions tried to distinguish themselves by flaunting their progressive outlook. One parent of a petitioner for his future daughter-in-law, who wanted to prove she would be joining a broadminded family, stated, "My wife was a good friend of a Japanese girl when in high school and I spent quite a bit of time in the South Pacific. So I'm sure we will get along swell."[71]

Other petitions at once pronounce and attempt to take advantage of the perception that America has a more hospitable climate with respect to race. This position seems ironic, given the *de jure* discrimination in the law the petitioners are trying to get around, and that the petitions seem to make a backhanded criticism of racism in other countries. CDJ petitioned for his half-English and half-Japanese fiancée's entry. The petitioner states "that because of her appearance and inability to speak fluent Japanese, she has never been accepted by the Japanese people as one of them, but rather has always been considered a foreigner".[72] Y and MM are the wife and daughter of an honorably discharged white veteran. In support of their petition to bring the baby to the US from Japan, a sponsor declares, "Because of her paternal heritage it is only just that the child should have every opportunity to grow up in America."[73] In a case involving a half-Korean and half-white infant adopted by an American couple in Korea, the baby's adoptive father describes her as "obviously an American child". He goes on to mention "that a white illegitimate child will suffer a horrible existence if it should be required to live its life among the Koreans. Its lack of conformity to the Korean racial characteristics immediately indicate its illegitimacy and it will literally suffer hell through life here".[74]

Nevertheless, the petitions also express an optimism, or romanticism, about the democratic ideals of America. Revealing the attitudes of a nation wanting to demonstrate an ideology free of race distinctions, SA's future

---

70. H.Rep. 81-2012 (1950).
71. H.Rep. 81-2421 (1950).
72. H.Rep. 81-1588 (1950).
73. H.Rep. 81-2553 (1950).
74. H.Rep. 81-2801 (1950). This petitioner refuses to acknowledge as a problem the role that he and his wife had in removing the child from the Korean couple who was raising the baby. The couple lost the baby because they were poor and they had approached the consulate seeking financial assistance to buy milk. The consulate, remembering the excellent care that Mrs S had provided another orphan, took the baby, in spite of the couple's reluctance to give her up. Pointing out the couple's role is not meant to discount the problems that mixed-race children of GIs faced.

father-in-law writes, "She has good charms, and dresses very well and has poise and appearance that anyone will take her as a 'Nisei' or second generation Japanese-American." Although his tone suggests xenophobia, he nevertheless seems to have elevated Japanese Americans over Japanese nationals.[75] In another petition, an occupation-army colonel in Japan writes to support one of his civilian employees who is trying to get a visa for his Japanese fiancée. He comments favorably on the young woman's character and then offers, "There is a good deal of publicity on the democratization of Japan; I know of no more impressive, practical test that liberality in American legislative or administrative channels to contribute [sic] to the personal happiness of a deserving war veteran."[76]

The petitions examined in this section honored individuals and at the same time endorsed and thereby helped to secure American democratic ideals and interests. War veterans epitomized the sense of attachment to the United States and to American ideals, and this status enabled them to criticize forcefully legal inequities based on race. Rather than making a case based on the benefits of diversity, the petitioners here erased difference by arguing that the American democratic principles that they had defended necessitated the construing of race as irrelevant.

CONCLUSION

Even though most of the petitioners in the post-World-War-II period were seeking something less than formal US citizenship, the petitioners and the members of Congress hearing their requests sometimes approached the petitions assuming that citizenship would be the ultimate goal. At the same time, the stakes involved in these individual requests were high; meaning that the petitioners felt they had a lot to lose if Congress denied their requests for relief. Thus, to increase their chances of success, they had to package their stories into a normative conception of citizenship.

At the time, political theorists, most prominently T.H. Marshall, were conceiving citizenship as a bundle of rights.[77] Full membership in society meant guaranteed access to civil, political, and social rights. A liberal democratic political community enabled people in the nation to access these rights. Accordingly, citizenship was conceived as a status based on rights, not on racial identity. And for a nation such as the United States, that believed its identity was centered on the notions of freedom and equality, the justifications for limiting access to this conception of

75. H.Rep. 81-1914 (1950).
76. H.Rep. 81-2207 (1950).
77. Will Kymlicka and Wayne Norman, "Return of the Citizen: A Survey of Recent Work on Citizenship Theory", *Ethics*, 104 (1994), pp. 352–381.

citizenship were problematic. The US citizens making claims to benefit their noncitizen family members thus had a strong argument.

Nevertheless, the law compelled the petitioners to do more than appeal to liberal sensibilities, and the contents of the private immigration bill-petitions show that the petitioners did go beyond substantiating an unjust limitation on access to citizenship status or immigration benefits. In addition to appealing to liberal ideals, they had to establish their worthiness for legal acceptance in the American community. By so doing, the petitioners masked the very characteristics they were trying to get Americans to accept. Consequently, instead of presuming that social rights would become available to the petitioners with their acceptance into the American community, the petitions demonstrated an individual responsibility that obviated the need for social rights. For example, petitioners like FG obtained relief from deportation by demonstrating economic self-reliance for their families.[78] And war bride petitions established the brides' dependence and reliance on their husbands in a suitably patriarchal social structure, where husbands took responsibility for wives' welfare. By declaring that aliens conformed to American religious, cultural, and (white) racial norms, the petitions also moderated the potential claims to civil rights.

Furthermore, the family represented and was a site of reinforcement of the petitioners' claims to assimilation. By portraying themselves as conforming to the notions of economic self-reliance and "American" cultural patterns, the petitioners did not threaten to taint or alter American citizenry. Instead, the petitions forecasted the beneficiaries to be ideal members of the American community, aliens whose identity would shift to America and who would embrace full membership. Paradoxically, in so doing, the alien petitioners simultaneously embody the attributes of American citizens and contribute to the conception of citizenship as distinct from membership in the American community.

The beneficiaries of the bills are aliens who technically do not have a representative in government. In a democracy, this lack of representation exemplifies noncitizen status. Thus the private bill petitions, while coming from "the people" and having some benefit for a citizen or would-be-citizen, are really about the potential citizen. The representation and acceptance of these potential citizens into American society nominally symbolizes a gradual "incorporation of previously excluded groups",[79] but that acceptance comes at the cost of obscuring their differences. Any subsequent deviation from the publicly declared American identity

---

78. H.Rep. 81-1764 (1950).
79. Linda Bosniak, "Universal Citizenship and the Problem of Alienage", *Northwestern University Law Review*, 94 (2000), pp. 963–982.

reinscribes outsider status on the petitioners, as well as on anyone else who might deviate from the norm.

Undoubtedly, there were many progressive attitudes behind, and positive effects arising from the private bill petitions. From a humanitarian perspective alone, the relief granted by the thousands of private bill petitions had positive effects on many more lives than were represented by the petitions. Additionally, the petitions had an impact on the revision of US immigration laws, by illuminating particular problems with race restrictions, which ultimately resulted in their elimination. But by disguising racial difference and by sanctioning the model nuclear family, the petitions illustrate the way that "progressive" social change is not so clearly progressive.

www.ingramcontent.com/pod-product-compliance
Ingram Content Group UK Ltd.
Pitfield, Milton Keynes, MK11 3LW, UK
UKHW042155280225
455719UK00001B/358